4th International Natural Language Generation Conference 2006

(INLG 06)

Held in conjunction with COLING/ACL 2006

Sydney, Australia
15-16 July 2006

ISBN: 978-1-61738-498-1

Printed from e-media with permission by:

Curran Associates, Inc.
57 Morehouse Lane
Red Hook, NY 12571
www.proceedings.com

Some format issues inherent in the e-media version may also appear in this print version.

Printed by Curran Associates, Inc. (2010)

Association for Computational Linguistics
209 N. Eighth Street
Stroudsburg, Pennsylvania 18360

Phone: 1-570-476-8006
Fax: 1-570-476-0860

acl@aclweb.org

Table of Contents

Preface

We are pleased to introduce the technical programme of the Fourth International Natural Language Generation Conference (INLG), the Biennial Meeting of SIGGEN, the ACL Special Interest Group in Natural Language Generation. INLG is the leading international conference on research into natural language generation. It has been held at Brockenhurst (UK) in 2004, in Harriman (New York, USA) in 2002, and in Mitzpe Ramon (Israel) in 2000. Prior to 2000, the INLG meetings were International Workshops, running every other year since 1980. The INLG conference provides a forum for the discussion, dissemination and archiving of research topics and results in the fiel of text generation. This year, INLG is being held as a COLING/ACL 2006 workshop. It takes place on the weekend prior to the main COLING/ACL 2006 conference, on July 15-16th 2006, in Sydney, Australia.

The INLG programme consists of substantial, original, and previously unpublished results on all topics related to natural language generation. This year, as in previous years, each submission was reviewed as a full paper by at least three members of an international programme committee of leading researchers in the field listed on the next page. We received 38 submissions (both long and short papers) from all over the world, from which we accepted 11 long papers (including two student papers) and f ve short papers. We would like to thank all who submitted papers and our programme committee for their hard work.

This year, the programme centers around a variety of research issues around the realisation component of a natural language system, including the use of statistical techniques. In particular, there are a substantial number of contributions on the generation of referring expressions. The programme also includes an invited talk by Professor Kathleen McKeown (Columbia University, New York, USA) entitled "Lessons Learned from Large Scale Evaluation from Systems that Produce Text: Nightmares and Pleasant Surprises" and a special session on "Sharing Data and Comparative Evaluation", organised by Dr Anja Belz (University of Brighton, UK) and Professor Robert Dale (Macquarie University, Australia).

We would like to thank the whole COLING/ACL 2006 committee, in particular: Suzanne Stevenson, the COLING/ACL 2006 Workshop Chair; Olivia Kwong, the Publications Chair; Priscilla Rasmussen, the ACL Business manager; and the local organising committee, including Judy Potter of Well Done Events, for their help and advice in organising INLG 2006. We are also grateful to the ACL Executive Committee and the SIGGEN board for their support and advice.

We welcome you to the conference and hope you will fin it to be a productive and enjoyable experience.

Nathalie Colineau
Cécile Paris
Stephen Wan
Robert Dale
INLG 2006 Programme Co-chairs

Organizers

Programme Co-Chairs:

Nathalie Colineau, CSIRO - ICT Centre, Australia
Cécile Paris, CSIRO - ICT Centre, Australia
Stephen Wan, CSIRO - ICT Centre and Macquarie University, Australia
Robert Dale, Macquarie University, Australia

Special Session Co-Chairs:

Anja Belz, University of Brighton, UK
Robert Dale, Macquarie University, Australia

Programme Committee:

Regina Barzilay, Columbia University, USA
Kalina Bontcheva, University of Sheffield UK
Joyce Y. Chai, Michigan State University, USA
Nathalie Colineau, CSIRO, Australia
Robert Dale, Macquarie University, Australia
Laurence Danlos, University of Paris 7, France
Noemie Elhadad, City College of New York, USA
Sabine Geldof, Namahn, Belgium
Graeme Hirst, University of Toronto, Canada
Kentaro Inui, Nara Institute of Science and Technology, Japan
Elena Not, IRST, Italy
Cecile Paris, CSIRO, Australia
Ehud Reiter, University of Aberdeen, UK
Norbert Reithinger, DFKI, Germany
Rolf Schwitter, Macquarie University, Australia
Donia Scott, Open University, UK
Mariet Theune, University of Twente, Netherlands
Keith Vander Linden, Calvin College, USA
Ingrid Zukerman, Monash University, Australia

Student Session Program Committee:

Bernd Bohnet, University of Stuttgart, Germany
Matt Huenerfauth, University of Pennsylvania, Philadelphia, USA
Eric Kow, Loria, France.
Tomasz Marciniak, Language Computer Corporation, Richardson, Texas.
Ani Nenkova, Columbia University, USA
David Reitter, University of Edinburgh, Scotland, UK
Stephen Wan, University of Macquarie, Australia

Invited Speaker:

Kathleen R. McKeown, Columbia University, USA

Conference Programme

Saturday, 15 July 2006

9:15–9:30	Opening Remarks
	Surface Realisation Session 1:
9:30–9:45	*A Generation-Oriented Workbench for Performance Grammar: Capturing Linear Order Variability in German and Dutch* Karin Harbusch, Gerard Kempen, Camiel van Breugel and Ulrich Koch
9:45–10:15	*CCG Chart Realization from Disjunctive Inputs* Michael White
10:15–10:30	*Overgeneration and Ranking for Spoken Dialogue Systems* Sebastian Varges
10:30–11:00	Morning Tea
	Surface Realisation Session 2:
11:00–11:30	*Individuality and Alignment in Generated Dialogues* Amy Isard, Carsten Brockmann and Jon Oberlander
11:30–12:00	*Using Distributional Similarity to Identify Individual Verb Choice* Jing Lin
12:00–12:15	*Adjective-to-Verb Paraphrasing in Japanese Based on Lexical Constraints of Verbs* Atsushi Fujita, Naruaki Masuno, Satoshi Sato and Takehito Utsuro
12:15–2:00	Lunch
	Referring Expressions Session 1:
2:00–2:30	*Generating References to Parts of Recursively Structured Objects* Helmut Horacek
2:30–3:00	*Overspecified Reference in Hierarchical Domains: Measuring the Benefits for Readers* Ivandré Paraboni, Judith Masthoff and Kees van Deemter
3:00–3:30	*Algorithms for Generating Referring Expressions: Do They Do What People Do?* Jette Viethen and Robert Dale
3:30–4:00	Afternoon Tea

Saturday, 15 July 2006 (continued)

	Special Session on Sharing Data and Comparative Evaluation:
4:00–4:15	Special Session Opening Remarks
4:15–4:30	*Evaluations of NLG Systems: Common Corpus and Tasks or Common Dimensions and Metrics?* Cécile Paris, Nathalie Colineau and Ross Wilkinson
4:30–4:45	*Building a semantically transparent corpus for the generation of referring expressions.* Kees van Deemter, Ielka van der Sluis and Albert Gatt
4:45–5:00	*Shared-task Evaluations in HLT: Lessons for NLG* Anja Belz and Adam Kilgarriff
5:00–5:15	*GENEVAL: A Proposal for Shared-task Evaluation in NLG* Ehud Reiter and Anja Belz
5:15–6:15	Open Mic Session Participants: Kees van Deemter, Albert Gatt, Ielka van der Sluis Michael White David Reitter and Charles Callaway Helmut Horacek Sebastian Varges Donia Scott and Johanna Moore .. and other contributions from the floo .

Sunday, 16 July 2006

9:00–10:30 Invited Talk

Lessons Learned from Large Scale Evaluation of Systems that Produce Text: Nightmares and Pleasant Surprises
Kathleen R. McKeown

10:30–11:00 Morning Tea

Referring Expressions Session 2:

11:00–11:30 *Group-Based Generation of Referring Expressions*
Kotaro Funakoshi, Satoru Watanabe and Takenobu Tokunaga

11:30–12:00 *Noun Phrase Generation for Situated Dialogs*
Laura Stoia, Darla Magdalene Shockley, Donna K. Byron and Eric Fosler-Lussier

12:00–12:15 *The Clarity-Brevity Trade-off in Generating Referring Expressions*
Imtiaz Hussain Khan, Graeme Ritchie and Kees van Deemter

12:15–1:45 Lunch

Session on Querying, Answering and Arguing:

1:45–2:15 *Generic Querying of Relational Databases using Natural Language Generation Techniques*
Catalina Hallett

2:15–2:45 *Generating Intelligent Numerical Answers in a Question-Answering System*
Véronique Moriceau

2:45–3:00 *Generating Multiple-Choice Test Items from Medical Text: A Pilot Study*
Nikiforos Karamanis, Le An Ha and Ruslan Mitkov

3:00–3:30 *Generation of Biomedical Arguments for Lay Readers*
Nancy Green

3:30–4:00 Afternoon Tea

Lessons Learned from Large Scale Evaluation of Systems that Produce Text: Nightmares and Pleasant Surprises

Kathleen R. McKeown
Department of Computer Science
Columbia University
New York, NY 10027
kathy@cs.columbia.edu

Extended Abstract

As the language generation community explores the possibility of an evaluation program for language generation, it behooves us to examine our experience in evaluation of other systems that produce text as output. Large scale evaluation of summarization systems and of question answering systems has been carried out for several years now. Summarization and question answering systems produce text output given text as input, while language generation produces text from a semantic representation. Given that the output has the same properties, we can learn from the mistakes and the understandings gained in earlier evaluations. In this invited talk, I will discuss what we have learned in the large scale summarization evaluations carried out in the Document Understanding Conferences (DUC) from 2001 to present, and in the large scale question answering evaluations carried out in TREC (e.g., the definition pilot) as well as the new large scale evaluations being carried out in the DARPA GALE (Global Autonomous Language Environment) program.

DUC was developed and run by NIST and provides a forum for regular evaluation of summarization systems. NIST oversees the gathering of data, including both input documents and gold standard summaries, some of which is done by NIST and some of which is done by LDC. Each year, some 30 to 50 document sets were gathered as test data and somewhere between two to nine summaries were written for each of the input sets. NIST has carried out both manual and automatic evaluation by comparing system output against the gold standard summaries written by humans. The results are made public at the annual conference. In the most recent years, the number of participants has grown to 25 or 30 sites from all over the world.

TREC is also run by NIST and provides an annual opportunity for evaluating the output of question-answering (QA) systems. Of the various QA evaluations, the one that is probably most illuminating for language generation is the definition pilot. In this evaluation, systems generated long answers (e.g., paragraph length or lists of facts) in response to a request for a definition. In contrast to DUC, no model answers were developed. Instead, system output was pooled and human judges determined which facts within the output were necessary (termed "vital nuggets") and which were helpful, but not absolutely necessary (termed "OK nuggets"). Systems could then be scored on their recall of nuggets and precision of their response.

DARPA GALE is a new program funded by DARPA that is running its own evaluation, carried out by BAE Systems, an independent contractor. Evaluation more closely resembles that done in TREC, but the systems' scores will be compared against the scores of human distillers who carry out the same task. Thus, final numbers will report percent of human performance. In the DARPA GALE evaluation, which is a future event at the time of this writing, in addition to measuring properties such as precision and recall, BAE will also measure systems' ability to find all occurrences of the same fact in the input (redundancy).

One consideration for an evaluation program is the feel of the program. Does the evaluation program motivate researchers or does it cause headaches? I liken Columbia's experience in DUC and currently in GALE to that of Max in *Where the Wild Things Are* by Maurice Sendak. We began with punishment (i.e., if you don't do well, your funding will be in jeopardy), encounter monsters along the way (seemingly arbitrary methods for

Proceedings of the Fourth International Natural Language Generation Conference
Sydney, July 2006.

measuring output quality), finally tame the monsters and sail back peacefully across time. DUC has reached the peaceful stage, but GALE has not. The TREC definition pilot had less of a threat of punishment.

Evaluation in all of these programs began at the request of the funders, with the goal of comparing how well different funded systems perform. Improvement over the years is also measured in order to determine if funding is well spent. This kind of goal creates anxiety in participants and makes it most important to get the details of the evaluation right; errors in how evaluation is carried out can have great consequences. Coming to agreement on the metrics used, the methodology for measuring output and the tasks on which performance is measured can be difficult; the environment does not feel friendly. Even if evaluation within the language generation community was not initiated with the same goals, I think it is reasonable to expect a certain amount of disagreement as the program gets off the ground.

However, over time, researchers come to agreement on some portion of the task and these features become accepted. At this point in time, it is possible to see the benefits of the program. Certainly, within DUC, we are at this stage. DUC has generated large amounts of data, including both input document sets and multiple models of good output for each input set, which has spurred studies both on evaluation and summarization. Halteren and Teufel, for example, provide a method for annotation of content units and study consensus across summarizers (van Halteren and Teufel, 2003; Teufel and van Halteren, 2004b). Nenkova studies significant differences across DUC04 systems (Nenkova, 2005) as well as the properties of human and system summaries (Nenkova, 2006). We can credit DUC with the emergence of automatic methods for evaluation such as ROUGE (Lin and Hovy, 2003; Lin, 2004) which allow quick measurement of systems during development and enable evaluation of larger amounts of data. We have seen the development of manual methods for evaluation developed both within DUC (Harman and Over, 2004) and without. The Pyramid method (Nenkova and Passonneau, 2004) provides a annotation method and metric that addresses the issues of reliability and stability of scoring. Thus, research on evaluation of summarization has become a field in its own right resulting in greater understanding of the effect of different metrics and methodologies.

¿From DUC and TREC, we have learned important characteristics of a large-scale evaluation, of which the top three might be:

- Output can be measured by comparison against a human model, but we know that this comparison will only be valid if multiple models are used. There are multiple good summaries of the same input and if system output is compared against just one, the results will be biased.

- If the task is appealing to a wide audience, the evaluation will spur research and motivate researchers to join in. We have seen this with growth of participation in DUC. One benefit of summarization and QA is that the task is domain-independent and thus, no one site has an advantage over others through experience with a particular domain.

- Given the different ways in which evaluation can be carried out and the fact that different researchers may be biased towards methods which favor their own approach, it is important the evaluation be overseen by a neutral party which is not deeply involved in research on the task itself. On the other hand, some knowledge is necessary if the evaluation is to be well-designed.

While my talk will focus on large scale evaluation programs that feature quantitative evaluation through comparison with a gold standard, there has been work on task-based evaluation of summarization (McKeown et al, 2005). Task-based evaluation is more intensive and to date, has not been done on a large scale across sites, but shows potential for indicating the usefulness of summarization systems.

In this brief abstract, I've suggested some of the topics that will be covered in my talk, which will tour the land of the wild things for evaluation, illuminating monsters and highlighting events that will allow more peaceful sailing. Evaluation can be a nightmare, but over time and particularly if carried out away from the influence of funding pressures, it can nurture a community of researchers with common goals.

Acknowledgments

This material is based upon work supported in part by the ARDA AQUAINT program (Contract No. MDA908-02-C-0008 and Contract No. NBCHC040040) and the Defense Advanced Research Projects Agency (DARPA) under Contract No. HR0011-06-C-0023 and Contract No. N66001-00-1-8919. Any opinions, findings and conclusions or recommendations expressed in this material are those of the author(s) and do not necessarily reflect the views of the DARPA or ARDA.

References

Harman, D. and Over, P. 2004. The effects of human variation in duc summarization evaluation. In *Text Summarization Branches Out Workshop, ACL 2004.*

Lin, C.-Y. 2003. Rouge: a package for automatic evaluation of summaries. In *Proceedings of the Workshop in Text Summarization, ACL'04.*

Lin, C.-Y. and Hovy, E. 2003. Automatic evaluation of summaries using n-gram co-occurance statistics. In *Proceedings of HLT-NAACL 2003.*

McKeown, K. and Passonneau, R.J. and Elson, D.K., and Nenkova, A., and Hirschberg, J. 2005. A Task-Based Evaluation of Multi-Document Summarization. In *Proceedings of SIGIR 2005.*

Nenkova, A. 2005. Automatic text summarization of newswire: Lessons learned from the Document Understanding Conference. In *Proceedings of AAAI 2004.*

Nenkova, A. 2006. Understanding the process of multi-document summarization: content selection, rewrite and evaluation. Ph.D Dissertation, Columbia University.

Nenkova, A. and Passonneau, R. 2004. Evaluating content selection in summarization: The pyramid method. In *Proceedings of HLT/NAACL 2004.*

Teufel, S. and van Halteren, H. 2004. Evaluating information content by factoid analysis: human annotation and stability. In *EMNLP-04.*

van Halteren, H. and Teufel, S. 2003. Examining the consensus between human summaries: initial experiments with factoid analysis. In *HLT-NAACL DUC Workshop.*

A generation-oriented workbench for Performance Grammar: Capturing linear order variability in German and Dutch

Karin Harbusch[1], Gerard Kempen[2,3], Camiel van Breugel[3], Ulrich Koch[1]

[1]Universität Koblenz-Landau, Koblenz
{harbusch, koch}@uni-koblenz.de

[2]Max Planck Institute for Psycholinguistics, Nijmegen
gerard.kempen@mpi.nl

[3]Department of Psychology, Leiden University
cvbreuge@liacs.nl

Abstract

We describe a generation-oriented workbench for the Performance Grammar (PG) formalism, highlighting the treatment of certain word order and movement constraints in Dutch and German. PG enables a simple and uniform treatment of a heterogeneous collection of linear order phenomena in the domain of verb constructions (variably known as Cross-serial Dependencies, Verb Raising, Clause Union, Extraposition, Third Construction, Particle Hopping, etc.). The central data structures enabling this feature are clausal "topologies": one-dimensional arrays associated with clauses, whose cells ("slots") provide landing sites for the constituents of the clause. Movement operations are enabled by unification of lateral slots of topologies at adjacent levels of the clause hierarchy. The PGW generator assists the grammar developer in testing whether the implemented syntactic knowledge allows all and only the well-formed permutations of constituents.

1 Introduction

Workbenches for natural-language grammar formalisms typically provide a parser to test whether given sentences are treated adequately — D-PATR for Unification Grammar (Karttunen, 1986) or XTAG for Tree-Adjoining Grammars (Paroubek *et al.,* 1992) are early examples. However, a parser is not a convenient tool for checking whether the current grammar implementation licenses all and only the strings qualifying as well-formed expressions of a given input. Sentence generators that try out all possible combinations of grammar rules applicable to the current input, are better suited.

Few workbenches in the literature come with such a facility. LinGO (Copestake & Flickinger, 2000), for Head-Driven Phrase Structure Grammar, provides a generator in addition to a parser. For Tree Adjoining Grammars, several workbenches with generation components have been built: InTeGenInE (Harbusch & Woch, 2004) is a recent example.

Finetuning the grammar such that it neither over- nor undergenerates, is a major problem for semi-free word order languages (e.g., German; cf. Kallmeyer & Yoon, 2004). Working out a satisfactory solution to this problem is logically prior to designing a generator capable of selecting, from the set of all possible paraphrases, those that sound "natural," i.e., the ones human speakers/writers would choose in the situation at hand (cf. Kempen & Harbusch, 2004).

Verb constructions in German and Dutch exhibit extremely intricate word order patterns (cf. Seuren & Kempen, 2003). One of the factors contributing to this complexity is the phenomenon of *clause union*, which allows constituents of a complement clause to be interspersed between those of the dominating clause. The resulting sequences exhibit, among other things, cross-serial dependencies and clause-final verb clusters. Further complications arise from all sorts of 'movement' phenomena such as fronting, extraction, dislocation, extraposition, scrambling, etc. Given the limited space available, we cannot describe the Performance Grammar (PG) formalism and the linearization algorithm that enables generating a broad range of linear order phenomena in Dutch, German, and English verb constructions. Instead, we refer to Harbusch & Kempen (2002), and Kempen & Harbusch (2002, 2003).

Proceedings of the Fourth International Natural Language Generation Conference
Sydney, July 2006. ©2006 Association for Computational Linguistics

Here, we present the generation-oriented PG Workbench (PGW), which assists grammar developers, among other things, in testing whether the implemented syntactic and lexical knowledge allows all and only well-formed permutations.

In Section 2, we describe PG's topology-based linearizer implemented in the PGW generator, whose software design is sketched in Section 3. Section 4 shows the PGW at work and draws some conclusions.

2 Linearization in PG and PGW

Performance Grammar (PG) is a fully lexicalized grammar that belongs to the family of tree substitution grammars and deploys disjunctive feature unification as its main structure building mechanism. It adheres to the ID/LP format (Immediate Dominance vs. Linear Precedence) and includes separate components generating the hierarchical and the linear structure of sentences. Here, we focus on the linearization component.

PG's hierarchical structures consist of unordered trees composed of elementary building blocks called *lexical frames*. Every word is head of a lexical frame, which specifies the subcategorization constraints of the word. Associated with every lexical frame is a *topology*. Topologies serve to assign a left-to-right order to the branches of lexical frames. In this paper, we will only be concerned with topologies for verb frames (clauses). We assume that clausal topologies of Dutch and German contain exactly nine slots — see (1).

(1) Wat wil je dat ik doe? / what want you that I do /'What do you want me to do?'

F1	M1	M2	…	M6	E1	E2
●	wil	je				●
↑						⇑
Wat	dat	ik			doe	

The slot labeled F1 makes up the Forefield (from Ger. *Vorfeld*); slots M1-M6 make up the Midfield (*Mittelfeld*); slots E1 and E2 define the Endfield (*Nachfeld*). Every constituent (subject, head, direct object, complement, etc.) has a small number of placement options, i.e. slots in the topology associated with its "own" clause.

How is the Direct Object NP *wat* 'what' 'extracted' from the complement clause and 'promoted' into the main clause? Movement of phrases between clauses is due to *lateral topology sharing*. If a sentence contains more than one verb, each of their lexical frames instantiates its own topology. This applies to verbs of any type — main, auxiliary or copula. In such cases, the topologies are allowed to *share* identically labeled lateral (i.e. left- and/or right-peripheral) slots, conditionally upon several restrictions (not to be explained here; but see Harbusch & Kempen, 2002)). *After two slots have been shared, they are no longer distinguishable; in fact, they are unified and become the same object.* In example (1), the embedded topology shares its F1 slot with the F1 slot of the matrix clause. This is indicated by the dashed borders of the bottom F1 slot. Sharing the F1 slots effectively causes the embedded Direct Object *wat* to be *preposed* into the main clause (black dot in F1 above the single arrow in (1)). The dot in E2 above the double arrow marks the position selected by the finite complement clause.

The overt surface order is determined by a *read-out module* that traverses the hierarchy of topologies in left-to-right, depth first manner. E.g., *wat* is already seen while the reader scans the higher topology.

3 A sketch of PGW's software design

The PGW is a computational grammar development tool for PG. Written in Java, it comes with an advanced graphical direct-manipulation user interface. All lexical and grammatical data have been encoded in a *relational database* schema. This contrasts with the predominance of *hierarchical databases* in present-day computational linguistics. Relational lexical databases tend to be easier to maintain and update than hierarchical ones, especially for linguists with limited programming experience. The software was designed with an eye toward easy cross-language portability of the encoded information. For German we developed a *lexicon converter* that maps the German *CELEX* database automatically to the PGW format (Koch, 2004).

4 Generating verb constructions in Dutch and German

In order to convey an impression of the capabilities of the PGW, we show it at work in generating verb constructions that involve rather delicate linearization phenomena: "Particle Hopping" in Dutch (2), and "Scrambling" in German (3).

The finite complement clause (2) includes the verb *meezingen* 'sing along with,' where *mee* 'with' is a preposition functioning as separable particle. The three other verbs are auxiliaries. According to a topology sharing rule for Dutch, clauses headed by auxiliaries are free to share 4, 5 or 6 left-peripheral slots of their own topology with that of its complement. The most restrictive sharing option is shown in (2).

(2) ... *dat ze dit (lied) zouden kunnen hebben meegezongen*
... that they this (song) would be-able-to have along-sung
'... that they might have sung along this (song)'

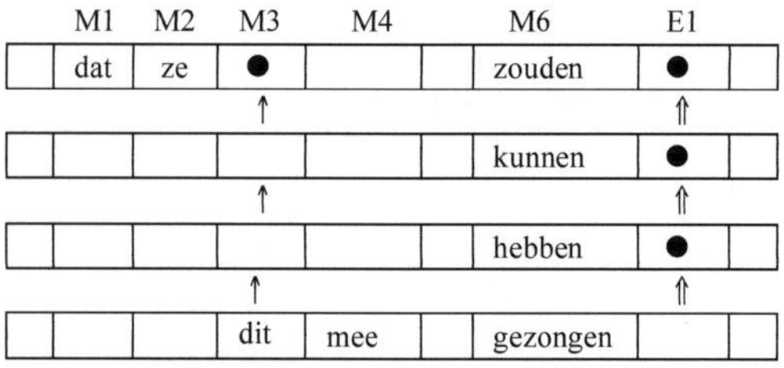

The Direct Object NP *dit (lied)* 'this (song)' lands in M3 of the lowest topology. As this slot belongs to the four left-peripheral ones, it is always shared and its content gets promoted all the way up into the highest clause (see single arrows). Particle *mee* always lands in the fifth slot (M4), i.e. in the optionally shared area. Hence, its surface position depends on the actual number of shared left-peripheral slots. In (2), with minimal slot sharing, *mee* stays in its standard position immediately preceding the head verb. In case of non-minimal topology sharing, the particle may move leftward until (but no farther than) the direct object, thus yielding exactly the set of grammatical placement options.

The quality of PGW's treatment of Scrambling in German can be assessed in terms of a set of 30 word order variations of sentence (3), discussed by Rambow (1994), who also provides grammaticality ratings for all members of the set. Seuren (2003) presents similar grammaticality judgments obtained from an independent group of native speakers. As the rating scores appeared to vary considerably (cf. (3a) and (3b)), we checked which permutations are actually generated by the PGW. It turned out easy to find a set of topology sharing values that generates all and only the paraphrases with high or satisfactory grammaticality scores.

In conclusion, although the performance data discussed here are very limited, we believe they justify positive expectations with respect to the potential of a topology-based linearizer to approximate closely the grammaticality judgments of native speakers and thus to avoid over- and undergeneration.

(3) a. ... *weil niemand das Fahrrad zu reparieren zu versuchen verspricht*
because nobody the bike to repair to try promises
'... because nobody promises to try to repair the bike'
b. *...*weil zu versuchen das Fahrrad niemand zu reparieren verspricht*

References

Copestake, A. and Flickinger, D. 2000. An open source grammar development environment and broad-coverage English grammar using HPSG. *Procs. of the 2nd Internat. Conf. on Language Resources and Evaluation (LREC),* Athens.

Harbusch, K. and Kempen, G. 2002 A quantitative model of word order and movement in English, Dutch and German complement constructions. *Procs. of the 19th Internat. Conf. on Computational Linguistics (COLING),* Taipei.

Harbusch, K. and Woch, J. 2004. Integrated natural language generation with Schema-TAGs. In: Habel, C., Pechmann, T. (eds.) *Language Production.* Berlin: Mouton De Gruyter.

Karttunen, L. 1986. D-PATR: A Development Environment for Unification Grammars. Tech. Rep. CSLI-86-61. CSLI, Stanford, CA.

Kempen, G. and Harbusch, K. 2002 Performance Grammar: A declarative definition. In Nijholt, A., Theune, M., Hondorp, H. (eds.), *Computational Linguistics in the Netherlands 2001.* Amsterdam: Rodopi, 146-162.

Kempen, G. and Harbusch, K. 2003. Dutch and German verb constructions in Performance Grammar. In Seuren & Kempen, 2003.

Koch, U. 2004. *The Specification of a German Performance Grammar from CELEX Data in Preparation for a German Performance Grammar Workbench,* Master's Thesis at the Computer Science Department, U. Koblenz-Landau.

Paroubek, P., Schabes, Y., and Joshi, A.K. 1992. XTAG – A Graphical Workbench for Developing Tree-Adjoining Grammars. *Procs. of the 3rd Applied Natural Language Processing Conference (ANLP)*, Trento, 216-223.

Rambow, O. 1994. *Formal and Computational Aspects of Natural Language Syntax.* Ph.D. Thesis, U. Pennsylvania, Philadelphia.

Seuren, P.A.M. 2003. Verb clusters and branching directionality in German and Dutch. In (Seuren & Kempen, 2003), 247-296.

Seuren, P. and Kempen, G. (eds.). 2003. *Verb Constructions in Dutch and German.* Amsterdam: Benjamins.

CCG Chart Realization from Disjunctive Inputs

Michael White
Department of Linguistics
The Ohio State University
Columbus, OH 43210 USA
http://www.ling.ohio-state.edu/~mwhite/

Abstract

This paper presents a novel algorithm for efficiently generating paraphrases from disjunctive logical forms. The algorithm is couched in the framework of Combinatory Categorial Grammar (CCG) and has been implemented as an extension to the OpenCCG surface realizer. The algorithm makes use of packed representations similar to those initially proposed by Shemtov (1997), generalizing the approach in a more straightforward way than in the algorithm ultimately adopted therein.

1 Introduction

In recent years, the generate-and-select paradigm of natural language generation has attracted increasing attention, particularly for the task of surface realization. In this paradigm, symbolic methods are used to generate a space of possible phrasings, and statistical methods are used to select one or more outputs from this space. To specify the desired paraphrase space, one may either provide an input logical form that underspecifies certain realization choices, or include *explicit disjunctions* in the input LF (or both). Our experience suggests that disjunctive LFs are an important capability, especially as one seeks to make grammars reusable across applications, and to employ domain-specific, *sentence-level* paraphrases (Barzilay and Lee, 2003).

Prominent examples of surface realizers in the generate-and-select paradigm include Nitrogen/Halogen (Langkilde, 2000; Langkilde-Geary, 2002) and Fergus (Bangalore and Rambow, 2000). More recently, generate-and-select realizers in the *chart realization* tradition (Kay, 1996) have appeared, including the OpenCCG (White, 2004) and LinGO (Carroll and Oepen, 2005) realizers. Chart realizers make it possible to use the same reversible grammar for both parsing and realization, and employ well-defined methods of semantic composition to construct semantic representations that can properly represent the scope of logical operators.

In the chart realization tradition, previous work has not generally supported disjunctive logical forms, with (Shemtov, 1997) as the only published exception (to the author's knowledge). Arguably, part of the reason that disjunctive LFs have not yet been embraced more broadly by those working on chart realization is that Shemtov's solution, while ingenious, is dauntingly complex. Looking beyond chart realizers, both Nitrogen/Halogen and Fergus support some forms of disjunctive input; however, in comparison to Shemtov's inputs, theirs are less expressive, in that they do not allow disjunctions across different levels of the input structure.

As an alternative to Shemtov's method, this paper presents a chart realization algorithm for generating paraphrases from disjunctive logical forms that is more straightforward to implement, together with an initial case study of the algorithm's efficiency. As discussed in Section 5, the algorithm makes use of packed representations similar to those initially proposed by Shemtov, generalizing the approach in a way that avoids the problems that led Shemtov to reject his preliminary method. The algorithm is couched in the framework of Steedman's (2000) Combinatory Categorial Grammar (CCG) and has been implemented as an extension to the OpenCCG surface realizer. Though the algorithm is well suited to CCG, it is expected to be applicable to other constraint-based grammatical frameworks as well.

Proceedings of the Fourth International Natural Language Generation Conference
Sydney, July 2006.

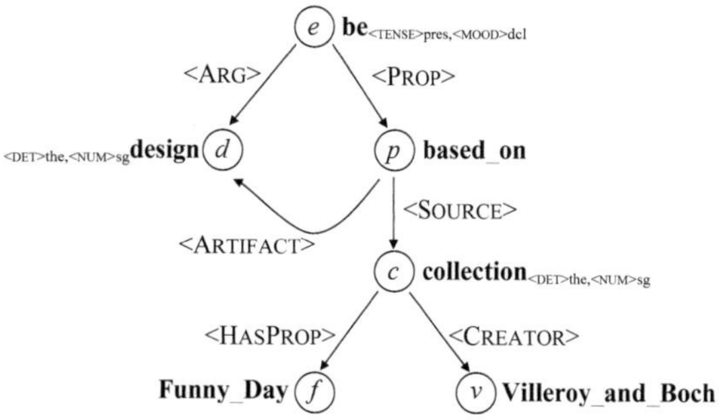

(a) Semantic dependency graph for *The design (is|'s) based on the Funny Day collection by Villeroy and Boch.*

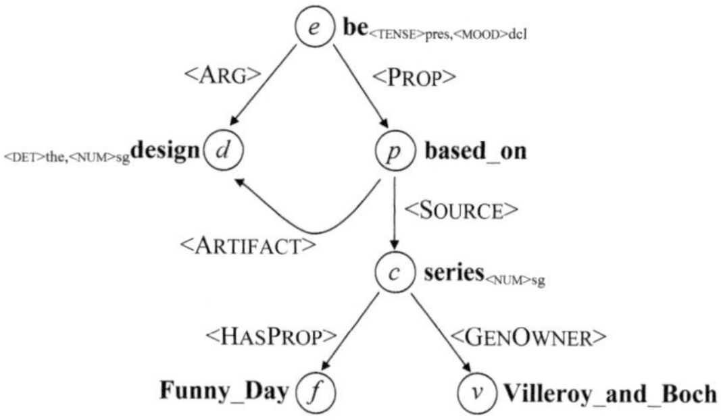

(b) Semantic dependency graph for *The design (is|'s) based on Villeroy and Boch's Funny Day series.*

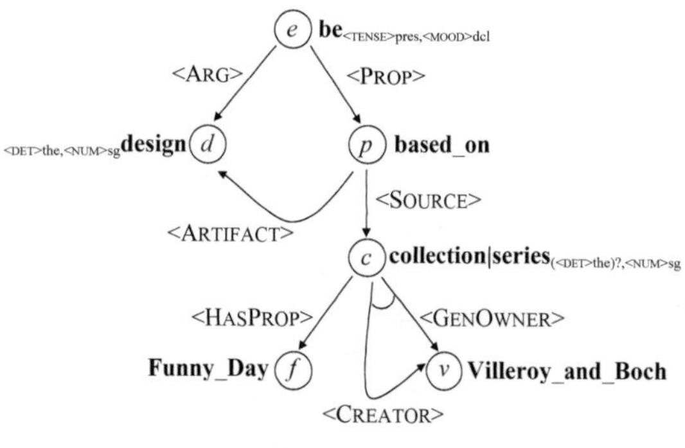

(c) Disjunctive semantic dependency graph covering (a)-(b), i.e. *The design (is|'s) based on (the Funny Day (collection|series) by Villeroy and Boch | Villeroy and Boch's Funny Day (collection|series)).*

Figure 1: Example semantic dependency graphs from the COMIC dialogue system.

$$
\begin{array}{l}
@_e(\mathbf{be} \wedge \langle \text{TENSE}\rangle \text{pres} \wedge \langle \text{MOOD}\rangle \text{dcl} \wedge \\
\quad \langle \text{ARG}\rangle(d \wedge \mathbf{design} \wedge \langle \text{DET}\rangle \text{the} \wedge \langle \text{NUM}\rangle \text{sg}) \wedge \\
\quad \langle \text{PROP}\rangle(p \wedge \mathbf{based\_on} \wedge \\
\qquad \langle \text{ARTIFACT}\rangle d \wedge \\
\qquad \langle \text{SOURCE}\rangle(c \wedge \mathbf{collection} \wedge \langle \text{DET}\rangle \text{the} \wedge \langle \text{NUM}\rangle \text{sg} \wedge \\
\qquad\quad \langle \text{HASPROP}\rangle(f \wedge \mathbf{Funny\_Day}) \wedge \\
\qquad\quad \langle \text{CREATOR}\rangle(v \wedge \mathbf{V\&B}))))
\end{array}
$$

(a)

⋮

$$
\begin{array}{l}
@_e(\mathbf{be} \wedge \langle \text{TENSE}\rangle \text{pres} \wedge \langle \text{MOOD}\rangle \text{dcl} \wedge \\
\quad \langle \text{ARG}\rangle(d \wedge \mathbf{design} \wedge \langle \text{DET}\rangle \text{the} \wedge \langle \text{NUM}\rangle \text{sg}) \wedge \\
\quad \langle \text{PROP}\rangle(p \wedge \mathbf{based\_on} \wedge \\
\qquad \langle \text{ARTIFACT}\rangle d \wedge \\
\qquad \langle \text{SOURCE}\rangle(c \wedge \langle \text{NUM}\rangle \text{sg} \wedge (\langle \text{DET}\rangle \text{the})? \wedge \\
\qquad\quad (\mathbf{collection} \,\underline{\vee}\, \mathbf{series}) \wedge \\
\qquad\quad \langle \text{HASPROP}\rangle(f \wedge \mathbf{Funny\_Day}) \wedge \\
\qquad\quad (\langle \text{CREATOR}\rangle \boxed{v} \,\underline{\vee}\, \langle \text{GENOWNER}\rangle \boxed{v})))) \\
\wedge\ @_v(\mathbf{Villeroy\_and\_Boch})
\end{array}
$$

(c)

Figure 2: HLDS for examples in Figure 1.

2 Disjunctive Logical Forms

As an illustration of disjunctive logical forms, consider the semantic dependency graphs in Figure 1, which are taken from the COMIC[1] multimodal dialogue system.[2] Graphs such as these constitute the input to the OpenCCG realizer. Each node has a lexical predication (e.g. **design**) and a set of semantic features (e.g. ⟨NUM⟩sg); nodes are connected via dependency relations (e.g. ⟨ARTIFACT⟩).

Given the lexical categories in the COMIC grammar, the graphs in Figure 1(a) and (b) fully specify their respective realizations, with the exception of the choice of the full or contracted form of the copula. To generalize over these alternatives, the disjunctive graph in (c) may be employed. This graph allows a free choice between the domain synonyms *collection* and *series*, as indicated by the vertical bar between their respective predications. The graph also allows a free choice between the ⟨CREATOR⟩ and ⟨GENOWNER⟩ relations—lexicalized via *by* and the possessive, respectively—connecting the head c (*collection* or *series*) with the dependent v (for

[1] http://www.hcrc.ed.ac.uk/comic/

[2] To simplify the exposition, the features specifying information structure and deictic gestures have been omitted, as have the semantic sorts of the discourse referents.

$$
\begin{aligned}
&@_e(\textbf{see} \wedge \langle \textsc{Arg0}\rangle(m \wedge \textbf{man}) \wedge \langle \textsc{Arg1}\rangle(g \wedge \textbf{girl}) \wedge \\
&\quad @_o(\textbf{on} \wedge \langle \textsc{Arg1}\rangle(h \wedge \textbf{hill})) \wedge @_w(\textbf{with} \wedge \langle \textsc{Arg1}\rangle(t \wedge \textbf{telescope})) \wedge \\
&\quad (((\langle \textsc{Mod}\rangle o \wedge @_h(\langle \textsc{Mod}\rangle w)) \veebar \\
&\quad\ (@_g(\langle \textsc{Mod}\rangle o) \wedge (@_g(\langle \textsc{Mod}\rangle w) \veebar @_h(\langle \textsc{Mod}\rangle w))) \veebar \\
&\quad\ ((\langle \textsc{Mod}\rangle w \wedge ((\langle \textsc{Mod}\rangle o \veebar @_g(\langle \textsc{Mod}\rangle o)))))
\end{aligned}
$$

Figure 3: Disjunctive LF for 5-way ambiguity in *A man saw a girl on the hill with a telescope.*

Villeroy and Boch); this choice is indicated by an arc between the two dependency relations. Finally, the determiner feature ($\langle$DET$\rangle$the) on c is indicated as optional, via the question mark.

It is worth pausing at this point to observe that in designing the COMIC grammar, the differences between (a) and (b) could perhaps have been collapsed. However, such a move would make it more difficult to reuse the grammar in other applications—and indeed, the core of the grammar is shared with the FLIGHTS system (Moore et al., 2004)—as it would presuppose that these paraphrases should always available in the same contexts. An example of a *sentence-level* paraphrase, whose context of applicability is more clearly limited, appears in (1):

(1) (This design | This one | This) (is|'s) (classic | in the classic style) | Here we have a (classic design | design in the classic style).

This example shows some of the phrasings that may be used in COMIC to describe the style of a design that has not been discussed previously. The example includes a top-level disjunction between the use of a deictic NP *this design* | *this one* | *this* (with an accompanying pointing gesture) followed by the copula, or the use of the phrase *here we have* to introduce the design. While these alternatives can function as paraphrases in this context, it is difficult to see how one might specify them in a single underspecified (and application-neutral) logical form.

Graphs such as those in Figure 1 are represented internally using Hybrid Logic Dependency Semantics (HLDS), as in Figure 2. HLDS is a dependency-based approach to representing linguistic meaning developed by Baldridge and Kruijff (2002). In HLDS, hybrid logic (Blackburn, 2000) terms[3] are used to describe dependency graphs. These graphs have been suggested as representations for discourse structure, and have their own underlying semantics (White, 2006).

In HLDS, as can be seen in Figure 2(a), each semantic head is associated with a nominal that identifies its discourse referent, and heads are connected to their dependents via dependency relations, which are modeled as modal relations. Modal relations are also used to represent semantic features. In (c), two new operators are introduced to represent periphrastic alternatives and optional parts of the meaning, namely $\veebar$ and $(\cdot)?$, for exclusive-or and optionality, respectively. To indicate that a nominal represents a reference to a node that is considered a shared part of multiple alternatives, the nominal is annotated with a box, as exemplified by $\boxed{v}$. As will be discussed in Section 3.1, this notion of shared references is needed during the logical form flattening stage of the algorithm in order to determine which elementary predications are part of each alternative.

As mentioned earlier, disjunctive LFs may contain alternations that are not at the same level. To illustrate, Figure 3 shows the representation (minus semantic features) for the 5-way ambiguity in *A man saw a girl on the hill with a telescope* (Shemtov, 1997, p. 45); in the figure, the nominal o (for *on*) can be a dependent of e (for *see*) or g (for *girl*), for example. As Shemtov explains, such packed representations can be useful in machine translation for generating ambiguity-preserving target language sentences. In a straight generation context, disjunctions that span levels enable one to compactly represent alternatives that differ in their head-dependent assumptions; for instance, to express contrast, one might employ the coordinate conjunction *but* as the sentence head, or the subordinate conjunction *although* as a dependent of the main clause head.

3 The Algorithm

As with the other chart realizers cited in the introduction, the OpenCCG realizer makes use of a chart and an agenda to perform a bottom-up dynamic programming search for signs whose LFs

[3] Hybrid logic extends modal logic with *nominals*, a new sort of basic formula that explicitly names states/nodes. Like propositions, nominals are first-class citizens of the object language, and thus formulas can be formed using propositions, nominals, and standard boolean operators. They may also employ the *satisfaction operator*, @. A formula $@_i(p \wedge \langle F\rangle(j \wedge q))$ indicates that the formulas p and $\langle F\rangle(j \wedge q)$ hold at the state named by i, and that the state j, where q holds, is reachable via the modal relation F; equivalently, it states that node i is labeled by p, and that node j, labeled by q, is reachable from i via an arc labeled F.

completely cover the elementary predications in the input logical form. The search for complete realizations proceeds in one of two modes, anytime or two-stage packing/unpacking. This section focuses on how the two-stage mode has been extended to efficiently generate paraphrases from disjunctive logical forms.

3.1 LF Flattening

In a preprocessing stage, the input logical form is flattened to an array of elementary predications (EPs), one for each lexical predication, semantic feature or dependency relation. When the input LF contains no exclusive-or or optionality operators, the list of EPs, when conjoined, yields a graph description that is equivalent to the original one. With disjunctive logical forms, however, more needs to be said. Our strategy is to keep track of the elementary predications that make up the alternatives and optional parts of the LF, as specified by the exclusive-or or optionality operators, and use these to enforce constraints on the elementary predications that may appear in any given realization. These constraints ensure that only combinations of EPs that describe a graph that is also described by the original LF are allowed.

To illustrate, the results of flattening the LF in Figure 2(c) are given below:

(2) $0{:}\ @_e(\mathbf{be}),\ 1{:}\ @_e(\langle\text{TENSE}\rangle\text{pres}),$
$2{:}\ @_e(\langle\text{MOOD}\rangle\text{dcl}),\ 3{:}\ @_e(\langle\text{ARG}\rangle d),$
$4{:}\ @_d(\mathbf{design}),\ 5{:}\ @_d(\langle\text{DET}\rangle\text{the}),$
$6{:}\ @_d(\langle\text{NUM}\rangle\text{sg}),$
$7{:}\ @_e(\langle\text{PROP}\rangle p),\ 8{:}\ @_p(\mathbf{based\_on}),$
$9{:}\ @_p(\langle\text{ARTIFACT}\rangle d),\ 10{:}\ @_p(\langle\text{SOURCE}\rangle c),$
$11{:}\ @_c(\langle\text{NUM}\rangle\text{sg}),\ 12{:}\ @_c(\langle\text{DET}\rangle\text{the}),$
$13{:}\ @_c(\mathbf{collection}),\ 14{:}\ @_c(\mathbf{series}),$
$15{:}\ @_c(\langle\text{HASPROP}\rangle f),\ 16{:}\ @_f(\mathbf{Funny\_Day}),$
$17{:}\ @_c(\langle\text{CREATOR}\rangle v),\ 18{:}\ @_c(\langle\text{GENOWNER}\rangle v),$
$19{:}\ @_v(\mathbf{Villeroy\_and\_Boch})$

(3) $\mathsf{alt}_{0,0} = \{13\};\ \mathsf{alt}_{0,1} = \{14\}$
$\mathsf{alt}_{1,0} = \{17, 19\};\ \mathsf{alt}_{1,1} = \{18, 19\}$
$\mathsf{opt}_0 = \{12\}$

In (2), the EPs are shown together with their array positions. Since the EPs are tracked positionally, it is possible to use bit vectors to represent the alternatives and optional parts of the LF. In (3), the first line shows the bit vectors[4] for the choice between **collection** (EP 13) and **series** (EP 14), as alternatives 0 and 1 in alternative group 0. On the second line, the bit vectors for the ⟨CREATOR⟩ (EP 17) and ⟨GENOWNER⟩ (EP 18) alternatives appear; note that both of these options also involve the shared EP 19. The bit vector for the optional determiner (EP 12) is shown on the third line.

The constraint associated with each group of alternatives is that in order to be valid, a collection of EPs must not intersect with the non-overlapping parts of more than one alternative. For example, for the second group of alternatives in (3), a valid collection could include EPs 17 and 19, or EPs 18 and 19, but it could not include EPs 17 and 18 together.

Flattening an LF to obtain the array of EPs, as in (2), just requires a relatively straightforward traversal of the HLDS formula. Obtaining the alternatives and optional parts of the LF is a bit more involved. To do so, during the traversal, the exclusive-or and optionality operators are handled by introducing a new alternative group or optional part, and then keeping track of which elementary predications fall under each alternative or under the optional part. Subsequently, the alternatives and optional parts are recursively propagated through any nominals marked as shared, collecting any further EPs that turn up along the way.[5] For example, with the second alternative group (second line) of (3), the initial traversal creates EPs 17 and 18 under alts $\mathsf{alt}_{1,0}$ and $\mathsf{alt}_{1,1}$, respectively. Since EPs 17 and 18 both include a nominal dependent v marked as shared in Figure 2(c), both alternatives are propagated through this reference, and thus EP 19 ends up as part of both $\mathsf{alt}_{1,0}$ and $\mathsf{alt}_{1,1}$. Determining which EPs have shared membership in multiple alternatives is essential for accurately tracking an edge's coverage of the input LF, a topic which will be considered next.

3.2 Edges

In the OpenCCG realizer, an *edge* is a data structure that wraps a CCG sign, which itself consists of a word sequence paired with a category (syntactic category plus logical form). An edge has bit vectors to record its coverage of the input LF and its indices, i.e. syntactically available nominals. In packing mode, a *representative* edge also maintains a list of alternative edges whose signs have equivalent categories (but different word sequences), so that a representative edge may effec-

[4]Only the positive bits are shown, via their indices.

[5]Though space precludes discussion, it is worth noting that the same propagation of membership applies to the LF chunks described in (White, 2006).

tively stand in for the others during chart construction.

To handle disjunctive inputs, an edge additionally maintains a list of active (i.e., partially completed) LF alternatives. It also makes use of a revised notion of input coverage and a revised equivalence relation. As in Shemtov's (1997, Section 3.3.2) preliminary algorithm, an edge is considered to cover an entire disjunction (alternative group) if it covers all the EPs of one of its alternatives. With optional parts of an LF, an edge that does not cover any EPs in the optional part can be extended to a new edge (using the same sign) that is additionally considered to cover all the EPs in the optional part. In this way, an edge can be defined to be *complete* with respect to the input LF if it covers all its EPs. For example, an edge for the sentence in Figure 1(b) would be considered complete, since (i) it would cover all the EPs in (2) except for 12, 13 and 17; (ii) 12 is optional; (iii) 14 completes $\mathsf{alt}_{0,1}$, and thus counts as covering 13, the other EP in the group; and (iv) 18 and 19 complete $\mathsf{alt}_{1,1}$, and thus count as covering EP 17.

As Shemtov points out, this extended notion of input coverage provides an appropriate way to form edge equivalence classes, as it can gather edges together that realize different alternatives in the same group. Thus, in OpenCCG, edge equivalence classes have been modified to include edges with the same syntactic category and coverage bit vector, but different word sequences and/or logical forms (as the latter varies according to which alternative is realized). The appropriate equivalence checks are efficiently carried out using a hash map with a custom hash function and equals method.

3.3 Lexical Instantiation

Once the input LF has been flattened, and the alternatives and optional parts have been identified, the next step is to access and instantiate lexical items. For each elementary predication, all lexical items indexed by the EP's lexical predicate or relation are retrieved from the lexicon.[6] Each such lexical item is then instantiated against the input EPs, starting with the one that triggered its retrieval, and incrementally extending successful instantiations until all the lexical item's EPs have been instantiated (otherwise failing). The lexical instantiation routine returns all instantiations that satisfy the alternative exclusion constraints. Associated with each instantiation is a bit vector that encodes the coverage of the input EPs. From each bit vector, the active (partially completed) LF alternatives are determined, and the bit vector is updated to include the EPs in any completed disjunctions. Finally, edges are created for the instantiated lexical items, which include the active alternatives and the updated coverage vector.

Continuing with example (2)-(3), the selected lexical edges in (4) below illustrate how lexical instantiation interacts with disjunctions:

(4)
a. {11,13,14} *collection* $\vdash \mathsf{n}_c$: $@_c(\mathbf{collection}) \wedge @_c(\langle\textsc{num}\rangle\mathrm{sg})$
b. {11,13,14} *series* $\vdash \mathsf{n}_c$: $@_c(\mathbf{series}) \wedge @_c(\langle\textsc{num}\rangle\mathrm{sg})$
c. {17} $\mathsf{alt}_{1,0}$ *by* $\vdash \mathsf{n}_c\backslash\mathsf{n}_c/\mathsf{np}_v$: $@_c(\langle\textsc{Creator}\rangle v)$
d. {18} $\mathsf{alt}_{1,1}$ *'s* $\vdash \mathsf{np}_c/\mathsf{n}_c\backslash\mathsf{np}_v$: $@_c(\langle\textsc{GenOwner}\rangle v)$
e. {19} $\mathsf{alt}_{1,0}$; $\mathsf{alt}_{1,1}$ *Villeroy_and_Boch* $\vdash \mathsf{np}_v$: $@_v(\mathbf{V\&B})$

The nouns in (a) and (b) complete $\mathsf{alt}_{0,0}$ and $\mathsf{alt}_{0,1}$, respectively, and thus they each count as covering EPs 11, 13 and 14. In (c) and (d), *by* and *'s* partially cover $\mathsf{alt}_{1,0}$ and $\mathsf{alt}_{1,1}$, respectively, and thus these alternatives are active for their respective edges. In (e), *V&B* partially covers both $\mathsf{alt}_{1,0}$ and $\mathsf{alt}_{1,1}$, and thus both alternatives are active.

3.4 Derivation

Following lexical instantiation, the lexical edges are added to the agenda, as is usual practice with chart algorithms, and the main loop is initiated. During each iteration of the main loop, an edge is moved from the agenda to the chart. If the edge is in the same equivalence class as an edge already in the chart, it is added as an alternative to the existing representative edge. Otherwise, it is combined with all applicable edges in the chart (via the grammar's combinatory rules), as well as with the grammar's unary rules, where any newly created edges are added to the agenda. The loop terminates when no edges remain on the agenda.

Before edge combinations are attempted, a number of constraints are checked, as detailed in (White, 2006). In particular, the edges' coverage bit vectors are required to not intersect, which ensures that they cover disjoint parts of the input LF. Since the coverage vectors are updated to cover all the EPs in a disjunction when one of the alternatives is completed, this check also ensures that the

[6] See (White, 2004; White, 2006) for discussion of how semantically null lexical items and unary type changing rules are handled.

1. $\{8\text{-}10\}$ *based_on* $\vdash \mathsf{s}_p\backslash\mathsf{np}_d/\mathsf{np}_c$
2. $\{12\}$ *the* $\vdash \mathsf{np}_c/\mathsf{n}_c$
3. $\{15, 16\}$ *Funny_Day* $\vdash \mathsf{n}_c/\mathsf{n}_c$
4. $\{11, 13, 14\}$ *collection* $\vdash \mathsf{n}_c$
   $\{11, 13, 14\}$ *series* $\vdash \mathsf{n}_c$
5. $\{17\}$ $\mathsf{alt}_{1,0}$ *by* $\vdash \mathsf{n}_c\backslash\mathsf{n}_c/\mathsf{np}_v$
6. $\{18\}$ $\mathsf{alt}_{1,1}$ *'s* $\vdash \mathsf{np}_c/\mathsf{n}_c\backslash\mathsf{np}_v$
7. $\{19\}$ $\mathsf{alt}_{1,0}; \mathsf{alt}_{1,1}$ *Villeroy_and_Boch* $\vdash \mathsf{np}_v$
8. $\{11, 13\text{-}16\}$ *FD [collection]* $\vdash \mathsf{n}_c$ (3 4 >)
9. $\{17\text{-}19\}$ *by V&B* $\vdash \mathsf{n}_c\backslash\mathsf{n}_c$ (5 7 >)
10. $\{17\text{-}19\}$ *V&B 's* $\vdash \mathsf{np}_c/\mathsf{n}_c$ (7 6 <)
11. $\{11, 13\text{-}19\}$ *FD [coll.] by V&B* $\vdash \mathsf{n}_c$ (8 9 <)
12. $\{11, 13\text{-}19\}$ *V&B 's FD [coll.]* $\vdash \mathsf{np}_c$ (10 8 >)
13. $\{11\text{-}19\}$ *the FD [coll.] by V&B* $\vdash \mathsf{np}_c$ (2 11 >)
    $\{11\text{-}19\}$ *V&B 's FD [coll.]* $\vdash \mathsf{np}_c$ (12 optC)
14. $\{8\text{-}19\}$ *b._on [the FD [coll.] ...]* $\vdash \mathsf{s}_p\backslash\mathsf{np}_d$ (1 13 >)

Figure 4: Part of realization chart for Figure 1(c).

exclusion constraints for the disjunction continue to be enforced. Thus, for example, no attempt will be made to combine the edges for *collection* and *series* in (4a) and (4b), since they both express EP 11 and since they contribute to different alternatives in group 0.

To enforce the constraints associated with active alternatives, a compatibility check is made to ensure that if the input edges have active alternatives in the same group, the intersection of these alternatives is non-empty. To illustrate, consider the edges for *by* and the possessive *'s* in (4c) and (4d). Since these edges have different alternatives active within group 1, the compatibility check fails, and thus their combination is not attempted. By contrast, the edge for *Villeroy and Boch* in (4e) will pass the compatibility check with both (4c) and (4d), as it shares an active alternative in common with each of these. When two edges succeed in combining, a new edge is constructed from the resulting sign by taking the union of the coverage bit vectors, determining the active alternatives, and updating the coverage vector to include the EPs in any completed disjunctions.

When the grammar's unary rules are applied to an edge, an operation is also invoked for creating an edge (for the same sign) with one or more optional parts marked as completed. This operation is invoked when it would complete the input LF, complete an alternative, or complete an LF chunk.[7] A constraint on its application is that the optional parts must be wholly missing from the input edge; additionally, in the case of completing an alternative or LF chunk, the optional parts must be part of the alternative or chunk in question.

Figure 4 demonstrates how the lexical edges in (4) are combined in the chart.[8] These lexical edges appear on lines 4-7. Note that the edge for *series* is added as an alternative edge to the one for *collection*, which acts as a representative for both; to highlight its role as a representative, *collection* is shown in square brackets from line 8 onwards. At the end of each line, the derivation of each (non-lexical) edge is shown in parentheses, in terms of its input edges and combinatory rule. On line 13, observe that the NP using the possessive is added as an alternative to the one using the *by*-phrase; the possessive version becomes part of the same equivalence class when the optional determiner is marked as covered, via the optional part completion operation.

3.5 Unpacking

Once chart construction has finished, the complete realizations are recursively unpacked bottom-up in a way that generalizes the approach of (Langkilde, 2000). Unpacking proceeds by multiplying out the alternative edges stored with the representative input edges; filtering out any duplicate edges resulting from spurious ambiguities; scoring the new edges with the scoring method configured via the API; and pruning the results with the configured pruning strategy. Note that since there is no need for checking grammatical or other constraints during the unpacking stage, new edges can be quickly and cheaply constructed using structure sharing.

To briefly illustrate the process, consider how the *Funny_Day collection* edge in line 8 of Figure 4 is unpacked. While the *Funny_Day* input edge has no alternative edges, the *collection* input edge has the *series* edge as an alternative, and thus a new *Funny_Day series* edge will be created and scored; as long as the pruning strategy keeps more than the single-best option, this edge will be added as an alternative, and both combinations will be propagated upwards through the edges in lines 11

[7] LF chunks serve to avoid propagating semantically incomplete phrases; see (White, 2006) for discussion.

[8] To save space, the figure only shows part of the normal form derivation, and the logical forms for the categories have been suppressed.

	10-best two-stage		1-best anytime	
	time	edges	time	edges
disjunctive	1.1	602	0.5	281
sequential	5.6	3550	4.1	2854

Table 1: Comparison of average run times (in seconds) and edges created vs. sequential realization

and 12.

4 Case Study

To examine the potential of the algorithm to efficiently generate paraphrases, this section presents a case study of its run times versus sequential realization of the equivalent top-level LF alternatives in disjunctive normal form. The study used the COMIC grammar, a small but not trivial grammar that suffices for the purposes of the system. In this grammar, there are relatively few categories per lexeme on average, but the boundary tone categories engender a great deal of non-determinism. With other grammars, run times can be expected to vary.

In anticipation of the present work, Foster and White (2004) generated disjunctive logical forms during sentence planning, then (as a stopgap measure) multiplied out the disjunctions and sequentially realized the top-level alternatives until an overall time limit was reached. Taking the previous logical forms as a starting point, 104 sentences from the evaluation in (Foster and White, 2005) were selected, and their LFs were manually augmented to cover a greater range of paraphrases allowed by the grammar.[9] To obtain the corresponding top-level LF alternatives, 100-best realization was performed, and the unique LFs appearing in the top 100 realizations were gathered; on average, there were 29 such unique LFs. We then compared the present algorithm's performance against sequential realization in producing 10-best outputs and single-best outputs. In the 10-best case, we used the two-stage packing/unpacking mode; for the single-best case, we used the anytime mode with 3-best pruning. With both cases, the run times include scoring with a trigram language model, and were measured on a 2.8GHz Linux PC. Realization quality was not assessed as part of the study, though manual inspection indicated that it was very high.

Table 1 shows the results of the comparison. The average run times of the present algorithm, with disjunctive LFs as input, appear on the first line, along with the average number of edges created; on the second line are the average aggregate run times and num. edges created of sequentially realizing the top-level alternatives (not including the time taken to produce these alternatives). As can be seen, realization from disjunctive inputs yields a 5-fold and 8-fold speedup over the sequential approach in the two cases, with corresponding reductions in the number of edges created. Additionally, the run times appear to be adequate for use in interactive dialogue systems (especially in the anytime, single-best case).

[9]Extending the COMIC sentence planner to produce these augmented LFs is left for future work.

5 Comparison to Shemtov (1997)

The present approach differs from Shemtov's in two main ways. First, since Shemtov developed his approach with the task of ambiguity preserving translation in mind, he framed the problem as one of generating from *ambiguous* semantic representations, such as one might find in a parse chart with unresolved ambiguities. Consequently, he devised a method for converting the meanings in a packed parse chart into an encoding where each fact (here, EP) appears exactly once, together with an indication of the meaning alternatives it belongs to, expressed as propositional formulas. While this *contexted facts* encoding may be suitable for MT, it is not very convenient as an input representation for systems which generate from non-linguistic data, as the formulas representing the contexts only make sense in reference to a parse chart. By contrast, the present approach takes as input disjunctive logical forms that should be reasonably intuitive to construct in dialogue systems or other NLG applications, since they are straightforwardly related to their non-disjunctive counterparts.

The second way in which the approach differs concerns the relative simplicity of the algorithms ultimately adopted. As part of his preliminary algorithm (Shemtov, 1997, Section 3.3.2), Shemtov proposed the extended use of coverage bit vectors that we embraced in Section 3.2. He then developed a refined version to handle disjunctions with intersecting predicates. However, he concluded that this refined version was arc-consistent but not path-consistent (p. 65, fn. 10), given that it checked combinations of contexted facts pairwise, without keeping track of which alternations such combinations were committed to. By contrast, the present approach does not suffer from this defect, because it checks the alternative exclusion constraints on all of a lexical edge's EPs at once (using bit vectors for both edge coverage and alternative membership), and also ensures that the active alternatives are compatible before combining edges during derivations. Shemtov does not appear to have considered a solution along the lines proposed here; instead, he went on to develop a sound but considerably more complex algorithm (his Section 3.4), where an edge's coverage bit vector is replaced with a contexted coverage array (an array of boolean conditions). With these arrays, it is no longer easy to group edges into equivalence classes, and thus during chart construction Shemtov is forced to group together edges which are not derivationally equivalent. Consequently, to prevent overgeneration, his algorithm has to solve during the enumeration phase a system of constraints (potentially exponential in size) formed from the conditions in the contexted coverage arrays—a process which is far from straightforward.

6 Conclusions

This paper has presented a new chart realization algorithm for efficiently generating surface realizations from disjunctive logical forms, and has argued that the approach represents an improvement over that of (Shemtov, 1997) in terms of both usability and simplicity. The algorithm has been implemented as an extension to the OpenCCG hybrid symbolic/statistical realizer, and has recently been employed to generate n-best realization lists for reranking according to their predicted synthesis quality (Nakatsu and White, 2006), as well as to generate dialogues exhibiting individuality and alignment(Brockmann et al., 2005; Isard et al., 2005). An initial case study has shown that the algorithm works many times faster than sequential realization, with run times suitable for use in dialogue systems; a more comprehensive study of the algorithm's efficiency is planned for future work.

Acknowledgements

The author thanks Mary Ellen Foster, Amy Isard, Johanna Moore, Mark Steedman and the anonymous reviewers for helpful feedback and discussion, and the University of Edinburgh's Institute for Communicating and Collaborative Systems for partially supporting this work.

References

Jason Baldridge and Geert-Jan Kruijff. 2002. Coupling CCG and Hybrid Logic Dependency Semantics. In *Proc. ACL-02*.

Srinivas Bangalore and Owen Rambow. 2000. Exploiting a probabilistic hierarchical model for generation. In *Proc. COLING-00*.

Regina Barzilay and Lillian Lee. 2003. Learning to paraphrase: An unsupervised approach using multiple-sequence alignment. In *Proc. of NAACL-HLT*.

Patrick Blackburn. 2000. Representation, reasoning, and relational structures: a hybrid logic manifesto. *Logic Journal of the IGPL*, 8(3):339–625.

Carsten Brockmann, Amy Isard, Jon Oberlander, and Michael White. 2005. Modelling alignment for affective dialogue. In *Proc. UM-05 Workshop on Adapting the Interaction Style to Affective Factors*.

John Carroll and Stefan Oepen. 2005. High efficiency realization for a wide-coverage unification grammar. In *Proc. IJCNLP-05*.

Mary Ellen Foster and Michael White. 2004. Techniques for Text Planning with XSLT. In *Proc. 4th NLPXML Workshop*.

Mary Ellen Foster and Michael White. 2005. Assessing the impact of adaptive generation in the COMIC multimodal dialogue system. In *Proc. IJCAI-05 Workshop on Knowledge and Representation in Practical Dialogue Systems*.

Amy Isard, Carsten Brockmann, and Jon Oberlander. 2005. Individuality and alignment in generated dialogues. In *Proc. INLG-06*. To appear.

Martin Kay. 1996. Chart generation. In *Proc. ACL-96*.

Irene Langkilde-Geary. 2002. An empirical verification of coverage and correctness for a general-purpose sentence generator. In *Proc. INLG-02*.

Irene Langkilde. 2000. Forest-based statistical sentence generation. In *Proc. NAACL-00*.

Johanna Moore, Mary Ellen Foster, Oliver Lemon, and Michael White. 2004. Generating tailored, comparative descriptions in spoken dialogue. In *Proc. FLAIRS-04*.

Crystal Nakatsu and Michael White. 2006. Learning to say it well: Reranking realizations by predicted synthesis quality. In *Proc. of COLING-ACL-06*. To appear.

Hadar Shemtov. 1997. *Ambiguity Management in Natural Language Generation*. Ph.D. thesis, Stanford University.

Mark Steedman. 2000. *The Syntactic Process*. MIT Press.

Michael White. 2004. Reining in CCG Chart Realization. In *Proc. INLG-04*.

Michael White. 2006. Efficient Realization of Coordinate Structures in Combinatory Categorial Grammar. *Research on Language & Computation*, on-line first, March.

Overgeneration and ranking for spoken dialogue systems

Sebastian Varges
Center for the Study of Language and Information
Stanford University
Stanford, CA 94305, USA
varges@stanford.edu

Abstract

We describe an implemented generator for a spoken dialogue system that follows the 'overgeneration and ranking' approach. We find that overgeneration based on bottom-up chart generation is well-suited to a) model phenomena such as alignment and variation in dialogue, and b) address robustness issues in the face of imperfect generation input. We report evaluation results of a first user study involving 20 subjects.

1 Introduction

Overgeneration and ranking approaches have become increasingly popular in recent years (Langkilde, 2002; Varges, 2002). However, most work on generation for practical dialogue systems makes use of generation components that work toward a single output, often using simple templates. In the following, we first describe our dialogue system and then turn to the generator which is based on the overgeneration and ranking paradigm. We outline the results of a user study, followed by a discussion section.

The dialogue system: Dialogue processing starts with the output of a speech recognizer (Nuance) which is analyzed by both a statistical dependency parser and a topic classifier. Parse trees and topic labels are matched by the 'dialogue move scripts' of the dialogue manager (DM) (Mirkovic and Cavedon, 2005). The dialogue system is fully implemented and has been used in restaurant selection and MP3 player tasks (Weng et al., 2004). There are 41 task-independent, generic dialogue rules, 52 restaurant selection rules and 89 MP3 player rules. Query constraints are built by dialogue move scripts if the parse tree matches input patterns specified in the scripts. For example, a request "I want to find an inexpensive Japanese restaurant that takes reservations" results in constraints such as `restaurant:Cuisine = restaurant:japanese` and `restaurant:PriceLevel = 0-10`. If the database query constructed from these constraints returns no results, various constraint modification strategies such as constraint relaxation or removal can be employed. For example, 'Japanese food' can be relaxed to 'Asian food' since cuisine types are hierarchically organized.

2 Overgeneration for spoken dialogue

Table 1 shows some example outputs of the system. The wording of the realizations is informed by a wizard-of-oz data collection. The task of the generator is to produce these verbalizations given dialogue strategy, constraints and further discourse context, i.e. the input to the generator is non-linguistic. We perform mild overgeneration of candidate moves, followed by ranking. The highest-ranked candidate is selected for output.

2.1 Chart generation

We follow a bottom-up chart generation approach (Kay, 1996) for production systems similar to (Varges, 2005). The rule-based core of the generator is a set of productions written in a production system. Productions map individual database constraints to phrases such as "open for lunch", "within 3 miles", "a formal dress code", and recursively combine them into NPs. This includes the use of coordination to produce "restaurants with a 5-star rating and a formal dress code", for example. The NPs are integrated into sentence templates, several of which can be combined

Proceedings of the Fourth International Natural Language Generation Conference
Sydney, July 2006.

	$\|result\|$	mod	example realization	f_{exp}
s1	0	no	I'm sorry but I found no restaurants on Mayfield Road that serve Mediterranean food .	0
s2	small: $> 0, < t_1$	no	There are 2 cheap Thai restaurants in Lincoln in my database : Thai Mee Choke and Noodle House .	61
s3	medium: $>= t_1, < t_2$	no	I found 9 restaurants with a two star rating and a formal dress code that are open for dinner and serve French food . Here are the first ones :	212
s4	large: $>= t_2$	no	I found 258 restaurants on Page Mill Road, for example Maya Restaurant , Green Frog and Pho Hoa Restaurant . Would you like to try searching by cuisine ?	300
s5	large	yes	I found no restaurants that ... However, there are NUM restaurants that ... Would you like to ...?	16
s6	(any)	yes/no	I found 18 items .	2

Table 1: Some system responses ('$|result|$': size of database result set, 'mod': performed modifications). Last column: frequency in user study (180 tasks, 596 constraint inputs to generator)

to form an output candidate turn. For example, a constraint realizing template "I found no [NP-original] but there are [NUM] [NP-optimized] in my database" can be combined with a follow-up sentence template such as "You could try to look for [NP-constraint-suggestion]". 'NP-original' realizes constraints directly constructed from the user utterance; 'NP-optimized' realizes potentially modified constraints used to obtain the actual query result. To avoid generating separate sets of NPs independently for these two – often largely overlapping – constraint sets, we assign unique indices to the input constraints, overgenerate NPs and check their indices.

The generator maintains state across dialogue turns, allowing it to track its previous decisions (see 'variation' below). Both input constraints and chart edges are indexed by turn numbers to avoid confusing edges of different turns.

We currently use 102 productions overall in the restaurant and MP3 domains, 38 of them to generate NPs that realize 19 input constraints.

2.2 Ranking: alignment & variation

Alignment Alignment is a key to successful natural language dialogue (Brockmann et al., 2005). We perform alignment of system utterances with user utterances by computing an ngram-based overlap score. For example, a user utterance "I want to find a Chinese restaurant" is presented by the bag-of-words {'I', 'want', 'to', 'find', ...} and the bag-of-bigrams {'I want', 'want to', 'to find', ...}. We compute the overlap with candidate system utterances represented in the same way and combine the unigram and bigram match scores. Words are lemmatized and proper nouns of example items removed from the utterances.

Alignment allows us to prefer "restaurants that serve Chinese food" over "Chinese restaurants" if the user used a wording more similar to the first. The Gricean Maxim of Brevity, applied to NLG in (Dale and Reiter, 1995), suggests a preference for the second, shorter realization. However, if the user thought it necessary to use "serves", maybe to correct an earlier mislabeling by the classifier/parse-matching patterns, then the system should make it clear that it understood the user correctly by using those same words. On the other hand, a general preference for brevity is desirable in spoken dialogue systems: users are generally not willing to listen to lengthy synthesized speech.

Variation We use a variation score to 'cycle' over sentence-level paraphrases. Alternative candidates for realizing a certain input move are given a unique alternation ('alt') number in increasing order. For example, for the simple move `continuation_query` we may assign the following alt values: "Do you want more?" (alt=1) and "Do you want me to continue?" (alt=2). The system cycles over these alternatives in turn. Once we reach alt=2, it starts over from alt=1. The actual alt 'score' is inversely related to recency and normalized to [0...1].

Score combination The final candidate score is a linear combination of alignment and variation scores:

$$score_{final} = \lambda_1 \cdot align_{uni,bi} + (1 - \lambda_1) \cdot variation \quad (1)$$

$$align_{uni,bi} = \lambda_2 \cdot align_{uni} + (1 - \lambda_2) \cdot align_{bi} \quad (2)$$

where $\lambda_1, \lambda_2 \in \{0...1\}$. A high value of λ_1 places more emphasis on alignment, a low value yields candidates that are more different from previously chosen ones. In our experience, alignment should be given a higher weight than variation, and, within alignment, bigrams should be weighted higher than unigrams, i.e. $\lambda_1 > 0.5$ and $\lambda_2 < 0.5$. Deriving weights empirically from corpus data is an avenue for future research.

3 User study

Each of 20 subjects in a restaurant selection task was given 9 scenario descriptions involving 3 constraints. We use a back-end database of 2500 restaurants containing the 13 attributes/constraints for each restaurant.

On average, the generator produced 16 output candidates for inputs of two constraints, 160 candidates for typical inputs of 3 constraints and 320 candidates for 4 constraints. For larger constraint sets, we currently reduce the level of overgeneration but in the future intend to interleave overgeneration with ranking similar to (Varges, 2002).

Task completion in the experiments was high: the subjects met all target constraints in 170 out of 180 tasks, i.e. completion rate was 94.44%. To the question "The responses of the system were appropriate, helpful, and clear." (on a scale where 1 = 'strongly agree', 5 = 'strongly disagree'), the subjects gave the following ratings: 1: 7, 2: 9, 3: 2, 4: 2 and 5: 0, i.e. the mean user rating is 1.95.

4 Discussion & Conclusions

Where NLG affects the dialogue system: Discourse entities introduced by NLG add items to the system's salience list as an equal partner to NLU.

Robustness: due to imperfect ASR and NLU, we relax completeness requirements when doing overgeneration, and reason about the generation input by adding defaults for missing constraints, checking ranges of attribute values etc. Moreover, we use a template generator as a fall-back if NLG fails to at least give some feedback to the user (s6 in table 1).

What-to-say vs how-to-say-it: the classic separation of NLG into separate modules also holds in our dialogue system, albeit with some modifications: 'content determination' is ultimately performed by the user and the constraint optimizer. The presentation dialogue moves do microplanning, for example by deciding to present retrieved database items either as examples (s4 in table 1) or as part of a larger answer list of items. The chart generator performs realization.

In sum, flexible and expressive NLG is crucial for the robustness of the entire speech-based dialogue system by verbalizing what the system understood and what actions it performed as a consequence of this understanding. We find that overgeneration and ranking techniques allow us to model alignment and variation even in situations where no corpus data is available by using the discourse history as a 'corpus'.

Acknowledgments This work is supported by the US government's NIST Advanced Technology Program. Collaborating partners are CSLI, Robert Bosch Corporation, VW America, and SRI International. We thank the many people involved in this project, in particular Fuliang Weng and Heather Pon-Barry for developing the content optimization module; Annie Lien, Badri Raghunathan, Brian Lathrop, Fuliang Weng, Heather Pon-Barry, Jeff Russell, and Tobias Scheideck for performing the evaluations and compiling the results; Matthew Purver and Florin Ratiu for work on the CSLI dialogue manager. The content optimizer, knowledge manager, and the NLU module have been developed by the Bosch Research and Technology Center.

References

Carsten Brockmann, Amy Isard, Jon Oberlander, and Michael White. 2005. Modelling alignment for affective dialogue. In *Proc. of the UM'05 Workshop on Adapting the Interaction Style to Affective Factors.*

Robert Dale and Ehud Reiter. 1995. Computational Interpretations of the Gricean Maxims in the Generation of Referring Expressions. *Cognitive Science*, 19:233–263.

Martin Kay. 1996. Chart Generation. In *Proceedings of ACL-96*, pages 200–204.

Irene Langkilde. 2002. An Empirical Verification of Coverage and Correctness for a General-Purpose Sentence Generator. In *Proc. of INLG-02.*

Danilo Mirkovic and Lawrence Cavedon. 2005. Practical Plug-and-Play Dialogue Management. In *Proceedings of the 6th Meeting of the Pacific Association for Computational Linguistics (PACLING).*

Sebastian Varges. 2002. Fluency and Completeness in Instance-based Natural Language Generation. In *Proc. of COLING-02.*

Sebastian Varges. 2005. Chart generation using production systems (short paper). In *Proc. of 10th European Workshop On Natural Language Generation.*

Fuliang Weng, L. Cavedon, B. Raghunathan, D. Mirkovic, H. Cheng, H. Schmidt, H. Bratt, R. Mishra, S. Peters, L. Zhao, S. Upson, E. Shriberg, and C. Bergmann. 2004. Developing a conversational dialogue system for cognitively overloaded users. In *Proceedings of the International Congress on Intelligent Transportation Systems (ICSLP).*

Individuality and Alignment in Generated Dialogues

Amy Isard and **Carsten Brockmann** and **Jon Oberlander**
School of Informatics, University of Edinburgh
2 Buccleuch Place
Edinburgh EH8 9LW, UK
{Amy.Isard, Carsten.Brockmann, J.Oberlander}@ed.ac.uk

Abstract

It would be useful to enable dialogue agents to project, through linguistic means, their individuality or personality. Equally, each member of a pair of agents ought to adjust its language (to a greater or lesser extent) to match that of its interlocutor. We describe CRAG, which generates dialogues between pairs of agents, who are linguistically distinguishable, but able to align. CRAG-2 makes use of OPENCCG and an over-generation and ranking approach, guided by a set of language models covering both personality and alignment. We illustrate with examples of output, and briefly note results from user studies with the earlier CRAG-1, indicating how CRAG-2 will be further evaluated. Related work is discussed, along with current limitations and future directions.

1 Introduction

A computer agent should be *individual*. Nass and collaborators find that users' responses to computer-agents are influenced by whether the agent's linguistic personality matches—or mismatches—the personality of the user (Moon and Nass, 1996; Nass and Lee, 2000). Similarly, characters in virtual environments should be distinctive (Ball and Breese, 2000; Rist et al., 2003). But an aspect of personality is how well you adjust to other people (and their language use): *alignment*. Pickering and Garrod's Interactive Alignment Model suggests that people tend to automatically converge on lexical and syntactic choices, via a low-level mechanism of interpersonal priming (Pickering and Garrod, 2004), and Brennan has shown that people will align their language towards that of computer agents (Brennan, 1996). But it is an open issue as to whether some people are better 'aligners' than others. Conversely, alignment is only visible and interesting (among computer agents) if they start out being individual.

We therefore set out to simulate *both* individuality and alignment. The paper briefly surveys the evidence for linguistic personality, for interpersonal alignment, and for interaction between them. It then sketches the current version of CRAG. CRAG-2 makes use of OPENCCG and an over-generation and ranking approach, guided by a set of language models for personality and alignment. We illustrate the differing linguistic behaviours that it generates, and briefly note promising results from user studies with the earlier CRAG-1 system, indicating how CRAG-2 will be further evaluated. Related work is discussed, along with possible directions for future work.

2 Background

2.1 Personality and Language

Current work on personality traits is dominated by Costa and McCrae's five-factor model (Costa and McCrae, 1992). The five factors, or dimensions, are: Extraversion; Neuroticism; Openness; Agreeableness; and Conscientiousness (Matthews et al., 2003). It has been shown that scores on these dimensions correlate with some aspects of language use (Scherer, 1979; Dewaele and Furnham, 1999). In studies of text, the focus has been on lexical choice, and Pennebaker and colleagues have analysed relative frequencies of use of word-stems in a dictionary structured into semantic and syntactic categories (Pennebaker et al., 2001). Amongst other results, they have shown that High Extraverts

Proceedings of the Fourth International Natural Language Generation Conference
Sydney, July 2006.

use: more social process talk, positive emotion words and inclusives; and fewer negations, tentative words, exclusives, causation words, negative emotion words, and articles (Pennebaker and King, 1999; Pennebaker et al., 2002).

Computational linguistic exploitation of such empirically-derived features has been limited. On the one hand, in generation, there has been work on personality-based generation. For instance, in developing embodied conversational agents, researchers have designed agents or teams of agents with distinguishable linguistic personalities (Ball and Breese, 2000; Rist et al., 2003; Piwek and van Deemter, 2003; Gebhard, 2005). However, the linguistic behaviour is usually informed by rules based on personality stereotypes, rather than on language statistics themselves. On the other hand, in interpretation, more empirical work has recently been carried out, to enable text classification. Argamon et al. (2005) attempted to classify authors as High or Low Extravert and High or Low Neurotic, using Pennebaker and King's (1999) data. They report classification accuracies of around 58% (with a 50% baseline). Oberlander and Nowson (2006) undertake a comparable task, using weblog data. They report classification accuracies of roughly 85% (Neuroticism) and 94% (Extraversion), and comparable figures for Agreeableness and Conscientiousness. Such studies can provide ordered lists of linguistic features which are useful for distinguishing language producers, and we will return to this, below.

2.2 Alignment and Language

People converge with their interlocutors in linguistic choices at a number of levels (Pickering and Garrod, 2004). The phenomena can be seen in both social and cognitive terms. On the social side, co-operative processes such as audience design are usually considered to be conscious, at least in part (Bell, 1984). But on the cognitive side, coordinative processes such as alignment are usually considered to be largely automatic (Garrod and Doherty, 1994). Alignment can be probed by psycholinguistic tests for interpersonal priming, establishing the extent to which participants are more likely to use a lexical item or syntactic construction after hearing their conversational partner use it. Syntactic priming experiments involve constructions such as passives, and ditransitives (Pickering and Branigan, 1998).

It is possible that some people are stronger aligners than others. Gill et al. (2004) probed syntactic priming for passives, and investigated whether levels of Extraversion or Neuroticism would affect the strength of priming effects. It was found that Extraversion has no effect, but that Neuroticism has a non-linear effect: both High and Low levels of Neuroticism led to weaker priming; Mid levels led to significantly stronger priming. Given this, if a generation system is going to simulate alignment, it is probably worth designing it so that it can simulate agents with differing propensities to align.

3 The CRAG System Overview

The system described in the following sections (CRAG-2) is the successor to CRAG-1 which is detailed in Isard et al. (2005). The system generates a dialogue between two computer agents on the subject of opinions about a film. CRAG-2 uses the OPENCCG parsing and generation framework (White, 2004; White, 2006). The realiser component takes a logical form as input and outputs a list of candidate sentences ranked using one or more language models. In CRAG-2, we use the OPENCCG generator to massively over-generate paraphrases, and the combination of n-gram models described in Section 4 to choose the best utterance according to a character's personality and agenda, and the dialogue history.

4 N-Grams: Personality and Alignment Modelling

4.1 N-Gram Language Models

The basic assumption underlying CRAG-2 is that personality, as well as alignment behaviour, can be modelled by the combination of a variety of n-gram language models.

Language models are trained on a corpus and subsequently used to compute probability scores of word sequences. An n-gram language model approximates the probability of a word given its history of the preceding $n-1$ words. According to the chain rule, probabilities are then combined by multiplication. Equation (1) shows a trigram model that takes into account two words of context to predict the probability of a word sequence w_1^n:

(1) $$P(w_1^n) \approx \prod_{i=1}^{n} P(w_i | w_{i-2}^{i-1})$$

4.2 Avoiding the Length Effect

Because word probabilities are always less than 1 and therefore each multiplication decreases the total, if we use this standard model, longer sentences will always receive lower scores (this is known as the length effect). We therefore calculate the probability of a sentence as the geometric mean of the probability of each word in the sentence as shown in (2):

(2) $$P(w_1^n) \approx \prod_{i=1}^{n} P(w_i|w_{i-2}^{i-1})^{1/n}$$

4.3 Linear Combination of Language Models

OPENCCG supports the linear combination of language models, where each model is assigned a weight. For uniform interpolation of two language models P_a and P_b, each receives equal weight:

(3) $$P(w_i|w_{i-2}^{i-1}) = \frac{P_a(w_i|w_{i-2}^{i-1}) + P_b(w_i|w_{i-2}^{i-1})}{2}$$

In the more general case, the language models are assigned weights λ_i, the sum of which has to be 1:

(4) $$P(w_i|w_{i-2}^{i-1}) = \lambda_1 P_a(w_i|w_{i-2}^{i-1}) + \lambda_2 P_b(w_i|w_{i-2}^{i-1})$$

For example, setting $\lambda_1 = 0.9$ and $\lambda_2 = 0.1$ assigns a high weight to the first language model.

4.4 OPENCCG N-Gram Ranking

In the OPENCCG framework, language models can be used to influence the chart-based realisation process. The agenda of edges is re-sorted according to the score an edge receives with respect to a language model. For CRAG-2, many paraphrases are generated from a given logical form, and they are then ranked in order of probability according to the combination of n-gram models appropriate for the character and stage of the dialogue.

5 CRAG-2 Personality and Alignment Models

We use the SRILM toolkit (Stolcke, 2002) to compute our language models. All models (except for the cache language model described in Section 5.4) are trigram models with backoff to bigrams and unigrams.

We have experimented with two strategies for creating personality models. Since we want to study the effects of alignment as well as personality, it is essential that the two characters in a dialogue be distinct from one another, so that the effects of alignment can be seen. The first strategy involves using typical language for each personality trait, and the second uses the language of one individual. In both cases, the language models described in the following sections are combined as described in Section 5.5.

5.1 Building a Personality

Nowson (2006) performed a study on language use in weblogs. The weblog authors were asked to complete personality questionnaires based on the five-factor model (see Section 2.1). All weblog authors scored High or Medium on the Openness dimension, so we have no data for typical Low Open language.

We divided the data into High, Medium and Low for each personality dimension, and trained language models so that we would be able to assess the probability of a word sequence given a personality type. This means that each individual weblog is used 5 times, once for each dimension.

For each personality dimension, the system simplifies a character's personality setting x by assigning a value of High ($x > 70$), Medium ($30 < x \leq 70$) or Low ($x \leq 30$). The five models corresponding to the character's assigned personality are uniformly interpolated to give the final personality model. If the character has been given a low Openness score, since we do not have a model for this personality type, we simply interpolate the other four models.

5.2 Borrowing a Personality

Our second strategy was to train n-gram models on language of the individuals from the CRAG-1 corpus (Isard et al., 2005) and to use one of these models for each character in the dialogue.

5.3 Base Language Model

In the case of building a personality, a base language model is obtained by combining a language model computed from the corpus collected for the CRAG-1 system and a general language model based on data from the Switchboard corpus (Stolcke et al., 2000). The combined base model alone would rank the utterances without any bias for personality or alignment. When we are borrowing a personality, the base model is calculated from the Switchboard corpus alone.

5.4 Cache Language Model

We simulate alignment by computing a cache language model based on the utterance that was generated immediately before. This dialogue history cache model is the uniform interpolation of word- and class-based n-gram models, where classes act as a backoff mechanism when there is no exact word match. Classes group together lexical items with similar semantic properties, e.g.:

- *good*, *bad*: `quality-adjective`
- *loved*, *hated*: `opinion-verb`

Details of this approach can be found in Brockmann et al. (2005).

5.5 Combining the Language Models

The system uses weights to combine all the models described above. First the base and personality models are interpolated to produce a base-personality model, and finally the cache model is introduced to add alignment effects.

6 Dialogue and Utterance Specifications

6.1 Character Specification

Two computer characters are parameterised for their personality by specifying values (on a scale from 0 to 100) for the five dimensions: Extraversion (E), Neuroticism (N), Openness (O), Agreeableness (A), and Conscientiousness (C). Their alignment behaviour is set to a value between 0 (low propensity to align) and 1 (high propensity to align). Also, each character receives an agenda of topics they wish to discuss, along with polarities (positive/negative) that indicate their opinion on the respective topic.

6.2 Utterance Design

The character with the higher Extraversion score begins the dialogue, and their first topic is selected. Once an utterance has been generated, the other character is selected, and the system applies the algorithm shown in (5) to decide which topic should come next. This process continues until there are no topics left on the agenda of the current speaker.

(5) **if** (A $<$ 46) or (C $<$ 46) or
(no. of utts about this topic $=$ 2)
then take next topic from own agenda
else continue on same topic

The system creates a simple XML representation of the character's utterance, using the specified topic and polarity. An example using the topic music and polarity negative is shown in Figure 1. At this point the system also decides which discourse connectives may be appropriate, based on the previous topic and polarity.

```
<utterance>
  <utt topic="music" polarity="dislike"
       opp-polarity="like" so="no" right="no"
       also="no" well="yes" and="no" but="no">
    <pred adj="bad"/>
    <opp-pred adj="good"/>
  </utt>
</utterance>
```

Figure 1: Simple Utterance Specification

6.3 OpenCCG Logical Forms

Following the method described in Foster and White (2004), the basic utterance specification is transformed, using stylesheets written in the XSL transformation language, into an OpenCCG logical form. We make use of the facility for defining optional and alternative inputs and underspecified semantics to massively over-generate candidate utterances. A fragment of the logical form which results from the transformation of Figure 1 is shown in Figure 2. We also include some fragments of canned text from the CRAG corpus in our OpenCCG lexicon.

We also add optional interjections (*i mean*, *you know*, *sort of*) and conversational markers (*right*, *but*, *and*, *well*) where appropriate given the discourse history.

When the full logical form is processed by the OpenCCG system, the output consists of sentences of the types shown below:

(I think) the music was bad.
(I think) the music was not (wasn't) good.
I did not (didn't) like the music.
I hated the music.
One thing I did not (didn't) like was the music.
One thing I hated was the music.

The fragmentary logical form in Figure 2 would create all possible paraphrases from:

(well) (you know) I (kind of) [liked/loved] the [music/score]

By using synonyms (e.g., plot=story, comedy=humour) and combining the sentence types

```
<node id="l1:opinion" pred="like" tense="past">
  <rel name="Speaker">
    <node id="p1:person" pred="pro1" num="sg"/>
  </rel>
  <rel name="Content">
    <node id="f1:cragtopic" pred="music"
          det="the" num="sg"/>
  </rel>
  <opt>
    <rel name="Modifier">
      <node id="w1:adv" pred="well"/>
    </rel>
  <opt>
  <opt>
    <rel name="HasProp">
      <node id="a2:proposition" pred="kind-of"/>
    </rel>
  </opt>
  <opt>
    <rel name="Modifier">
      <node id="a1:adv" pred="you-know"/>
    </rel>
  </opt>
</node>
```

Figure 2: Fragment of Logical Form

Stan: E:53 N:48 A:57 C:46 O:65
agenda: film(neg), dialogue(neg), music(pos)
other opinions: plot(neg), comedy(neg)

Eddie: E:51 N:43 A:57 C:41 O:65
agenda: plot(neg), comedy(neg), dialogue(neg)
other opinions: music(pos), film(neg)

Figure 3: Stan and Eddie

and optional expressions, we create up to 3000 possibilities per utterance, and the best candidate is chosen by the specific combination of n-gram models appropriate for the given personality and dialogue history, as described in Section 4.

Our OPENCCG lexicon is based on the core English lexicon included with the system and we have added vocabulary appropriate to the movie domain, and extended the range of grammatical constructions where necessary.

7 Output and Evaluation

7.1 Output

In this section, we provide some example outputs from the CRAG-2 system, using characters based on participants from our corpus (see Section 5.2). Stan is higher on the Extraversion, Neuroticism, and Conscientiousness scales than Eddie. The characters' personalities and agendas are summarised in Figure 3.

We show three example dialogues between Stan and Eddie. In the first (Figure 4) neither character aligns with the other at all, while in the second (Figure 5) Stan has a slight tendency towards alignment and in the third (Figure 6) a more pronounced tendency. In system terms, this means that in the first dialogue the cache model was given weight 0, while in the second and third the cache model was given weights 0.05 and 0.1 respectively for Stan's utterances. It can be seen that in the first dialogue, Eddie's use of *humour* in utterance 4 is followed by Stan's *comedy*, and *dialogue* in utterance 6 is followed by *script*. In the second dialogue, Stan aligns his first lexical choice with Eddie's but not his second, while in the third dialogue he aligns both. The syntactic structures of Stan's utterances in the second and third dialogue also mirror Eddie's progressively more closely.

1. Stan: I didn't think much of the film you know.
2. Eddie: I mean I didn't like kind of like the story.
3. Stan: Yeah there were so many little pathways that they didn't take you know.
4. Eddie: I mean I didn't think the humour was really funny.
5. Stan: Yeah you know the comedy was a bit dull.
6. Eddie: I mean I didn't like kind of like the dialogue.
7. Stan: I mean the script was a bit dull.

Figure 4: Zero Alignment

1. Stan: I didn't think much of the film you know.
2. Eddie: I mean I didn't like kind of like the story.
3. Stan: Yeah there were so many little pathways that they didn't take you know.
4. Eddie: I mean I didn't think the humour was really funny.
5. Stan: I mean the humour was a bit dull.
6. Eddie: I mean I didn't like kind of like the dialogue.
7. Stan: I mean the script was a bit dull.

Figure 5: Little Alignment from Stan

1. Stan: I didn't think much of the film you know.
2. Eddie: I mean I didn't like kind of like the story.
3. Stan: I mean the story was a bit dull.
4. Eddie: I mean I didn't think the humour was really funny.
5. Stan: I mean the humour was a bit dull.
6. Eddie: I mean I didn't like kind of like the dialogue.
7. Stan: I mean the dialogue was a bit dull.

Figure 6: More Alignment from Stan

To further illustrate the differences between the dialogues with and without alignment, we provide some utterance rankings. We show candidates for the fifth utterance in each dialogue. Table 1 shows sentences from the example generated without alignment, corresponding to utterance 5 (Stan)

1	.03317	Yeah you know the comedy was a bit dull.
3	.03210	Yeah you know the humour was a bit dull.
6	.03083	Yeah to be honest I didn't think that the comedy was very good either.
15	.02938	I didn't think much of the comedy either.
24	.02861	I thought that the comedy was a bit dull too you know.

Table 1: Ranked Sentences with Zero Alignment

1	.05384	I mean the humour was a bit dull.
8	.05239	The humour wasn't really funny you know.
15	.04748	I mean I didn't think that the humour was very good either.
19	.04518	I didn't think much of the humour either you know.
21	.04478	I thought the humour was a bit dull too you know.

Table 2: Ranked Sentences with Little Alignment from Stan

from Figure 4. We show the first five occurrences of different sentence structures (see Section 6.3), with their rank and their geometric mean adjusted scores.

Table 2 shows the the top five sentences from the fifth utterance from Figure 5 (little alignment), and Table 3 those from Figure 6 (more alignment). It can be seen that when more alignment is present, the syntactic structure used by the previous speaker rises higher in the rankings.

7.2 Evaluation

We have not evaluated CRAG-2. However, we have evaluated CRAG-1. The method was to generate a set of dialogues, systematically contrasting characters with extreme settings for the personality dimensions (High/Low Extraversion, Neuroticism, and Psychoticism[1]).

[1] CRAG-1 used the simpler PEN three factor personality model.

1	.07081	I mean the humour was a bit dull.
2	.06432	The humour wasn't really funny you know.
15	.05516	I mean I didn't think that the humour was really funny either.
27	.05000	I thought the humour was a bit dull too you know.
36	.04884	I mean I didn't think much of the humour either.

Table 3: Ranked Sentences with More Alignment from Stan

Human subjects were asked to fill in a questionnaire to determine their personality. They were then given a selection of dialogues to read. After each dialogue, they were asked to rate their perception of the interaction and of the characters involved by assigning scores to a number of adjectives related to the personality dimensions.

It was found that subjects could recognise differences in the Extraversion level of the language. Also, the personality setting of a character influenced the perception of its and its dialogue partner's personality (Kahn, 2006).

We plan a similar evaluation for CRAG-2 to be able to compare human raters' impressions of dialogues generated by the two systems. We also plan to evaluate CRAG-2 internally by varying the weight given to the underlying language models, and observing the effects this has on the resulting ranking of the generated utterances.

8 Related Work

Related work in NLG involves either personality or alignment. So far as we can tell, there is little work on the latter. Varges (2005) suggests that "a word similarity-based ranker could align the generation output (i.e. the highest-ranked candidate) with previous utterances in the discourse context", but there is no report yet on an implementation of this proposal. A rather different approach is suggested by Bateman and Paris (2005), who discuss initial work on alignment, mediated by a process of register-recognition. Regarding generation with personality, the most influential work is probably Hovy's PAULINE system, which varies both content selection and realisation according to an individual speaker's goals and attitudes (Hovy, 1990). In her extremely useful survey of work on affective (particularly, emotional) natural language generation, Belz (2003) notes that the complexity of PAULINE's rule system means that numerous rule interactions can lead to unpredictable side effects. In response, Paiva and Evans (2004) take a more empirical line on style generation, which is closer to that pursued here. Other relevant work includes Loyall and Bates (1997), who explicitly propose that personality and emotion could be used in generation, but Belz observes that technical descriptions of Hap and the Oz project suggest that the proposals were not implemented. Walker et al.'s (1997) system produces linguistic behaviour which is much more varied than our current system is capable of; but there, variation is driven by a model of social relations (based on Brown and Levinson), rather than on personality. The NECA project subsequently developed methods for generating scripts for pairs of dialogue agents (Piwek and van Deemter, 2003), supported by the MIAU platform (Rist et al., 2003). The VIRTUALHUMAN project is a logical successor to this work, and its ALMA platform provides an integrated approach to affective generation, covering emotion, mood and personality (Gebhard, 2005).

9 Conclusion and Next Steps

Our current system takes a much coarser-grained approach to semantics and discourse goals than the recent projects described above, in order to take advantage of empirically-derived relations between language and personality. It should be feasible in principle to move to a more sophisticated semantics, but still retain the massive overgeneration and ranking method. However, to support more perceptible variation, we need to exploit much larger personality-corpus resources than have been available up to now, and our current priority is to obtain a corpus at least an order of magnitude larger than what is currently available. This interest in individual differences and what corpora can (and cannot) tell us about them is one we share with Reiter and colleagues (Reiter and Sripada, 2004).

We also plan to integrate techniques from CRAG-1 and CRAG-2, by passing the ranked output of CRAG-2 through further processing and ranking stages. Furthermore, we intend to investigate longer-ranging alignment processes, taking into account more than one previous utterance, with reduced weight by distance, to emulate memory effects.

With these enhancements, we will take further steps towards our goal of simulating both individuality and alignment in believable computer agents.

10 Acknowledgements

This research has been funded by Scottish Enterprise through the Edinburgh-Stanford Link project "Critical Agent Dialogue" (CRAG). We would like to thank Michael White and Scott Nowson for their assistance and our anonymous reviewers for their helpful comments.

References

Shlomo Argamon, Sushant Dhawle, Moshe Koppel, and James W. Pennebaker. 2005. Lexical predictors of personality type. In *Proceedings of the 2005 Joint Annual Meeting of the Interface and the Classification Society of North America*.

Gene Ball and Jack Breese. 2000. Emotion and personality in a conversational agent. In J. Cassell, J. Sullivan, S. Prevost, and E. Churchill, editors, *Embodied Conversational Agents*, pages 189–219. MIT Press, Cambridge, MA, USA.

John A. Bateman and Cécile L. Paris. 2005. Adaptation to affective factors: architectural impacts for natural language generation and dialogue. In *Proceedings of the Workshop on Adapting the Interaction Style to Affective Factors at the 10th International Conference on User Modeling (UM-05)*, Edinburgh, UK.

Allan Bell. 1984. Language style as audience design. *Language in Society*, 13(2):145–204.

Anja Belz. 2003. And now with feeling: Developments in emotional language generation. Technical Report ITRI-03-21, Information Technology Research Institute, University of Brighton, Brighton.

Susan E. Brennan. 1996. Lexical entrainment in spontaneous dialog. In *Proceedings of the 1996 International Symposium on Spoken Dialogue (ISSD-96)*, pages 41–44, Philadelphia, PA.

Carsten Brockmann, Amy Isard, Jon Oberlander, and Michael White. 2005. Modelling alignment for affective dialogue. In *Proceedings of the Workshop on Adapting the Interaction Style to Affective Factors at the 10th International Conference on User Modeling (UM-05)*, Edinburgh, UK.

Paul T. Costa and Robert R. McCrae, 1992. *Revised NEO Personality Inventory (NEO-PI-R) and NEO Five-Factor Inventory (NEO-FFI): Professional Manual*. Odessa, FL: Psychological Assessment Resources.

Jean-Marc Dewaele and Adrian Furnham. 1999. Extraversion: The unloved variable in applied linguistic research. *Language Learning*, 49:509–544.

Mary Ellen Foster and Michael White. 2004. Techniques for Text Planning with XSLT. In *Proc. of the 4th NLPXML Workshop*.

Simon Garrod and Gwyneth Doherty. 1994. Conversation, co-ordination and convention: an empirical investigation of how groups establish linguistic conventions. *Cognition*, 53(3):181–215.

Patrick Gebhard. 2005. Alma: a layered model of affect. In *AAMAS '05: Proceedings of the Fourth International Joint Conference on Autonomous Agents and Multiagent Systems*, pages 29–36, New York, NY, USA. ACM Press.

Alastair J. Gill, Annabel J. Harrison, and Jon Oberlander. 2004. Interpersonality: Individual differences and interpersonal priming. In *Proceedings of the 26th Annual Conference of the Cognitive Science Society*, pages 464–469.

Eduard Hovy. 1990. Pragmatics and natural language generation. *Artificial Intelligence*, 43.

Amy Isard, Carsten Brockmann, and Jon Oberlander. 2005. Re-creating dialogues from a corpus. In *Proceedings of the Workshop on Using Corpora for Natural Language Generation at Corpus Linguistics 2005 (CL-05)*, pages 7–12, Birmingham, UK.

Adam S. Kahn. 2006. Master's thesis, Stanford University.

A. Bryan Loyall and Joseph Bates. 1997. Personality-rich believable agents that use language. In J. Lewis and B. Hayes-Roth, editors, *Proceedings of the 1st International Conference on Autonomous Agents (Agents'97)*. ACM Press.

Gerald Matthews, Ian J. Deary, and Martha C. Whiteman. 2003. *Personality Traits*. Cambridge University Press, Cambridge, 2nd edition.

Youngme Moon and Clifford Nass. 1996. How "real" are computer personalities? *Communication Research*, 23:651–674.

Clifford Nass and Kwan Min Lee. 2000. Does computer-generated speech manifest personality? an experimental test of similarity-attraction. In *Proceedings of CHI 2000, The Hague, Amsterdam, 2000*, pages 329–336.

Scott Nowson. 2006. *The Language of Weblogs: A study of genre and individual differences*. Ph.D. thesis, University of Edinburgh.

Jon Oberlander and Scott Nowson. 2006. Whose thumb is it anyway? Classifying author personality from weblog text. In *Proceedings of COLING/ACL-06: 44th Annual Meeting of the Association for Computational Linguistics and 21st International Conference on Computational Linguistics*, Sydney.

Daniel S. Paiva and Roger Evans. 2004. A framework for stylistically controlled generation. In *Proceedings of the 3rd International Conference on Natural Language Generation*, pages 120–129.

James W. Pennebaker and Laura King. 1999. Linguistic styles: Language use as an individual difference. *Journal of Personality and Social Psychology*, 77:1296–1312.

James W. Pennebaker, Martha E. Francis, and Roger J. Booth. 2001. *Linguistic Inquiry and Word Count 2001*. Lawrence Erlbaum Associates, Mahwah, NJ.

James W. Pennebaker, Matthias R. Mehl, and Kate G. Neiderhoffer. 2002. Psychological aspects of natural language use: Our words, our selves. *Annual Review of Psychology*, 54:547–577.

Martin J. Pickering and Holly P. Branigan. 1998. The representation of verbs: Evidence from syntactic priming in language production. *Journal of Memory and Language*, 39(4):633–651.

Martin J. Pickering and Simon Garrod. 2004. Towards a mechanistic psychology of dialogue. *Behavioral and Brain Sciences*, 27:169–225.

Paul Piwek and Kees van Deemter. 2003. Dialogue as discourse: Controlling global properties of scripted dialogue. In *Proceedings of the AAAI Spring Symposium on Natural Language Generation in Spoken and Written Dialogue*.

Ehud Reiter and Somayajulu Sripada. 2004. Contextual influences on near-synonym choice. In *Proceedings of the Third International Conference on Natural Language Generation*, pages 161–170.

Thomas Rist, Elisabeth André, and Stephan Baldes. 2003. A flexible platform for building applications with life-like characters. In *IUI '03: Proceedings of the 8th International Conference on Intelligent User Interfaces*, pages 158–165, New York, NY, USA. ACM Press.

Klaus Scherer. 1979. Personality markers in speech. In K. R. Scherer and H. Giles, editors, *Social Markers in Speech*, pages 147–209. Cambridge University Press, Cambridge.

Andreas Stolcke, Harry Bratt, John Butzberger, Horacio Franco, Venkata Ramana Rao Gadde, Madelaine Plauché, Colleen Richey, Elizabeth Shriberg, Kemal Sönmez, Fuliang Weng, and Jing Zheng. 2000. The SRI March 2000 Hub-5 conversational speech transcription system. In *Proceedings of the 2000 Speech Transcription Workshop*, College Park, MD.

Andreas Stolcke. 2002. SRILM – an extensible language modeling toolkit. In *Proceedings of the 7th International Conference on Spoken Language Processing (ICSLP-02)*, pages 901–904, Denver, CO.

Sebastian Varges. 2005. Spatial descriptions as referring expressions in the MapTask domain. In *Proceedings of the 10th European Workshop on Natural Language Generation*.

Marilyn A. Walker, Janet E. Cahn, and Steve J. Whittaker. 1997. Improvising linguistic style: Social and affective bases for agent personality. In J. Lewis and B. Hayes-Roth, editors, *Proceedings of the 1st International Conference on Autonomous Agents (Agents'97)*, pages 96–105. ACM Press.

Michael White. 2004. Reining in CCG Chart Realization. In *Proceedings of the 3rd International Conference on Natural Language Generation*, pages 182–191.

Michael White. 2006. Efficient Realization of Coordinate Structures in Combinatory Categorial Grammar. *Research on Language & Computation*, online first, March.

Using Distributional Similarity to Identify Individual Verb Choice

Jing Lin
Department of Computing Science
University of Aberdeen
jlin@csd.abdn.ac.uk

Abstract

Human text is characterised by the individual lexical choices of a specific author. Significant variations exist between authors. In contrast, natural language generation systems normally produce uniform texts. In this paper we apply distributional similarity measures to help verb choice in a natural language generation system which tries to generate text similar to individual author. By using a distributional similarity (DS) measure on corpora collected from a recipe domain, we get the most likely verbs for individual authors. The accuracy of matching verb pairs produced by distributional similarity is higher than using the synonym outputs of verbs from WordNet. Furthermore, the combination of the two methods provides the best accuracy.

1 Introduction

Human text is characterised by the individual lexical choices of the specific author. It varies from author to author. Individual authors use different verbs to describe the same action. Natural language generation (NLG) systems, in contrast, normally produce uniform outputs without considering other lexical possibilities. Consider the following example from our corpora that are the BBC corpus and the Recipes for health eating corpus.

1. *BBC Corpus: Finely grate the ginger and squeeze out the juice into a shallow non-metallic dish. (BBC online recipes)*

2. *Author2: Extract juice from orange and add this with the water to the saucepan. (Recipes for health eating).*

Here, we can see that the two authors express the same type of action with different verbs, 'squeeze' and 'extract'. In fact, when expressing this action, the BBC corpus always use the verb 'squeeze', and Author2 only uses the verb 'extract'. Therefore, we can assume that Author2 considers the verb 'extract' to describe the same action as the verb 'squeeze' used by the BBC corpus. The purpose of our research is to develop a NLG system that can detect these kinds of individual writing features, such as the verb choice of individual authors, and can then generate personalised text.

The input of our personalised NLG system is an unseen recipe from the BBC food website. Our system, then, translates all sentences into the style of a personal author based on features drawn from analysing an individual corpus we collected. In this paper, we address the verb choice of the individual author in the translation process.

Our system defines the writing style of an individual author by analysing an individual corpus. Therefore, our system is a corpus-based NLG system. Lexical choice for individual authors is predicted by analysing the distributional similarity between words in a general large recipe corpus that is used to produce the verbs as the action representation and words in a specific indi-

Proceedings of the Fourth International Natural Language Generation Conference
Sydney, July 2006.

vidual recipe corpus. Firstly, we collected a large corpus in the recipe domain from the BBC online website. This large recipe corpus is used to extract feature values, for example verb choice, by analysing an individual corpus. Secondly, we collected our individual corpora for a number of individual authors. Each of them is used to extract feature values that may define the individual writing style. The individual author may choose the same or a different verb to describe cooking actions. The question is how can we identify the individual choice? For example, Author2 uses the verb 'extract' instead of the verb 'squeeze'. However, if the author does express the action by a different verb, the problem is how our system picks out verbs according to the individual choice of an author.

One way to solve this problem is to access large-scale manually constructed thesauri such as WordNet (Fellbaum, 1998), Roget's (Roget, 1911) or the Macquarie (Bernard, 1990) to get all synonyms and choose the most frequent one in the individual corpus. Another possible way is to use a lexical knowledge based system, like VerbNet (Kipper et al., 2000) to get more possible lexical choices. However, both methods only provide a number of pre-produced lexical choices that may or may not be the words that the individual author would choose. In other words, the lexical choice of an author may not be based on the synonyms extracted from one of the thesauri or may not even belong to the same semantic class. In our example, 'squeeze' and 'extract' are neither synonyms nor Coordinate Terms in WordNet. In a small domain, it is possible to manually build a verb list so that each action is described by a set of possible verbs. The drawback is that this is expensive. Furthermore, it still cannot catch verbs that are not included in the list. Is it possible to predict the individual verbs automatically?

The distributional hypothesis (Harris, 1968) says the following:

> The meaning of entities, and the meaning of grammatical relations among them, is related to the restriction of combinations of these entities relative to other entities.

Over recent years, many applications (Lin, 1998), (Lee, 1999), (Lee, 2001), (Weeds et al., 2004), and (Weeds and Weir, 2006) have been investigating the distributional similarity of words. Similarity means that words with similar meaning tend to appear in similar contexts. In NLG, the consideration of semantic similarity is usually preferred to just distributional similarity. However, in our case, the most important thing is to capture the most probable choice of a verb of an individual author for expressing an action. The expression of an action can be either the same verb, synonyms, or Coordinate terms to the verb in the big corpus, or any verbs that an individual author chooses for this action. If we check an individual corpus, there are a set of verbs in our list that do not occur. If these actions occur in the individual corpus, the individual author must use different verbs. Distributional similarity technology helps us to build the links between verbs in our list and the verbs in an individual corpus.

The rest of this paper is organised as follows. In Section 2, we describe the recipe domain, our corpora and our verb list. Section 3 disscuss our baseline system. In Section 4, we present the distributional similarity measures that we are proposing for analysing our corpora. The combination method is disscussed in Section5. In Section 6, we present an evaluation of our results. In Section 7, we draw conclusions and discuss future work.

2 The Recipe Domain and our Corpora

To find the most expressive verb pairs, we have to have corpora to be analysed. Therefore, the selection of a corpus is very important. As the research of authorship attribution (AA) shows (Burrow, 1987), (Holmes and Forsyth, 1995), (Keuelj et al., 2003), (Peng, 2003), and (Clement and Sharp, 2003), there can be style variations of an individual author. This happens even with the same topic and genre, and for the same action expressions. Firstly, a person's writing style can change as time, genre, and topic change. Can and Patton (Can and Patton, 2004) have drawn the conclusion:

> A higher time gap may have positive impact in separation and categorization.

Even within one text, the style may not be uniform. (Burrow, 1987) has pointed out that, for example, in fiction:

> The language of its dialogue and that of its narrative usually differ from each other in some obvious and many less obvious ways.

These problems require us to collect high-quality corpora. The recipe domain is a good start in this case. Sentences in it are narrative, imperative and objective, compared with other normal human text. For example, journal articles normally contain a large number of quotations, and they are more subjective. Furthermore, journal articles are more varied in content, even within the same topic. Secondly, most large corpora are not author-categorised. This requires us to collect our own individual corpora.

2.1 Our Corpora

As we mentioned before, we collected a general corpus in the recipe domain from the BBC food website. To make recipes varied enough, this corpus contains different cooking styles from western to eastern, different courses, including starters, main courses and desserts, and a number of recipes of famous cooks, such as Ainsley Harriott. Since recipes are widely-available both from the Internet and from publications, it is easy to collect author-categorised corpora. Our individual recipe corpora include four individual authors so far. Two of them are from two published recipe books, and another two we collected online. Recipe books are useful, because they are written in an unique style. Table 1 shows information about both our individual corpora and our large general corpus.

Our Corpora	**Number of Recipes**	**Total Lines**	**Total Words**
Large corpus (BBC online recipes)	823	6325	85594
Recipes for Health Eating	76	961	9212
Food for Health	113	1347	11791
CM (www.cooks.com)	48	537	6432
Jo Pratt (www.bbc.co.uk)	91	904	15417

Table 1: Our corpora information

Although we are focusing on a small domain, verb variation between individual authors is a common phenomenon. Here are a few further examples from our corpora, which we want to capture.

1. *BBC corpus: Preheat the oven to 200C/400F/Gas 6. (BBC online food recipes)*
2. *Author2: Switch on oven to 200C, 400F or Gas Mark 6 and grease a $\frac{1}{2}$ litre ovenproof serving dish. (Recipes for Healthy Eating)*
3. *Author3. Put the oven on. (Food for Health)*

1. *BBC corpus: Sift the flour, baking powder and salt into a large bowl. (BBC online Recipes)*
2. *Author2: Sieve the flour, baking powder and bicarbonate of soda into a large mixing bowl. (Recipes for Health Eating)*
3. *Author3: Sieve the flour in, one-third at a time. (Food for Health)*

2.2 Our Verb List

```
...
squeeze==(10) squash, crush, squelch, mash,
squeeze -- (to compress with violence, out of
natural shape or condition; "crush an aluminum
can"; "squeeze a lemon")
...
```

Figure 1: The information of the verblist

We manually built a verb list with 146 verbs in total from our BBC corpus. Each verb represents an unique cooking action, associated with definitions and synonyms extracted from WordNet. For example, the verb 'squeeze' contains the following information shown in Figure 1. The BBC Corpus also contains a number of synonyms, such as the verb sift and the verb sieve. In this case, we only pick up the most frequent verb, which is the verb sift in this case, as an cooking action, and we record its synonyms, such as the verb sieve, in the late part of our verb list.

2.3 Using RASP in our corpora

Our data consists of verb-object pairs for verbs obtained from our BBC Corpus using RASP (Briscoe and Carroll, 2002). To derive reliable results, we deal with our data by the following rules. To avoid the sparse data problem and parsing mistakes, we removed a number of verbs that occur less than 3 times in our large corpus, and a set of mistake verbs made by the parser. We consider both direct objects and indirect objects together at the same time.

3 The Baseline Method - WordNet Synonyms

After the individual corpus is parsed, there are a number of main verbs appearing only in the BBC recipe corpus, but not in the individual corpus. This kind of main verbs is called *missing verb* in a corpus. For example, verbs such as 'roast', 'insert', 'drizzle' appear in the BBC corpus, but not in the Food for Health corpus. We say they are missing verbs in the Food for Health corpus. In this case, if the individual author expresses actions in the missing verb group, other verbs must be chosen instead. Our purpose is to find alternatives used by the individual author. To solve this problem, our baseline measure is the WordNet synonyms. If the missing verb contains synonyms in the verb list, we pick one as the candidate verb, called an *available candiate*. The following ways decide the verb alternatives for a missing verb. If there is more than one candidate verb for one missing verb, the most frequent synonym of the missing verb in the individual corpus is chosen as the alternative. The chosen synonym also has to be a main verb in the individual corpus. If the missing verb does not have a synonym or all available candidates do not appear in the individual corpus, we assign no alternative to this missing verb. In this case, we say there is no available alternative for the missing verb. The number of available alternatives for the missing verb and the accuracy is shown in Table 2, and Figure 2.

4 Distributional Similarity Measure

In this section, we introduce the idea of using distributional similarity measures, and discuss how this methodology can help us to capture verbs from individual authors.

By calculating the co-occurrence types of target words, distributional similarity defines the similarity between target word pairs. The *co-occurrence types* of a target word (*w*) are the context, *c*, in which it occurs and these have associated frequencies which may be used to form probability estimates (Weeds et al., 2004). In our case, the target word is main verbs of sentences and the co-occurrence types are objects. In section 6, similarity between verbs is derived from their objects, since normally there is no subject in the recipe domain. We are using the Additive t-test based Co-occurrence Retrieval Model of (Weeds and Weir, 2006). This method considers for each word *w* which co-occurrence types are retrieved. In our case, objects have been extracted from both the BBC Corpus and an individual corpus. Weeds and Weir use the the co-occurrence types as the features of word *(w)*, *F(w)*:

$$F(w) = \{c : D(w, c) > 0\}$$

where *D(w, c)* is the weight associated with word *w* and co-occurrence type *c*. T-test is used as a weight function, which is listed later.

Weeds and Weir use the following formula to describe the set of True Positives of co-occurrence types, which *w1* and *w2* are considered main verbs in copora:

$$TP(w_1, w_2) = F(w_1) \cap F(w_2)$$

They use the t-test from (Manning and Schütze, 1999) as the weight formula $D_t(w, c)$:

$$D_t(w, c) = \frac{p(c, w) - P(c)P(w)}{\sqrt{\frac{P(c,w)}{N}}}$$

Weeds and Weir then calculate the precision by using the proportion of features of *w1* which occurs in both words, and the recall by using the proportion of features of *w2* which occur in both words. In our experiment, precision is relative to

Individual Corpora	Total Numbers of Missing Verbs	Available Candidates by WordNet	Available Candidates by DS	Available Candidates by Combination	Correct Alternatives by (DS VS. WordNet VS. Combination)
Recipes for Health Eating	56	A = 36	A = 47	A = 52	8 VS. 10 VS. 17
Food for Health	57	A = 34	A = 52	A = 54	12 VS. 18 VS. 27
CM (www.cooks.com)	58	A = 25	A = 44	A = 51	10 VS. 4 VS. 14
Jo Pratt (www.bbc.co.uk)	26	A = 13	A = 22	A = 24	4 VS. 5 VS. 8

Table 2: The number of available missing verbs by the Distributional Similarity (DS) and by WordNet and by combination of DS and WordNet. ('A' means the total number of missing verbs in the individual corpus that have candidate alternatives in an individual corpus from methods.)

the BBC Corpus, and the recall is relative to an individual corpus.

$$P^{add}(w_1, w_2) = \frac{\sum_{TP(w_1,w_2)} D(w_1, c)}{\sum_{F(w_1)} D(w_1, c)}$$

$$R^{add}(w_1, w_2) = \frac{\sum_{TP(w_1,w_2)} D(w_2, c)}{\sum_{F(w_2)} D(w_2, c)}$$

Finally, Weeds and Weir combine precision and recall together by the following formulas:

$$m_h(P(w_1, w_2), R(w_1, w_2)) =$$

$$\frac{2.P(w_1, w_2).R(w_1, w_2)}{P(w_1, w_2) + R(w_1, w_2)}$$

$$m_a(P(w_1, w_2), R(w_1, w_2)) =$$

$$\beta.P(w_1, w_2) + (1 - \beta).R(w_1, w_2)$$

$$sim(w_1, w_2) = r.m_h(P(w_1, w_2), R(w_1, w_2))$$

$$+(1 - r).m_a(P(w_1, w_2), R(w_1, w_2))$$

where both r, β are between $[0, 1]$. In our experiments, we only assigned r=1. However, further performs can be done by assigning different values to r and β.

4.1 The Distributional Similarity method

Each missing verb in the BBC corpus is assigned the most likely verb as the available candidate from the individual corpus. The most likely verb is always chosen according to the largest similarity using the DS measure. In our case, if the largest similarity of the verb pair is larger than a certain value (-5.0), we say the missing verb has an *available candidate*. Otherwise, there is no available candidate existing in the individual corpus. For instance, DS suggests verb 'switch' is the most likely-exchangable verb for missing verb 'preheat' in the Recipes for Health Eating corpus. 'switch' appears 33 times in the individual corpus, in which there are 33 times that 'switch' has the same object as 'preheat'. Meanwhile, 'preheat' shows 191 times in total in the BBC corpus, with the same objects as 'switch' 176 times. By using the DS formulas, the similarity value between 'preheat' and 'switch' is 11.99. The number of available candidates of the missing verbs and the accuracy are shown in Table 2, and Figure 2.

There is only one corpus in the DS measures. In our case, *w1* and *w2* are from different corpora. For example, verb 'preheat' is from the BBC corpus, and verb 'switch' is in the Recipes for Health Eating. Although the co-occurence type is objects of the main verb, the precision is for the general corpus ——the BBC corpus, and the recall is for the individual corpus in our experiments.

5 The Combination method

We also combine the baseline and the DS method together in the combination method. The combination method tries the baseline first. For each missing verb, if the baseline returns an available alternative, this is the final available alternative of the combination method. If not, the available alternative is calculated by the DS method. If there is still no candidate for the missing verb, there is no available alternative in this case.

6 Evaluation

To justify accuracy of results by both the baseline method and the DS method, we manually judge whether or not the alternatives are inter changeable for the missing verbs. Table 2 shows the total number of missing verbs for each individual corpus and numbers of available alternatives as well. Also, it presents the number of correct alternatives for cases where both methods return answers, and results of a combination of two methods. In the future, we would like to evaluate the accuracy by more judges.

From Table 2, accuracies of distributional similarity are higher than WordNet synonyms in most cases, except in the individual corpus CM. The reason that CM got worse results is probably that the corpus size is not big enough. Since CM is the only individual corpus that has less than 50 recipes, this could lead to unreliable accuracy. In table 2, 'A' means the total number of missing verbs in the individual corpus that have candidate alternatives in an individual corpus from methods. It is obvious that distributional methods produce more available verbs than the synonyms of WordNet. In this case, we assume that WordNet is not very productive to provide alternative verb choices for individual authors compared with distributional similarity in a domain.

Figure 2 represents the accuracies of all methods. In Figure 2, we can see the overall accuracy of WordNet is not as good as the distributional similarity method. Moreover, we calculate the accuracy for the available verb pairs from the combination method of both the distributional similarity and WordNet. We can see that all combination accuracies are significantly better than accuracies of either distributional similarity or WordNet synonyms. In this case, distributional similarity and WordNet find different types of verbs. In other words, the similarity distributional method is very useful to find verbs that are not synonyms but represent the same type of action in individual corpora. And the type of verbs found by distributional similarity could not be pre-predicted, which makes the verb choice personalised.

In our verb pair outputs from distributional similarity, one problem is that we got similar verb pairs, for instances the verb 'simmer' matches to 'fry'. This is a common problem with distributional similarity, since it is not based on semantic meaning. This problem can perhaps be solved by building some hierarchical relationships between verbs. For instance, roast is one type of cooking.

The following examples are correct cases of verb pairs that are captured by distributional similarity. In each example, the semantic meanings of sentences are different, but the representation of action are the same.

roast (BBC Corpus) - cook (Food for Health):

1. *BBC Corpus: Season generously and roast for 30 minutes until softened and a little charred. (BBC online recipes)*

2. *Author2: Cover with a lid or foil and cook in the centre of the oven for 20 minutes, then turn down the oven to Reg 3 or 160C and continue cooking for 1 hour or until the kidneys are cooked. (Food for Health)*

saute (BBC Corpus) - fry (Food for Health):

1. *BBC Corpus: Melt the butter in a small to medium ovenproof pan and saute the cashew nuts for 2-3 minutes. (BBC online recipes)*

2. *Author2: Add the carrots and fry quickly for 5 minutes, stirring continuously. (Food for Health)*

preheat (BBC Corpus) - switch on (Food for Health):

1. *BBC Corpus: Preheat the oven to 200C/400F/Gas 6. (BBC online recipes)*

2. *Author2: Switch on oven to 190C, 375F or Gas Mark 5. (Food for Health)*

So far distributional similarity cannot capture the prepositions such as *on* in the third example. This is our future work.

7 Conclusion

In this paper, we used a distributional similarity method to help us to find matching verbs in

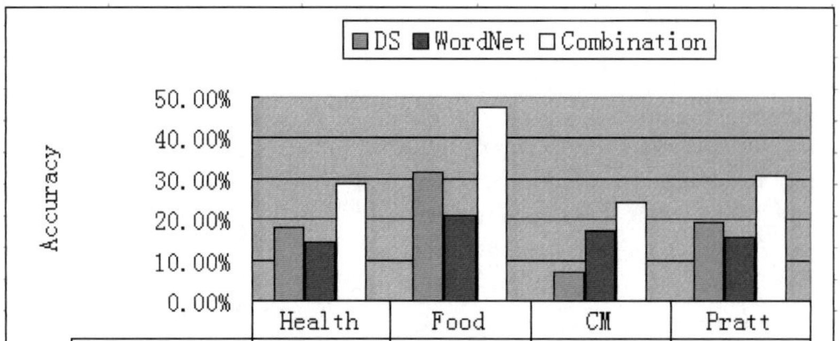

	Health	Food	CM	Pratt
DS	17.86%	31.58%	6.90%	19.23%
WordNet	14.29%	21.05%	17.24%	15.38%
Combination	28.57%	47.37%	24.14%	30.77%

Figure 2: The Accuracy for Missing Verbs in Individual Corpora

an individual corpus. We have compared the result between the distributional similarity method and WordNet and the overall accuracy of distributional similarity is better than WordNet. Furthermore, the combination of the distributional similarity method and WordNet achieved the best accuracy. This suggests that distributional similarity is very helpful in choosing the proper verbs for individual authors. It is especially useful to find verbs that are not synonyms but represent the same type of action in individual corpora. This means distributional similarity can capture unpredicted verb preferences of individual authors from the individual corpora.

References

John R.L Bernard. 1990. *The Macquarie Encyclopedic Thesaurus*. The Macquarie Library, Sydney, Australia.

Edward Briscoe and John Carroll. 2002. Robust Accurate Statistical Annotation of General Text. In *Proceedings of the LREC-2002*, pages 1499–1504.

John F. Burrow. 1987. Word-patterns and Story-shapes: the Statistical Analusis of Narrative style. *Literary and Linguistic Computing*, 2(2):61–70.

Fazli Can and Jon M. Patton. 2004. Change of Writing Style with Time. *Computers and Humanities*, 38:61–82.

R. Clement and D. Sharp. 2003. Ngram and Bayesian Classification of Documents for Topic and Authorship. *Literary and Linguistic Computing*, 18(4):423–447.

Christiance Fellbaum, editor. 1998. *WordNet: An Electronic lexical Database*. MIT Press.

Zelig S. Harris. 1968. *Mathematical Structures of Language*. John Wiley.

D. I Holmes and R.S Forsyth. 1995. The Federalist Revisited: New Directions in Authoriship attribution. *Literary and Linguistic Computing*, 10(2):111–127.

V. Keuelj, F. C. Peng, N. Cercone, and C. Thomas. 2003. N-Gram-Based Author Profiles for Authorship Attribution. In *Proceedings the Pacific Association for Computational Linguistics.*

Karin Kipper, Hoa Trang Dang, and Martha Palmer. 2000. Class-Based Construction of a Verb Lexicon. In *Proceedings the AAAI/IAAI*, pages 691–696.

Lillian Lee. 1999. Measure of Distributional Similarity. In *Proceedings of the Association for Computational Linguistics (ACL).*

Lillian Lee. 2001. On the Effectiveness of the Skew Divergence for Statistical Language. In *AIR*.

Dekang Lin. 1998. Automatic Retrieval and Clustering of Similar Words. In *Proceedings of the COLING-ACL.*

Christopher D. Manning and Hinrich Schütze. 1999. *Foundations of Statistical Natural Language Processing*. The MIT Press.

F. C. Peng. 2003. Language Independent Authorship Attribution using Character Level Language Models. In *Proceedings of the European Association for Computational Linguistics (ACL)*.

Peter Roget. 1911. *Thesaurus of English Words and Phrases*. Longmans.

Julie Weeds and David Weir. 2006. Co-occurrence Retrieval: A Flexible Framework for lexical Distributional Similarity. *Computational Linguistics*, 31(4):440–475.

Julie Weeds, David Weir, and Diana McCarthy. 2004. Charactersing Measures of Lexical Distributional Similarity. In *Proceedings of the COLING*.

Adjective-to-Verb Paraphrasing in Japanese Based on Lexical Constraints of Verbs

Atsushi Fujita[†] **Naruaki Masuno**[††] **Satoshi Sato**[†] **Takehito Utsuro**[‡]
[†]Graduate School of Engineering, Nagoya University
[††]IBM Engineering & Technology Services, IBM Japan, Ltd.
[‡]Graduate School of Systems and Information Engineering, University of Tsukuba

Abstract

This paper describes adjective-to-verb paraphrasing in Japanese. In this paraphrasing, generated verbs require additional suffixes according to their difference in meaning. To determine proper suffixes for a given adjective-verb pair, we have examined the verbal features involved in the theory of Lexical Conceptual Structure.

1 Introduction

Textual expressions that (roughly) convey the same meaning are called paraphrases. Since generating and recognizing paraphrases has a potential to contribute to a broad range of natural language applications, such as MT, IE, and QA, many researchers have done a lot of practices on automatic paraphrasing in the last decade.

Most previous studies have addressed paraphrase phenomena where the syntactic category is not changed: e.g., noun-to-noun ("document" ⇔ "article"), verb-to-verb ("raise" ⇔ "bring up"). In these *inner-categorial paraphrasing*, only limited types of problems arise when replacing words or phrases with their synonymous expressions. On the other hand, this paper focuses on *inter-categorial paraphrasing*, such as adjective-to-verb ("attractive" ⇔ "attract") that leads to novel type of problems due to the prominent differences in meaning and usage. In other words, calculating those differences is more crucial to determine how they can or cannot be paraphrased.

The aim of this study is to clarify what lexical knowledge is required for capturing those differences, and to explore where such a knowledge can be obtained from. Recent work in lexical semantics has shown that syntactic behaviors and semantic properties of words provide useful information to explain the mechanisms of several classes of paraphrases. More specifically, lexical properties involved in the theory of *Lexical Conceptual Structure* (LCS) (Jackendoff, 1990) have seemed to be beneficial because each verb does not function idiosyncratically. However, in the literature, there have been less studies for other syntactic categories than verbs. To the best of our knowledge, the Meaning-Text Theory (MTT) (Mel'čuk and Polguère, 1987) is one of the very few frameworks. In MTT, lexical properties and inter-categorial paraphrasing are realized with a unique semantic representation irrespective of syntactic categories and what are called lexical functions, e.g., $S_0(\textit{receive}) = \textit{reception}$.

To make out how the recent advances in lexical semantics for verbs can be extended to other syntactic categories, we assess LCS for inter-categorial paraphrasing. We choose adjectives as a counterpart of paraphrasing because they behave relatively similar to verbs compared with other categories: both adjectives and verbs have inflection and function as predicates, adnominal elements, etc. Yet, we speculate that their difference in meaning and usage reveal intriguing generation problems. To put it briefly, adjective-to-verb paraphrasing in Japanese requires verbal suffixes such as "*ta* (past / attributive)" in example (1)[1]:

(1) s. ***furui*** *otera-no* *jushoku-o* *tazune-ta*.
be old temple-GEN priest-ACC to visit-PAST
I visited a priest in the old temple.

t. ***furubi-ta*** *otera-no* *jushoku-o* *tazune-ta*.
to olden-ATTR temple-GEN priest-ACC to visit-PAST
I visited a priest in the olden(ed) temple.

2 Preliminary investigation

To make an investigation into the variation and distribution of required verbal suffixes, we collected a set of paraphrase examples through the following semi-automatic procedure:

Step 1. We handcrafted adjective-verb pairs based on JCore (Sato, 2004), which classifies Japanese words into five-levels of readability. Our 128 pairs (for 85 adjectives) contain only those sharing first few phonemes (reading)

[1]For each example, "s" and "t" denote an original sentence and its paraphrase, respectively.

Proceedings of the Fourth International Natural Language Generation Conference
Sydney, July 2006.

Table 1: Distribution of verbal suffixes used.

Verbal suffix	C_{ad_c}	C_{pr_1}	C_{pr_2}
ru	9	16	0
tei-ru	5	42	0
re-ru	14	8	0
re-tei-ru	2	5	0
ta	57	0	7
tei-ta	2	0	2
re-ta	6	0	1
re-tei-ta	0	0	1
both *ta* and *tei-ru*	4	0	0
both *ta* and *ru*	1	0	0
tea-ru	0	2	0
Total	100	73	11

where
ru: base form
tei: progressive / perfective
re: passive / potential
ta: past / attributive
tea: perfective

and characters (*kanji*), and either of adjective or verb falls into the easiest three levels.

Step 2. Candidate paraphrases for a given sentence collection are automatically generated by replacing adjectives with their corresponding verbs. Multiple candidates are generated for adjectives that correspond to multiple verbs.

Step 3. The correctness of each candidate paraphrase is judged by two human annotators. The basic criterion for judgement is that *two sentences are regarded as paraphrases if and only if they share at least one interpretation.* In this step, the annotators are allowed to revise candidates: (i) append verbal suffixes, (ii) change of case markers, and (iii) insert adverbs. Finally, candidates that both annotators judge correct qualify as paraphrases.

Assuming that the variation and distribution of verbal suffixes vary according to the usage of adjectives, we separately collected paraphrase examples for adnominal and predicative usages.

Adnominal usages: For 960 sentences randomly extracted from a one-year newspaper corpus, Mainichi 1995, we obtained 165 examples for 142 source sentences. We then divided them into two portions: 12 adjectives that appeared only once and at least one examples for the other adjectives were kept unseen (C_{ad_o}), while the remaining examples (C_{ad_c}) were used for our investigation.

Predicative usages: For 157 example sentences within IPAL adjective dictionary (IPA, 1990), we generated candidate paraphrases. 84 candidates for 70 sentences qualified as paraphrases. They are then divided into two portions according to the tense of adjectives: C_{pr_1} consists of examples where adjectives appear in base form and C_{pr_2} is for "*ta*" form (past tense).

Table 1 shows the distribution of verbal suffixes used for given *adjective-verb pairs* in each portion of example collections. We confirmed that their distribution was fairly different. In the remaining sections, we focus on adnominal usages because examples of predicative usages have displayed a degree of compositionality. Which of "*ru*" or "*ta*" must be used is given by the input: if a given adjective accompanies past tense, the resultant verbal suffix is necessarily that for present tense followed by "*ta*."

3 Determining verbal suffixes

The task we address here is to determine verbal suffixes for a given input, a pair of an adnominal usage of adjective in a certain context and a candidate verb given by our adjective-verb list.

From the viewpoint of language generation, this task can be thought of as generating verbal expressions where options are already given in Table 1. A straightforward way for determining verbal suffixes is to make use of lexical properties of verbs as constraints on generation. To manifest them, in particular aspectual properties involved in LCS, we first designed seven types of linguistic tests shown in Table 2. They are derived from a classical analysis of verb semantics in Japanese (Kageyama, 1996) and some ongoing projects on constructing LCS dictionaries (Kato et al., 2005; Takeuchi et al., 2006). We then manually examined 128 verbs in Section 2 under those tests. To determine the word sense in which the derivative relationship hold good, example sentences in IPAL verb dictionary (IPA, 1987) for each verb were used. For a verb which was out of the dictionary, we manually gave a sample sentence.

Since our aim is to explain why a certain verbal suffix is used for a given input, we have not feverishly applied a machine learning algorithm to the task. Instead, we have manually created a rule-based model shown in Table 3 using C_{ad_c}, where each *if-then rule* assigns either of verbal suffixes in Table 1 to a given input based on verbal features in Table 2 and some other features below:

- D: affix pair of the adjective and the candidate verb: e.g., "A_shii-V_mu" for "*kuyashii* (be regretful)" ⇔ "*kuyamu* (to regret)"
- N: disjunction of semantic classes in a thesaurus (The Natural Institute for Japanese Language, 2004) for the modified noun
- C: whether the adjective is head of clause

4 Experiment and discussion

By conducting an empirical experiment with C_{ad_c} and C_{ad_o}, we evaluate how our model (***RULE***) properly determines verbal suffixes. A comparison with a simple baseline model (***BL***) is also done. ***BL*** selects the most frequently used suffix (in this experiment "*ta*") for any given input.

Table 2: Linguistic tests for verbs derived from Lexical Conceptual Structure (Kageyama, 1996).

Label	Description
V_a	whether the verb allows accusative case
V_b	whether the verb can co-occur with a temporal adverb "*ichi-jikan* (for one hour)" or its variant
V_c	whether the verb can co-occur with a temporal adverb "*ichi-jikan-de* (in one hour)" or its variant
V_d	whether the verb can be followed by "*tearu* (perfective)" when its accusative case is moved to nominative
V_e	interpretation of the verb followed by "*tei-ru* (progressive / perfective)"
V_f	when followed by "*ta*," whether the verb can have the perfective interpretation or just past tense
V_g	whether the verb can co-occur with a sort of adverb which indicates intention of the action: e.g. "*wazato* (purposely)" and "*iyaiya* (reluctantly)"

Table 3: The rule-set for determining verbal suffixes, where "(non)" indicates non-paraphrasable.

Order	Condition (conjunction of "feature label =" value")	Verbal suffix
1	V_a="yes" ∧ V_b="yes" ∧ V_f="no" ∧ N="except *Human* (1.10)" ∧ D="A_ui–V_bumu" ∨ "A_i–V_mu" ∨ "A_asii–V_u"	*re-ru*
2	V_a="yes" ∧ V_b="yes" ∧ V_f="no" ∧ V_d="no" ∧ N="*Mind: mind, attitude* (1.303)"	*ta*
3	V_a="no" ∧ V_g="yes"	*ta*
4	V_a="no" ∧ V_f="yes" ∧ D="A_i–V_migakaru"	*ta / tei-ru*
5	C="clause" ∧ D="A_i–V_maru"	*ru*
6	V_a="no" ∧ V_f="yes"	*ta*
7	V_a="no" ∧ V_b="yes" ∧ V_f="no"	*ta*
8	V_b="yes" ∧ V_f="no" ∧ V_c="yes" ∧ V_d="yes" ∧ V_e="progressive" ∧ N="*Subject* (1.2)"	*tei-ru*
9	*	(non)

Table 4 shows the experimental results, where recall and precision are calculated with regard to input adjective-verb pairs. Among rules in Table 3, rules 1 (for "*re-ru*"), 3, 6, and 7 (for "*ta*" where V_a="no") performed much better than the other rules. This indicates that these rules and features in their conditions properly reflect our linguistic intuition. For instance, rule 6 reflects that a change-of-state intransitive verb expresses resultative meaning as adjectives when it modifies *Theme* of the event via "*ta*" (Kageyama, 1996) as shown in (1), and rule 2 does that a psychological verb modifies a nouns with "*re-ru*" when the noun arouses the specific emotion, such as regretting mistakes (e.g., "*kuyashii* (be regretful)" ⇔ "*kuyama-re-ru* (be regretted)"). The aspectual property captured by the tests in Table 2 is used to classify verbs into these semantic classes.

On the other hand, the rules for the other types are immature due to lack of examples: we cannot find out even necessary conditions to be "*ru*," "*tei-ru*," etc. What is required to induce proper conditions for these suffixes is a larger example collection and discovering another semantic property and a set of linguistic tests for capturing it.

5 Conclusion and future work

In this paper, we focused on inter-categorial paraphrasing and reported on our study on an issue in adjective-to-verb paraphrasing. Two general-purpose resources and a task-specific rule-set have been handcrafted to generate proper verbal suffixes. Although the rule-based model has achieved better performance than a simple baseline model, there is a plenty of room for improvement.

Table 4: Recall and precision of determining verbal suffix for given adjective-verb pairs.

	C_{ad_c}		C_{ad_o}	
Verbal suffix	Recall	Precision	Recall	Precision
ta (V_a="yes")	3/13	3/3	1/6	1/1
ta (V_a="no")	42/44	42/63	18/18	18/29
re-ru	12/14	12/19	7/13	7/11
ru	3/9	3/6	0/2	0/5
tei-ru	1/5	1/7	2/8	2/6
ta / tei-ru	2/4	2/2	1/2	1/1
No rule	for 11 inputs		for 7 inputs	
Total (***RULE***)	63/100 (63%)	63/100 (63%)	29/56 (52%)	29/53 (55%)
BL	57/100 (57%)	57/148 (39%)	24/56 (43%)	24/83 (29%)

Future work includes (i) to enlarge our two resources as in (Dorr, 1997; Habash and Dorr, 2003) evolving an effective construction method, (ii) intrinsic evaluation of those resources, and, of course, (iii) to enhance the paraphrasing models through further experiments with a larger test-set.

References

B. J. Dorr. 1997. Large-scale dictionary construction for foreign language tutoring and interlingual machine translation. *Machine Translation*, 12(4):271–322.

N. Habash and B. J. Dorr. 2003. A categorial variation database for English. In *Proceedings of the 2003 Human Language Technology Conference and the North American Chapter of the Association for Computational Linguistics (HLT-NAACL)*, pages 17–23.

IPA. 1987. *IPA Lexicon of the Japanese language for computers (Basic Verbs)*. Information-technology Promotion Agency. (in Japanese).

IPA. 1990. *IPA Lexicon of the Japanese language for computers (Basic Adjectives)*. Information-technology Promotion Agency. (in Japanese).

R. Jackendoff. 1990. *Semantic structures*. The MIT Press.

T. Kageyama. 1996. *Verb semantics*. Kurosio Publishers. (in Japanese).

T. Kato, S. Hatakeyama, H. Sakamoto, and T. Ito. 2005. Constructing Lexical Conceptual Structure dictionary for verbs of Japanese origin. In *Proceedings of the 11th Annual Meeting of the Association for Natural Language Processing*, pages 871–874. (in Japanese).

I. Mel'čuk and A. Polguère. 1987. A formal lexicon in meaning-text theory (or how to do lexica with words). *Computational Linguistics*, 13(3-4):261–275.

S. Sato. 2004. Identifying spelling variations of Japanese words. In *Information Processing Society of Japan SIG Notes, NL-161-14*, pages 97–104. (in Japanese).

K. Takeuchi, K. Inui, and A. Fujita. 2006. Construction of compositional lexical database based on Lexical Conceptual Structure for Japanese verbs. In T. Kageyama, editor, *Lexicon Forum No.2*. Hitsuji Shobo. (in Japanese).

The Natural Institute for Japanese Language. 2004. *Word list by semantic principles, revised and enlarged edition*. Dainippon Tosho. (in Japanese).

Generating References to Parts of Recursively Structured Objects

Helmut Horacek
Universität des Saarlandes
FB 6.2 Informatik
horacek@cs.uni-sb.de

Abstract

Algorithms that generate expressions to identify a referent are mostly tailored towards objects which are in some sense conceived as holistic entities, describing them in terms of their properties and relations to other objects. This approach may prove not fully adequate when referring to components of structured objects, specifically for abstract objects in formal domains, where scope and relative positions are essential features. In this paper, we adapt the standard Dale and Reiter algorithm to specifics of such references as observed in a corpus about mathematical proofs. Extensions incorporated include an incremental specialization of property values for metonymic references, local and global positions reflecting group formations and implicature-based scope preferences to justify unique identification of the intended referent. The approach is primarily relevant for domains where abstract formal objects are prominent, but some of its features are also useful to extend the expressive repertoire of reference generation algorithms in other domains.

1 Introduction

Over the past two decades, a number of algorithms for generating referring expressions have been proposed. Almost all of these algorithms conceive objects in some sense as holistic entities, describing them in terms of their properties and relations to other objects, but not treating components of an object as objects in their own rights. This approach may yield inadequate results for references to

Consider, for instance, a Rubic's cube where one side is currently visible, and reference is intended to a square consisting of the visible squares of four white subcubes, which are the only white elements on the visible side. The best way to refer to this composed structure is the concise "the white square", which exploits a preference for maximum scope objects, typical for such recursive structures. However, most reference generation algorithms would attempt to disambiguate the intended referent from its four components, producing an unnecessarily long expression, such as "the big white square" or "the white square which is composed of four squares". These expressions are not really bad, especially the first one, but things might turn out really awkward for more complex structural compositions, where the maximum scope preference often allows the identification in a surprisingly concise form.

In this paper, we address this problem by examining referring expressions produced by humans in domains with recursively structured objects playing a prominent role. Specifically, we have studied referring expressions in a corpus of simulated human-computer dialogs about tutoring mathematical problem-solving (Wolska et al. 2004, with recent additions in this paper). We express the criteria and preferences observed in a way compatible with the incremental reference generation algorithm of Dale and Reiter (1995), and we extend their algorithm by adapting the property selection and discrimination testing criteria accordingly.

This paper is organized as follows. First, we motivate our approach. Then we describe our corpus and the relevant phenomena observed in it. Next, we present extensions to the incremental algorithm that allow the generation of this kind of referring expressions. Finally, we illustrate how some examples from the corpus are handled and discuss our achievements.

Proceedings of the Fourth International Natural Language Generation Conference
Sydney, July 2006.

2 Previous Work

Within this paper, we adopt Dale's terminology (1988). A *referential description* (Donellan 1966) serves the purpose of letting the hearer or reader identify a particular object or set of objects in a situation. Referring expressions to be generated are required to be *distinguishing descriptions*, that is, descriptions of the entities being referred to, but not to any other object in the *context set*. A context set is defined as the set of the entities the addressee is currently assumed to be attending to – this is similar to the concept of focus spaces of the discourse focus stack in Grosz' & Sidner's (1986) theory of discourse structure. Moreover, the *contrast set* (the set of *potential distractors* (McDonald 1981)) is defined to entail all elements of the *context set* except the *intended referents*.

Generating referring expressions is pursued since the eighties (e.g., (Appelt 1985), among several others). Subsequent years were characterized by a debate about computational efficiency versus minimality of the elements appearing in the resulting referring expression (Dale 1988, Reiter 1990, and several others). In the mid-nineties, this debate seemed to be settled in favor of the incremental approach (Dale and Reiter 1995) – motivated by results of psychological experiments (e.g., Levelt 1989), certain non-minimal expressions are tolerated in favor of adopting the fast strategy of incrementally selecting ambiguity-reducing attributes from a domain-dependent preference list. Complementary activities include the generation of vague descriptions (van Deemter, 2000) and extensions to multimodal expressions (Van der Sluis 2005). Recently, algorithms have also been developed to the identification of sets of objects rather than individuals (Bateman 1999, Stone 2000, Krahmer, v. Erk, and Verweg 2001), and the repertoire of descriptions has been extended to boolean combinations of attributes, including negations (van Deemter 2002). To avoid the generation of redundant descriptions what incremental approaches typically do, Gardent (2002) and Horacek (2003) proposed exhaustive resp. best-first searches.

All these procedures more or less share the design of the knowledge base which bears influence on the descriptor selection. Objects are conceived as atomic entities, which can be described in terms of sets of attributes and relations to other objects. In such a setting, a structured object can be represented, among others, by a set of relations to its components, which are themselves conceived as objects. An exception to this method is the work by Paraboni and van Deemter (2002) who use hierarchical object representations to refer to parts of a book (figures, sections., etc.). Reference to such a component is made identifiable by iteratively adding a description of embedding structures until obtaining uniqueness. There are, however, no approaches addressing identification of objects or their components when the structures in these objects are of a *recursive* nature. Objects of this kind are mostly abstract ones, such as formulas, but also some sorts of geometric objects. Typical applications where such objects are prominent include scientific-technical documentation and tutoring systems. As we will see in the next section, naturally observed references to such objects have a number of particularities which are not addressed by existing generation algorithms.

3 A Corpus with References to Formulas

In this paper, we analyze some phenomena in the context of references to mathematical formulas and their components, as observed in a corpus on simulated man-machine tutoring dialogs (Wolska et al., 2004). These dialogs constitute the result of Wizard-of-Oz experiments in teaching students mathematical theorem proving in naive set theory resp. mathematical relations. In these experiments, a human wizard took the role of the tutor, with constraints on tutoring strategy and on use of natural language, although the constraints on natural language use were relaxed to encourage natural behavior on behalf of the student.

In the corpus obtained this way, a number of quite particular expressions referring to components of recursively structured objects – the formulas – showed up. Consequently, it is our goal to automate the production of these kinds of referring expressions in a more elaborate version of the simulated tutoring system, with full-fledged natural language generation.

Representative examples originating from our corpus appear in Figure 1. Each example consists of two parts: 1. a student utterance, mostly a formula, labeled by (#a), which is the context for interpreting subsequent referring expressions, the intended referent appearing in

1. Reference to the typographic order

(1a) $(R\circ S)^{-1} = \mathbf{\{(x,y) \mid (y,x) \in R\circ S\} = \{(x,y) \mid \exists z\, (z \in M \wedge (x,z) \in R^{-1} \wedge (z,y) \in S^{-1})\}} = R^{-1}\circ S^{-1}$

(1b) Das geht ein wenig schnell. Woher nehmen Sie *die zweite Gleichheit*?
(That was a little too fast. How did you find *the second equality*?)

(2a) Nach 9 $\Rightarrow ((y,z) \in R \wedge (z,\mathbf{y}) \in S)$

(2b) Fast korrekt. *Das zweite Vorkommen von y* muß durch x ersetzt werden.
Almost correct. *The second occurrence of y* must be replaced by x.

(3a) $(R \cup S)\circ T$ ist dann $\{(x,y) \mid \exists z\, (z \in M \wedge ((x,y) \in R \vee (x,y) \in S)\ \mathbf{\wedge\ (y,z) \in T)}\}$

(3b) Nicht korrekt. Vermutlich liegt der Fehler *nach der letzten 'und'-Verknüpfung*
Not correct. The mistake is probably located *after the last 'and'-operation*

2. Reference by exploiting default scope and metonymic relations

(4a) $(R\circ S)^{-1} = \mathbf{\{(x,y) \mid \exists z\, (z \in M \wedge (y,z) \in R^{-1} \wedge (z,x) \in S^{-1})\}} \supseteq S^{-1}\circ R^{-1}$

(4b) Nein, das ist nicht richtig! Vergleichen Sie *den zweiten Term* mit Ihrer vorhergehenden Aussage!
No, this is not correct! Compare *the second term* with your previous assertion!

(5a) $\{(x,y) \mid (y,x) \in (R\circ S)\} = \mathbf{\{(x,y) \mid (x,y) \in \{(a,b) \mid \exists z\, (z \in M) \wedge (a,z) \in R \wedge (z,b) \in S\}\}}$

(5b) Das stimmt so nicht. Die *rechte Seite* wäre identisch mit $R\circ S$.
This is not correct. The *right side* would be identical to $R\circ S$.

(6a) $\{(x,y) \mid \exists z\, (z \in M) \wedge ((x,z) \in R \vee (x,z) \in S) \wedge (z,y) \in S\} =$
$\{(x,y) \mid \exists z\, (z \in M) \wedge (z,y) \in S \wedge ((x,z) \in R \vee (x,z) \in S)\} \Leftrightarrow \mathbf{((y,z) \in S \wedge (z,y) \in S)}$

(6b) Auf der *rechten Seite* ist *z* nicht spezifiziert
On the *right side*, *z* is not specified

(7a) $\mathbf{\{(x,y) \mid \exists z\, (z \in M) \wedge ((x,z) \in R \vee (x,z) \in S) \wedge (z,y) \in S\}} = \{(x,y) \mid \exists z\, (z \in M) \wedge$
$(z,y) \in S \wedge ((x,z) \in R \vee (x,z) \in S)\} \Leftrightarrow \mathbf{\exists z\, (z \in M \wedge ((y,z) \in S \wedge (z,y) \in S))}$

(7b) Diese Aussagen scheinen nicht gleichwertig zu sein. Ein *z*, das die Bedingung der *rechten Aussage* erfüllt, muß nicht die Bedingung der *linken Menge* erfüllen.
These assertions do not seem to be of equal range. A *z* which fulfills the condition of the *right assertion* does not necessarily fulfill the condition of the *left set.*

3. Reference by exploiting default scope for building groups of objects

(8a) $K((A \cup B) \cap (C \cup D)) = \mathbf{K(A \cup B)} \cup \mathbf{K(C \cup D)}$

(8b) De Morgan Regel 2 auf *beide Komplemente* angewendet.
De Morgan Rule 2, applied to *both complements.*

(9a) $\mathbf{(T^{-1}\circ S^{-1})^{-1}} \cup \mathbf{(T^{-1}\circ R^{-1})^{-1}} = \{(x,y) \mid (y,x) \in (T^{-1}\circ S^{-1}) \wedge (y,x) \in (T^{-1}\circ R^{-1})\}$

(9b) Dies würde dem Schnitt *der beiden Mengen* entsprechen.
This would correspond to the intersection of *both sets.*

4. Reference to regions by expressions involving vagueness

(10a) Also ist $(R \cup S)\circ T = \{(x,z) \mid \exists v\, (((x,v) \in R \vee (x,v) \in S) \wedge \mathbf{(z,v) \in T)}\}$

(10b) Fast richtig. *Am Ende der Formel* ist ein Fehler.
Almost correct. At *the end of the formula*, there is a mistake.

(11a) Wegen der Formel für die Komposition folgt $(R \cup T)\circ(S \cup T) =$
$\{(x,z) \mid \exists z\, ((x,z) \in R \wedge (z,y) \in T) \vee \mathbf{\exists z\, ((x,z) \in R \wedge (z,y) \in T)}\}$

(11b) Fast richtig. In *der zweiten Hälfte der Formel* ist ein Fehler.
Almost correct. In *the second half of the formula*, there is a mistake.

Figure 1: References to components of mathematical objects in dialog fragments of our corpus

bold, and 2. a tutor response labeled by (#b), with at least one referring expression, in italics. Texts are given in the original German version, accompanied by a translation into English.

The examples are partitioned into four categories. The first one, (examples 1 to 3), illustrate references by the typographical position, from left to right. Items referred to in this manner are qualified by their formal category. (1) refers to an equality – two terms joined by an equal sign – in a sequence of three equalities. (2) refers to an instance of a variable, *y*, which must be further qualified by its position to distinguish it from another occurrence. (3) refers to the last occurrence of the *and* operator. Distinct surface forms are used for objects referred to by category ("second equality") resp. by name ("second *occurrence* of y").

The second category, the only one specific to recursively structured objects, comprises references which look similar to the previous ones, but they do not reflect the *typographical* position but *structural* embeddings. Objects referred to by this kind of expressions are found on the top level of the embedding object or close to it. In most cases, references to the embedding level where the intended referent is to be found are left unexpressed, which carries the implicit meaning that the referent appears at the top most level in which the referred category can be found. In (4), for example, the entire formula contains many terms as its components, in various levels of embedding, so that orientation on typographic positions is not clear. However, on top level of the inequation chain, there are only three terms and the order among these is perfectly clear. (5) and (6) illustrate the role of incompleteness – only "right side" is mentioned, leaving the object whose right side is meant implicit. Consequently, this must be the right side of the whole formula. The last example in this category, (7) shows the reference to different levels of embedding in one sentence. While "right assertion" refers to the expression on the right side of the equivalence on top level, "left set" refers to the left of the two sets in the equation on the left side of that equivalence.

The third category, which features the reference to sets of objects, shows the interpretation of the embedding level in which the intended referent is to be found on the basis of number constraints. In precise terms, this is an instance of implicature (Grice 1975): if the number of objects that are on top level of the embedding object and satisfy the description, exceeds the cardinality specified, identification of the intended referents is transferred to one of the embedded substructures. In (8), three subexpressions satisfy the metonymic description "complement", but the expression refers only to two. Consequently, the intended referents must be found in one of the substructures where a precise cardinality match is present – here, the right side of the equation. Due to the implicature, expressing this additional qualification is not required. An additional complication arises in the context of interference across referring expressions in one sentence. In (9), "both sets" would be resolved to the two sides of the equation, without the context of the whole sentence. However, since "this" refers to the result of the preceeding assertion, that is, the right side of the equation, this part is in some sense excluded from the context for resolving the next referring expressions. Hence, the left side of the equation yields the two sets on top level as interpretation.

The fourth category comprises examples of references which are in some sense associated with vagueness. In references to formulas, we consider the *end* (example (10)) – which means the region towards the end, as a vague expression, but also the *second half* (example (11)), since it is not entirely clear whether this expression must be interpreted structurally or typographically, and a precise interpretation of "half" in the typographical sense is pointless.

In the following, we present methods for the automated generation of referring expressions of the kind illustrated in Figure 1 – concise ones. We address the following phenomena:

- Implicit scope interpretation
- Incomplete or metonymic expressions
- Implicatures of category and cardinality

We do, however, restrict our task to the generation of single referring expressions with precise references. Hence, we do not address vagueness issues, since the meaning of expressions as occurring in (10) and (11) is not fully clear. Moreover, we do not accommodate the context due to previously generated referring expressions as in (9), which we assume to be done by the embedding process.

3 Operationalization

In this section, we describe an operationalization of generating referring expressions of the kind discussed in the previous section. This operationalization is realized in terms of extensions to the algorithm by Dale and Reiter (1995). This algorithm assumes an environment with three interface functions: *BasicLevelValue*, accessing basic level categories of objects (Rosch 1978), *MoreSpecificValue* for accessing incrementally specialized attribute values according to a taxonomic hierarchy, and *UserKnows* for judging whether the user is familiar with the attribute value of an object. In a nutshell, *MakeReferringExpression* (Figure 2, including our extensions) iterates over the attributes P of an intended referent r (or a set of referents). In *FindBestValue*, a value is chosen that is known to the user and maximizes discrimination (*RulesOut*) – this value describes the intended referent and rules out at least one potential distractor in C. If existing, such values are iteratively collected in L, until P is empty or a distinguishing description is found. The value V of an attribute A is chosen within an embedded iteration, starting with the basic level value attributed to r, after which more specific values also attributed to r and assumed to be known to the user are tested for their discriminatory power. Finally, the least specific value that excludes the largest number of potential distractors and is known to the user is chosen.

The extensions to handle particularities for our concerns comprise several components:

- The knowledge representation of objects is enh…
- The value selection for context-dependent descrip…
- The discriminatory power in the subprocedure *RulesOut* is interpreted [illegible] contexts for attributes expressing position.
- Termination criteria include a test whether a card…

Group(x) ::=
  $G \equiv \{y \mid \exists z\, (\forall y \text{ dominates}(z,y))\} \wedge G \supseteq x$

T-group-items :: =
  $\{x \mid \exists y\, (\neg\exists z \text{ dominates}(z,y) \wedge \forall x \text{ dominates}(y,x))\}$

L1-items :: =
  $\{x \mid \exists y\, (y \in \text{T-group-items} \wedge \text{dominates}(y,x))\}$

Group-pref($Group,N,V$) :: =
  $|(r \cup C) \cap Group| = N \wedge$
  $\forall x \in ((r \cup C) \cap Group)$: Position($x,Group,N$) = V

T-group-pref(N,V) ::=
  Group-pref(T-group-items,N,V)

L1-group-pref(x,N,V) ::= $\neg$T-Group-pref(N,V) $\wedge$
  L1-items $\supseteq$ Group(x) $\wedge$ Group-pref(x,N,V) $\wedge$
  ($\forall y$ (Group(y) $\wedge$ L1-items $\supseteq$ Group(y)):
    ($x \neq y \rightarrow \neg$Group-pref($y,N,V$)))

Figure 2: Definitions with group components

In order to precisely define the extensions, we introduce some predicates and formal definitions for them (Figure 2). Composition in recursively structured objects is built on *dominates(x,y)*, expressing that component y is part of component x; chained compositions of *dominates* are acyclic. On that basis, groups of items are built according to local contexts. A *Group* which some items x belong to is the set of items dominated by one same item, if existing. Otherwise, *Group* is empty. A special group is the set of items on top level, *T-group-items*, which are all dominated by the entire structure, the root item, which is not dominated by any item. These items also build a group. In contrast, *L1-items*, which comprise the items one level below the *T-group-items*, are not all in one group. Intersection with the *Group* predicate yields subsets, where each element in these sets is dominated by one and the same *T-group-item* (see the definition of *L1-group-pref*). A central definition is *Group-pref* (group preference), used for testing the effect of implicatures. It is defined for the set of relevant items to be used within the algorithm ($r \cup C$), that is, the intended referents and still existing distractors, in relation to a *Group*, in the context of cardinality N and position V, which apply to the set of items. For that group to be preferred, the relevant items falling into that group must match the given cardinality and the position description (see the definition of *Position* in the next paragraph). On that basis, *T-group-pref* expresses

```
              MakeReferringExpression (r,C,P)
L ← { }, Ctotal ← C                                      [1]
for each member A_i of list P do
case A_i of                                              [2]
 cardinality: V ← |r|                                    [3]
 global-position: V ← Position(r,Ctotal,|r|)             [4]
 local-position: V ← Position(r,Group(r),|r|)            [5]
 other: V = FindBestValue(r,A_i,BasicLevelValue(r,A_i))
end case
if RulesOut(<A_i,V>,C) ≠ nil then
 if metonymic(A_i,X) and <type,X> ∈ L for some X         [6]
    and RulesOut(<A_i,V>,Ctotal) ⊒                        [7]
         RulesOut(<type,X>,Ctotal)                       [8]
   then L ← L \ {<type,X>} ∪ {<type,V>}                  [9]
   else L ← L ∪ {<A_i,V>} end if
 C ← C - RulesOut(<A_i,V>,C)                             [10]
end if
if C = { } or Preference-by-Implicature then             [11]
 if <type,X> ∈ L for some X
   then return L           (an identifying description)
   else return L ∪ {<type,BasicLevelValue(r,type)>}
 end if end if
end for
return L                   (a non-identifying description)

              FindBestValue (r,A,initial-value)
if UserKnows(r,<A,initial-value>) = true
then value ← initial-value
else value ← no-value end if
if (spec-value ← MoreSpecificValue(r,A,value)) ≠ nil ∧
(new-value ← FindBestValue(r,A,spec-value)) ≠ nil ∧
(|RulesOut(<A,new-value>,C)| >
 |RulesOut(<A,value>,C)|)                                [12]
then value ← new-value end if
return value

          RulesOut (<A,V>,C)                             [13]
if V = no-value then return nil
else case A_i of                                         [14]
 cardinality: return C ∩ ⋃ Group(c) c ∈ C,
                  where |Group(c) ∩ C| < V               [15]
 global-position: return {x : x ∈ C ∧ Position(x,Ctotal,|r|) ≠ V  [16]
 local-position: return {x : x ∈ C ∧ Position(x,Group(x),|r|) ≠ V
 other: return {x: x ∈ C ∧ UserKnows(x,<A,V>) = false}
end case end if

          Preference-by-Implicature                      [17]
V ← any, N ← any
if <global-position,V> ∈ L ∨ <local-position,V> ∈ L ∨
   <cardinality,N> ∈ L then                              [18]
 return (T-group-pref(|r|,V) ∧ T-group-items ⊒ r ) ∨
      (L1-items ⊒ r ∧ L1-group-pref(r,|r|,V))            [19]
else return false end if
```

Figure 3: The algorithm in pseudo-code

preference for top-group items, when bound to Group, and *L1-group-pref* expresses preference for such a group with x one level below.

The knowledge representation of objects is enriched by some properties which are not intrinsic to an object itself. These properties comprise descriptors *cardinality*, *position*, and the meta-property *metonymic*. The predicate *metonymic(x,y)* expresses the acceptability of a metonymic reference of a descriptor x for a category y (e.g., an operator for a formula, in mathematical domains). The descriptor *cardinality* easily fits in the standard schema of the procedure. However, it only contributes to the discrimination from potential distractors in the context of effects of implicature. The most complex addition is the descriptor *position*, which expresses some sort of relative position of an object considered within the context of a set of comparable objects (e.g., first, second). There are two dimensions along which such descriptors are meaningful in the domain of mathematical formulas and in similar domains with recursively structured objects: (1) the typographical position within the entire object, referred to by the descriptor *global-position*, and (2) the position within the structural level where the object in question resides, referred to by the descriptor *local-position*. Moreover, that position also depends on the number of objects considered, if subgroups of objects are built prior to checking their position within the entire group (e.g,: the first *two* items). This information is encapsulated in the function *Position(x,y,n)*, where x denotes the object or set of objects whose position within group y is the value of that function, where subgroups of n objects are formed. In order to yield a proper result, x must be a subset of y and the position value within y must be the same for all elements of x. Otherwise, the value is undefined. For example, for a group G=<1,2,3,4, 5,6>, *Position({3},G,1)* = 3, *Position({3},G,2)* = 2, and *Position({2,3},G,2)* = undefined. In some sense, this handling of positions is a generalization of the ordering for vague descriptors in (van Deemter 2006). Also in accordance with van Deemter, we separate descriptor selection from surface form determination, yielding, for example, "left set" for {<type,set>, <local-position,first>}, the first part of an equation, and "second occurrence of x" for {<type,x>, <local-position,second>}.

In order to process these enhanced representations adequately, we have incorporated appropriate modifications in the procedure *MakeReferringExpression* (labeled by [#] in Figure 3). First, the original set of potential distractors is stored for computations within a global context [1]. Then the value selection for the attribute currently considered is done [2], which is different from the usual call to *FindBestValue* for *cardinality* [3], *global-position* [4], and *local-position* [5]; the latter two are realized by the function *Position*, with appropriate instantiations for the group parameter. Next, the treatment for the inclusion of metonymic properties in the description is addressed. If the metonymic descriptor fits to the object category [6], and its discriminatory power [7] dominates that associated with the type descriptor [8], the descriptor values are conflated by overwriting the type value by that of the metonymic descriptor [9]. The two calls to *RulesOut* involved in the above test ([7] and [8]) are the only references to *Rules Out* where effects on the original, entire set of distractors are tested. Therefore, the parameter *C* is added in the definition of *RulesOut* [13] and in all other places where that procedure is called [10], [12]. Similarly to the inclusion of attribute-value pairs in the description, the exclusion tests in *RulesOut* are specific for non-intrinsic attributes [14]. For *cardinality*, those distractors are excluded which belong to a group where the number of still relevant distractors (those consistent with the partial description built so far) is below that cardinality [15]. Similarly, for testing position values, those distractors are picked for which the values returned by the function *Position,* in dependency of the relevant scope – the group the intended referent(s) belong to, are not consistent with value of the attribute considered (*global-position* resp. *local-position*) [16]. Finally, the termination criterion [11] is enhanced, by taking into account the effect of implicatures through cardinality and position descriptors, by the function *Preference-by-implicature* [17]. In this function, the values of *cardinality* and *global-position* or *local-position* are instantiated, provided they appear in the description *L* [18]. The return value is the result of a test whether there exists preference for the top-level, or for that level 1 group which contains the intended referents [19].

4 Examples

In this section, we illustrate how particularities of our application domain are modeled and how the procedure behaves in generating the referring expressions observed in our corpus. The ordered list of attributes, *P*, consists of <type, form, cardinality, global-order, local-order> for atomic items and of <type, operator, cardinality, local-order, dominated-by> for the composed expressions – dominated-by is the inverse of dominates. The meta-predicate *metonymic* is instantiated for pairs <variable, form>, <expression, local-order>, and <term, operator> for producing expressions such as "x" referring to variable x, "left side" referring to the left part of an assertion or equation, and "complement" referring to a term with complement as top level operator.

We show the generation of two examples.

1. example: "Left set" in (7) in Figure 1. It is generated by choosing "set" as the *type*, followed by unsuccessful attempts to pick an *operator* attribute (there is none defined for that set), and a *cardinality* (which yields no discrimination). Then "first" is chosen for *local-ordering*, yielding unique identification (the embedding is left implicit), and this value is expressed by "left" on the surface.

2. example: "both complements" in (8). It is generated by choosing "term" as the *type*, followed by "complement" as the *operator*, which overwrites "term" due to its specification as metonymic with respect to that category. Then "2" is chosen for *cardinality*, which yields unique identification since a subgroup preference for level one is present.

Altogether, the algorithm is able to generate the expressions occurring in our corpus, or quite similar ones, assisted by the application-specific tailored list *P*. Exceptions constitute reference to regions related to some formula component, such as (3) in Figure 1, effects of interference of scope across several referring expressions, such as (9), and expressions involving vague region descriptors, such as (10) and (11). While the last set of examples comprises more than referring expressions, the first two can be handled, but the generated expressions are typically a bit cumbersome, such as "the third term in the condition of the set" instead of "after the last 'and'-operation" in (3) and "both sets on the left side" instead of simply "both sets" in (9).

5 Conclusion and Discussion

In this paper, we have presented an approach to generating referring expressions that identify components of recursively structured objects. Known techniques are enhanced by measures building metonymic expressions, descriptors expressing positions relative to some subgroup of object components, and exploiting the effect of implicatures due to cardinality and position descriptors. Concise expressions can be generated, in accordance with those in our corpus.

While our elaborations are domain-specific to a certain extent, several parts of our method are also much broader applicable. Metonymic expressions are quite common, and we think that building them within the task of reference generation is superior to doing this in a process thereafter, because this enables an easy computation of the discrminatory power of both alternatives, the implicit and the explicit one. Another aspect of broader relevance concerns the effect of implicatures in connection with object subgroups. While the group building itself, which is based on compositions of the relation *dominates,* is specific to our environment, the techniques to establish preferences among groups and deriving identification from that pertain to other environments. For instance, when a subgroup of two items of some kind is visually identifiable in the context of a few other subgroups with different cardinalities, "the two X's" would lead to the identification of the subgroup in focus, through the effect of implicature, the group formation being based on local proximity. Thus, only the group formation schema needs to be changed.

References

Appelt, D. 1985. Planning English Referring Expressions. *Artificial Intelligence* 26, pp. 1-33.

Bateman, J. 1999. Using Aggregation for Selecting Content when Generating Referring Expressions. In Proc. of the *37th Annual Meeting of the Association for Computational Linguistics (ACL-99)*, pp. 127-134, University of Maryland.

Dale, R. 1988. Generating Referring Expressions in a Domain of Objects and Processes. PhD Thesis, Centre for Cognitive Science, Univ. of Edinburgh.

Dale, R., and Reiter, E. 1995. Computational Interpretations of the Gricean Maxims in the Generation of Referring Expressions. *Cognitive Science* 18, pp. 233-263.

Donellan, K. 1966. Reference and Definite Description. *Philosophical Review* 75, pp. 281-304.

Gardent, C. 2002. Generating Minimal Definite Descriptions. In Proc. of the *40th Annual Meeting of the Association for Computational Linguistics (ACL-2002)*, pp. 96-103, Philadelphia, Pennsylvania.

Grice, H. 1975. Logic and Conversation. In Syntax and Semantics: Vol. 3, Speech Acts, pp. 43-58, Academic Press.

Grosz, B., and Sidner, C. 1986. Attention, Intention, and the Structure of Discourse. *Computational Linguistics* 12, pp. 175-206.

Horacek, H. 2003. A Best-First Search Algorithm for Generating Referring Expressions. In Proc. of the *10th Conference of the European Chapter of the Association for Computational Linguistics (EACL-2003)*, Conference Companion (short paper), pp. 103-106, Budapest, Hungary.

Krahmer, E., v. Erk, S., and Verleg, A. 2001. A Meta-Algorithm for the Generation of Referring Expressions. In Proc. of the 8th European Workshop on Natural Language Generation (*EWNLG-2001)*, pp. 29-39, Toulouse, France.

Levelt, W. 1989. *Speaking: From Intention to Articulation*. MIT Press.

McDonald, D. 1981. Natural Language Generation as a Process of Decision Making under Constraints. PhD thesis, MIT.

Reiter, E. 1990. The Computational Complexity of Avoiding Conversational Implicatures. In Proc. of the *28th Annual Meeting of the Association for Computational Linguistics (ACL-90)*, pp. 97-104, Pittsburgh, Pennsylvania.

Rosch, E. 1978. Principles of Categorization. In E. Rosch and B. Llyod (eds.) *Cognition and Categorization*, pp. 27-48, Hillsdale, NJ: Lawrence Erlbaum.

Stone, M. 2000. On Identifying Sets. In Proc. of the *First International Conference on Natural Language Generation (INLG-2000),* pp. 116-123, Mitzpe Ramon, Israel.

van Deemter, K. 2000. Generating Vague Descriptions. In Proc. of the *First International Natural Language Generation Conference (INLG-2000),* pp. 179-185, Mitzpe Ramon, Israel.

Paraboni, I., and van Deemter, K. 2002. Generating Easy References: the Case of Document Deixis. In Proc. of the *Second International Natural Language Generation Conference (INLG-2002)*, pp. 113-119, Harriman, NY, USA.

van Deemter, K. 2002. Generating Referring Expressions: Boolean Extensions of the Incremental Algorithm. *Computational Linguistics*, 28(1), pp. 37-52.

van Deemter, K. 2006. Generating Referring Expressions that Involve Gradable Properties. *Computational Linguistics*, to appear.

van der Sluis, I. 2005. Multimodal Reference. Dissertation, Tilburg University.

Wolska, M., Vo, B., Tsovaltzi, D., Kruijff-Korbayová, I., Karagjosova, E., Horacek, H., Gabsdil, M., Fiedler, A., and Benzmüller, C. 2004. An Annotated Corpus of Tutorial Dialogs on Mathematical Theorem Proving. In Proc. of the *4th International Conference on Language Resources and Evaluation*, pp. 1007-1010, Lisbon, Portugal.

Overspecified reference in hierarchical domains: measuring the benefits for readers

Ivandré Paraboni
University of Sao Paulo
EACH - Av.Arlindo Bettio, 1000
03828-000 Sao Paulo, Brazil
ivandre@usp.br

Judith Masthoff
University of Aberdeen
Dep.of Computing Science
Aberdeen AB24 3UE, Scotland, UK
jmasthoff@csd.abdn.ac.uk

Kees van Deemter
University of Aberdeen
Dep.of Computing Science
Aberdeen AB24 3UE, Scotland, UK
kvdeemte@csd.abdn.ac.uk

Abstract

It is often desirable that referring expressions be chosen in such a way that their referents are easy to identify. In this paper, we investigate to what extent identification becomes easier by the addition of logically redundant properties.We focus on hierarchically structured domains, whose content is not fully known to the reader when the referring expression is uttered.

Introduction

Common sense suggests that speakers and writers who want to get their message across should make their utterances easy to understand. Broadly speaking, this view is confirmed by empirical research (Deutsch 1976, Mangold 1986, Levelt 1989, Sonnenschein 1984, Clark 1992, Cremers 1996, Arts 2004, Paraboni and van Deemter 2002, van der Sluis, 2005). The present paper follows in the footsteps of Paraboni and van Deemter (2002) by focussing on hierarchically structured domains and asking whether any benefits are obtained when an algorithm for the generation of referring expressions (GRE) builds logical redundancy into the descriptions that it generates. Where Paraboni and van Deemter (2002) reported on the results of a simple experiment in which subjects were asked to say which description they *preferred* in a given context, the present paper describes a much more elaborate experiment, measuring how difficult it is for subjects to find the referent of a description.

1 Background

Let us distinguish between two aspects of the 'understanding' of a referring expression, which we shall denote by the terms interpretation and resolution. We take *interpretation* to be the process whereby a hearer/reader determines the meaning or logical form of the referring expression; we take *resolution* to be the identification of the referent of the expression once its meaning has been determined. It is resolution that will take centerstage in our investigation.

Difficulty of resolution and interpretation do not always go hand in hand. Consider sentences (1a) and (1b), uttered somewhere in Brighton but not on Lewes Road.

(1a) *968 Lewes Road*
(1b) *number 968*

Assume that (1a) refers uniquely. If other streets in Brighton do not have numbers above 900, then even (1b) is a unique description – but a pretty useless one, since it does not help you to find the house unless your knowledge of Brighton is exceptional. The description in (1a) is longer (and might therefore take more time to read and interpret) than (1b), but the additional material in (1a) makes *resolution* easier once interpretation is successfully completed. We explore how an GRE program should make use of logically redundant properties so as to simplify resolution (i.e., the identification of the referent).

In corpus-based studies, it has been shown that logically redundant properties tend to be included when they fulfill one of a number of pragmatic functions, such as to indicate that a property is of particular importance to the speaker, or to highlight the speaker's awareness that the referent has the property in question (Jordan 2000). However, redundancy has been built into GRE algorithms

Proceedings of the Fourth International Natural Language Generation Conference
Sydney, July 2006.

only to a very limited extent. Perhaps the most interesting account of overspecification so far is the one proposed by Horacek (2005), where logically redundant properties enter the descriptions generated when the combined *certainty* of other properties falls short of what is contextually required. Uncertainty can arise, for example, if the hearer does not know about a property, or if she does not know whether it applies to the target referent.

Our own work explores the need for overspecification in situations where each of the properties in question is unproblematic (i.e., certain) in principle, but where the reader has to make an effort to discover their extension (i.e., what objects are truthfully described by the property). We ask how a generator can use logically redundant information to reduce the search space within which a reader has to 'find' a referent. (Cf., Edmonds 1994 for a related set of problems.)

2 Hierarchical domains

Existing work on GRE tends to focus on fairly simple domains, dominated by one-place properties. When relations (i.e., two-place properties) are taken into account at all (e.g., Dale and Haddock 1991, Krahmer and Theune 2002), the motivating examples are kept so small that it is reasonable to assume that speaker and hearer know all the relevant facts in advance. Consequently, search is not much of an issue (i.e., resolution is easy): the hearer can identify the referent by simply intersecting the denotations of the properties in the description. While such simplifications permit the study of many aspects of reference, other aspects come to the fore when larger domains are considered.

Interesting questions arise, for example, when a large domain is hierarchically ordered. We consider a domain to be hierarchically ordered if its inhabitants can be structured like a tree in which everything that belongs to a given node n belong to at most one of n's children, while everything that belongs to one of n's children belongs to n. Examples include countries divided into provinces which, in turn, may be divided into regions, etc.; years into months then into weeks and then into days; documents into chapters then sections then subsections; buildings into floors then rooms. Clearly, hierarchies are among our favourite ways of structuring the world.

A crucial question, in all such cases, is what knowledge is shared between speaker and hearer at utterance time. It will be convenient to start by focussing on the extreme case where, before the start of resolution, knows nothing about the domain. When the utterance is made, the hearer's blindfold is removed, so to speak, and resolution can start. No similar assumption about the speaker is made: we assume that the speaker knows everything about the domain, and that he knows that the hearer can achieve the same knowledge. Many of our examples will be drawn from a simple model of a University campus, structured into buildings and rooms; the intended referent will often be a library located in one of the rooms. The location of the library is not known to the hearer, but it is known to the speaker. Each domain entity r will be

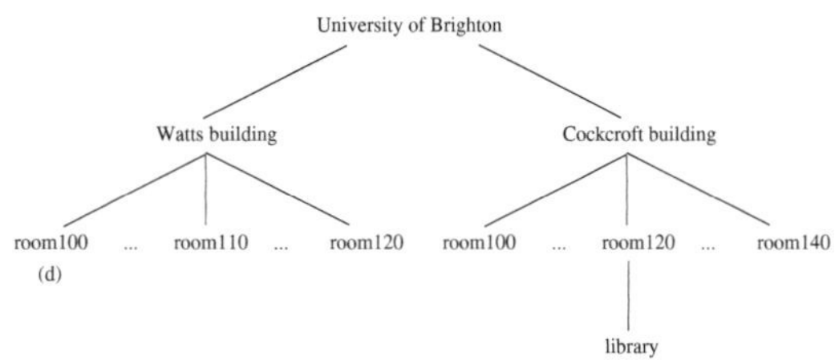

Figure 1: A hierarchically structured domain.

associated with a TYPE (e.g., the type 'room'), and with some additional attributes such as its ROOM NUMBER or NAME, and we will assume that it is always possible to distinguish r from its siblings in the tree structure by using one or more of these properties. (For example, 'R.NUMBER=102' identifies a room uniquely within a given building) [1].

3 Obstacles for resolution

Generating a uniquely referring expression is not always enough, because such an expression can leave the hearer with an unnecessarily large search space. But the issue is an even starker one, especially when the locations of speaker and hearer are taken into account. (For simplicity, we assume that the locations coincide.)

Suppose a hierarchically-ordered domain D contains *only one* entity whose TYPE is LIBRARY. Consider the following noun phrases, uttered in the position marked by d in Figure 1. (The first three have the same intended referent.)

[1]This is a useful assumption, since the existence of a distinguishing description cannot be otherwise guaranteed.

(2a) *the library, in room 120 in the Cockcroft bld.*
(2b) *the library, in room 120*
(2c) *the library*
(2d) *room 120*

Utterances like (2a) and (2b) make use of the hierarchical structure of the domain. Their content can be modelled as a list

$$L = \langle (x_1, P_1), (x_2, P_2)...(x_n, P_n) \rangle,$$

where $x_1 = r$ is the referent of the referring expression and, for every $j > 1$, x_j is an ancestor (not necessarily the parent) of x_{j-1} in D. For every j, P_j is a set of properties that jointly identify x_j within x_{j+1} or, if $j = n$, within the whole domain. For example, (2a) is modelled as

$$L = \langle (r, \{type = library\}), (x_2, \{type = room, r.number = 120\}), (x_3, \{type = building, name = Cockcroft\}) \rangle$$

We focus on the search for x_n because, under the assumptions that were just made this is the only place where problems can occur (since no parent node is available).

Even though each of (2a)-(2d) succeeds in characterising their intended referent uniquely, some of these descriptions can be problematic for the hearer. One such problem occurs in (2d). The expression is logically sufficient. But, intuitively speaking, the expression creates an expectation that the referent may be found nearby, within the Watts building whereas, in fact, a match can only be found in another building. In this case we will speak of *Lack of Orientation* (LO).

Even more confusion might occur if another library was added to our example, e.g., in Watts 110, while the intended referent was kept constant. In this case, (2c) would fail to identify the referent, of course. The expression (2b), however, would succeed, by *mutually* using two parts of the description ('the library' and 'room 120') to identify another: there are two libraries, and two rooms numbered 120, but there is only one pair (a, b) such that a is a library and b is a room numbered 120, while a is located in b. Such cases of mutual identification are unproblematic in small, transparent, domains where search is not an issue, but in large hierarchical domains, they are not. For, like (2d), (2b) would force a reader to search through an unnecessarily large part of the domain; worse even, the search 'path' that the reader is likely to follow leads via an obstacle, namely room 120 Watts, that matches a part of the description, while not being the intended referent of the relevant part of the description (i.e., room 120 Cockcroft). Confusion could easily result. In cases like this, we speak of a *Dead End* (DE).

In section 5 we will present evidence suggesting that instances of Dead End and Lack of Orientation may disrupt search in a sufficiently large or complex domain. For a theoretical discussion we refer to Paraboni and van Deemter (2002).

4 Generation algorithms

What kinds of expression would existing GRE algorithms produce in the situations of interest? Since hierarchies involve relations, the first algorithm that comes to mind is the one proposed by Dale and Haddock (1991). Essentially, this algorithm combines one- and two-place predicates, until a combination is found that pins down the target referent. A standard example involves a domain containing two tables and two bowls, while only one of the two tables has a bowl on it. In this situation, the combination $\{bowl(x), on(x, y), table(y)\}$ identifies x (and, incidentally, also y) uniquely, since only one value of x can be used to verify the three predicates; this justifies the description *'the bowl on the table'*. This situation can be 'translated' directly into our university domain. Consider Figure 2, with one additional library in room 110 of the Watts building. In this situation, the com-

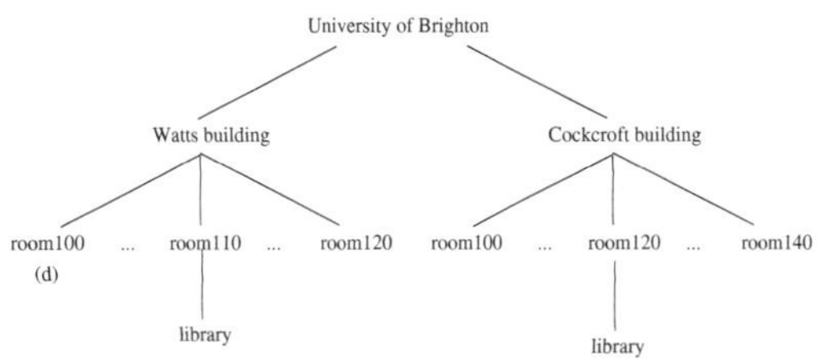

Figure 2: A university campus with two libraries.

bination $\{library(x), in(x, y), room(y), room-number(y) = 2\}$ identifies x (and, incidentally, also y) uniquely, because no other library is located in a room with number 120 (and no other room numbered 120 contains a library). Thus, the standard approach to relational descriptions allows precisely the kinds of situation that we have described as DE. Henceforth, we shall describe this as the Minimal Description (MD) approach to reference because, in the situations of interest, it uses the minimum number of properties by which the referent can be distinguished.

Paraboni and van Deemter (2002) have sketched two GRE algorithms, both of which are guaranteed to prevent DE and LO by including logically redundant information into the generated descriptions so as to reduce the reader's search space. These algorithms, called *Full Inclusion* (FI) and *Scope-Limited* (SL), are not the only ways in which resolution may be aided, but we will see that they represent two natural options. Both take as input a hierarchical domain D, a location d where the referring expression will materialise, and an intended referent r.

Briefly, the FI algorithm represents a straightforward way of reducing the length of search paths, without particular attention to DE or LO. It lines up properties that identify the referent uniquely within its parent node, then moves up to identify this parent node within its parent node, and so on until reaching a subtree that includes the starting point d [2]. Applied to our earlier example of a reference to room 120, FI first builds up the list

$$L = \langle (r, \{type = room, r.number = 120\}) \rangle,$$

then expands it to

$$L = \langle (r, \{type = room, r.number = 120\}), (x1, \{type = building, buildingname = Cockcroft\}) \rangle.$$

Now that Parent(X) includes d , r has been identified uniquely within D and we reach STOP. L might be realised as e.g., 'room 120 in Cockcroft'.

FI gives maximal weight to ease of resolution. But something has to give, and that is brevity: By conveying logical redundancy, descriptions are lengthened, and this can have drawbacks. The second algorithm in Paraboni and van Deemter (2002), called SCOPE-LIMITED (SL), constitutes a compromise between brevity and ease of resolution. SL prevents DE and LO but opts for brevity when DE and LO do not occur. This is done by making use of the notion of SCOPE, hence the name of the algorithm.

[2] The idea behind not moving up beyond this subtree is a natural extension of Krahmer and Theune's treatment of salience in GRE: see Paraboni and van Deemter (2002).

The *difference* between FI and SL becomes evident when we consider a case in which the minimally distinguishing description does not lead to DE or LO. For example, a reference to r = library would be realised by FI as 'the library in room 120 in Cockcroft'. By using SL, however, the same description would be realised by the SL algorithm simply as 'the library', since there is no risk of DE or LO. With the addition of a second library in the Watts building, the behaviour of the SL algorithm would change accordingly, producing 'the library in Cockcroft'. Similarly, had we instead included the second library under another room of Cockcroft, SL would describe r as 'the library in room 120 of Cockcroft', just like FI. For details of both algorithms we refer to Paraboni and van Deemter (2002).

5 The new experiment

In Paraboni and van Deemter (2002) an experiment was described to find out what types of references are favoured by human judges when their opinion about these references is asked. As an example of a hierarchically ordered domain, the experiment made use of a document structured in sections and subsections. This allowed Paraboni and van Deemter (2002) to show their subjects the domain itself, rather than, for example, a pictorial representation (as it would be necessary in most other cases such as that of a University campus, which motivated many of our examples so far).

The experiment investigated the choice of so-called *document-deictic* references, such as 'the picture in part x of section y' made by authors of documents to check whether they choose to avoid potential DE and LO situations by adding redundant properties (favouring ease of resolution) and, conversely, whether they choose shorter descriptions when there is no such risk (favouring ease of interpretation). The results suggested that human authors often prefer logically redundant references, particularly when DE and LO can arise.

While this approach had the advantage that subjects could compare different expressions (perhaps balancing ease of interpretation with ease of resolution), the method is limited in other respects. For example, meta-linguistic judgements are sometimes thought to be an unreliable predictor of people's linguistic behaviour (e.g., van Deemter 2004). Perhaps more seriously, the experiment fails to tell us how difficult a given type of reference (for example, one of the DE type) would actually be for a reader. Therefore, in this paper we report on a second experiment investigating the effect of the presence or absence of logical redundancy on the performance of readers. We are primarily interested in understanding the search process, so resolution rather than interpretation.

5.1 Experiment design

Subjects: Forty-two computing science students participated in the experiment, as part of a scheduled practical.

Procedure: A within-subjects design was used. Each subject was shown twenty on-line documents, in a random order. The entire document structure was always visible, and so was the content of the current document part. A screenshot of an example document providing this level of information is shown in Figure 3. Each document was

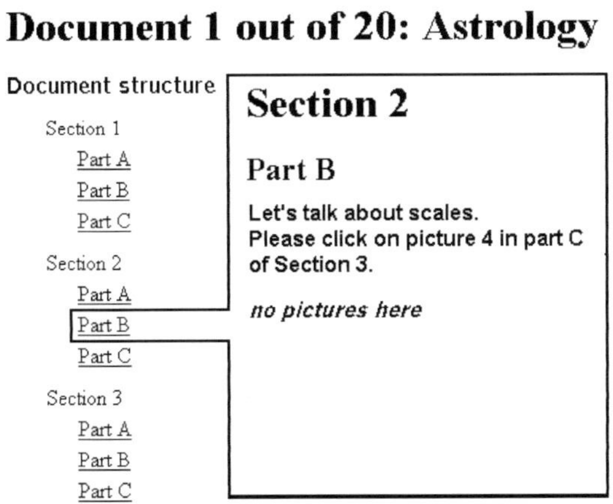

Figure 3: Fragment of the experiment interface.

initially opened in Part B of either Section 2 or 3, where a task was given of the form "Let's talk about [topic]. Please click on [referring expression]" . For instance "Let's talk about elephants. Please click on picture 5 in part A". Subjects could navigate through the document by clicking on the names of the parts (e.g. Part A as visible under Section 3). As soon as the subject had correctly clicked on the picture indicated, the next document was presented. Subjects were reminded throughout the document about the task to be accomplished, and the location at which the task was given. All navigation actions were recorded. At the start of the experiment, subjects were instructed to try to accomplish the task with a minimal number of navigation actions.

We assume that readers do not have *complete* knowledge of the domain. So, they do not know which pictures are present in each part of each section. If readers had complete knowledge, then a minimal description would suffice. We do, however, not assume readers to be completely ignorant either[3]: we allowed them to see the current document part (where the question is asked) and its content, as well as the hierarchical structure (sections and parts) of the remainder of the document as in Figure 3 above.

Research Questions: We want to test whether longer descriptions indeed help resolution, particularly in so-called problematic situations. Table 1 shows the types of situation (potential DE, LO, and non-problematic)[4], reader and referent location, and descriptions used.

> **Hypothesis 1:** In a problematic (DE/LO) situation, the number of navigation actions required for a long (FI/SL) description is smaller than that required for a short (MD) description.

We will use the DE and LO situations in Table 1 to test this hypothesis, comparing for each situation the number of navigation actions of the short, that is, minimally distinguishing (MD) and long (FI/SL) expressions. In Paraboni and van Deemter (2002) there was an additional hypothesis about non-problematic situations, stating that MD descriptions would be preferred to long descriptions in non-problematic situations. We cannot use this hypothesis in this experiment, as it is highly unlikely that a shorter description will lead to *fewer* navigation actions. (Note that the experiment in Paraboni and van Deemter (2002) looked at the combination of interpretation and resolution, while we are now focussing on resolution only). Instead, we will look at *gain*: the number of navigation actions required for a short description minus the number required for a long description.

[3]Readers will always have some knowledge: if in Part B of Section 2, then they would know (by convention) that there will also be a Section 1, and a Part A in Section 2 etc.

[4]In DE situations, there is another picture with the same number as the referent, but not in a part with the same name as the part in which the referent is. In LO situations, there is no other picture with the same number as the referent, and the reader location contains pictures. In non-problematic situations, there is another picture with the same number as the referent, but not in a part with the same name as the part in which the referent is.

Sit.	Type	Reader Loc.	Referent Loc.	Short (MD)	Long (FI/SL)	Long (other)
1	DE	Part B Sec 3	Part A Sec 2	Pic 3 in Part A	Pic 3 in Part A Sec 2	
2	DE	Part B Sec 2	Part C Sec 3	Pic 4 in Part C	Pic 4 in Part C Sec 3	
3	LO	Part B Sec 3	Part A Sec 3	Pic 5	Pic 5 in Part A	Pic 5 in Part A Sec 3
4	LO	Part B Sec 2	Part C Sec 2	Pic 4	Pic 4 in Part C	Pic 4 in Part C Sec 2
5	LO	Part B Sec 3	Part A Sec 4	Pic 5	Pic 5 in Part A Sec 4	Pic 5 in Part A
6	LO	Part B Sec 2	Part C Sec 1	Pic 4	Pic 4 in Part C Sec 1	Pic 4 in Part C
7	NONE	Part B Sec 2	Part A Sec 2	Pic 3 in Part A		Pic 3 in Part A Sec 2
8	NONE	Part B Sec 3	Part C Sec 3	Pic 4 in Part C		Pic 4 in Part C Sec 3

Table 1: Situations of reference

Hypothesis 2: The gain achieved by a long description over an MD description will be larger in a problematic situation than in a non-problematic situation.

We will use the DE and non-problematic situations in Table 1 to test this hypothesis, comparing the gain of situation 1 with that of situation 7, and the gain of situation 2 with that of situation 8.

Longer descriptions may always lead to fewer navigation actions, and it can be expected that complete descriptions of the form picture x in Part y of Section z will outperform shorter descriptions in any situation. So, from a resolution point of view, an algorithm that would always give a complete description may produce better results than the algorithms we proposed, which do not always give complete descriptions (e.g. situation 3 in Table 1). The aim of our algorithms is to make the descriptions complete enough to prevent DE and LO in *resolution*, but not overly redundant as this may affect *interpretation*. We would like to show that the decisions taken by FI and SL are sensible, i.e. that they produce descriptions that are neither too short nor too long. Therefore:

S1: We want to consider situations in which FI and SL have produced an incomplete description, and investigate how much gain could have been made by using a complete description in those cases. We would like this gain to be negligible. We will use situations 3 and 4 for this, calculating the gain of the long, complete descriptions (namely, long (other) in Table 1) over the short, incomplete descriptions generated by our algorithms (long (FI/SL) in Table 1).

S2: We want to consider situations in which FI and SL have produced a complete description, and investigate how much gain has been made by using this compared to a less complete description that is still more complete than MD. We would like this gain to be large. We will use situations 5 and 6 for this, calculating the gain of the long complete descriptions generated by our algorithms (long (FI/SL) in Table 1) over the less complete descriptions (long (other) in Table 1).

Introducing separate hypotheses for cases $S1$ and $S2$ poses the problem of defining when a gain is 'negligible' and when a gain is 'large'. Instead, we will compare the gain achieved in $S1$ with the gain achieved in $S2$, expecting that the gain in $S2$ (which we believe to be large) will be larger than the gain in $S1$ (which we believe to be negligible).

Hypothesis 3: The gain of a complete description over a less complete one will be larger for situations in which FI and SL generated the complete one, than for situations in which they generated the less complete one.

Materials: Twenty on-line documents were produced, with the same document structure (sections 1 to 5 with parts A to C) and containing 10 pictures. Documents had a unique background colour, title and pictures appropriate for the title. The number of pictures in a section or part varied per document. All of this was done to prevent subjects relying on memory.

Documents were constructed specifically for the experiment. Using real-world documents might have made the tasks more realistic, but would have posed a number of problems. Firstly, documents needed to be similar enough in structure to allow a fair comparison between longer and shorter descriptions. However, the structure should not allow subjects to learn where pictures are likely to be (for instance, in patient information leaflets most pictures tend to be at the beginning). Secondly, the content of documents should not help subjects find a picture: e.g., if we were using a real document on animals, subjects might expect a picture of a tiger to be near to a picture of a lion. So,

		Short		Long (FI/SL)		Long (Other)	
Sit.	Type	Mean	STDEV	Mean	STDEV	Mean	STDEV
1	DE	3.58	2.14	1.10	0.50		
2	DE	3.85	3.28	1.30	1.31		
3	LO	5.60	4.84	1.93	1.29	1.23	1.27
4	LO	2.50	1.97	1.60	1.28	1.38	2.07
5	LO	8.53	4.15	1.15	0.53	5.65	6.74
6	LO	7.38	5.49	1.25	1.03	4.08	2.35
7	NONE	1.58	0.98			1.63	2.61
8	NONE	1.48	0.96			1.05	0.32

Table 2: Number of clicks used to complete the tasks.

Sit.	Type	Mean	STDEV
1	DE	2.48	2.24
7	NONE	-0.05	2.77
2	DE	2.55	3.62
8	NONE	0.43	1.04

Table 3: Gain as used for Hypothesis 2.

Sit.	FI Decision	Mean	STDEV
3	NOT COMPLETE	0.70	1.40
5	COMPLETE	4.50	6.67
4	NOT COMPLETE	0.23	2.51
6	COMPLETE	2.83	2.16

Table 4: Gain as used for Hypothesis 3.

we do not want subjects to use semantic information or their background knowledge of the domain. Thirdly, real documents might not have the right descriptions in them, so we would need to change their sentences by hand.

5.2 Results and discussion

Forty subjects completed the experiment. Table 2 shows descriptive statistics for the number of clicks subjects made to complete each task. To analyse the results with respect to Hypothesis 1, we used a General Linear Model (GLM) with repeated measures. We used two repeated factors: Situation (sit. 1 to 6) and Description Length (short and long(FI/SL)). We found a highly significant effect of Description Length on the number of clicks used to complete the task ($p<.001$). In all potential problematic situations the number of clicks is smaller for the long than for the short description. This confirms Hypothesis 1.

Table 3 shows descriptive statistics for the gain as used for Hypothesis 2. We again used a GLM with repeated measures, using two repeated factors: Descriptions Content (that of situations 1 and 7, and that of situations 2 and 8) and Situation Type (potential DE and non-problematic). We found a highly significant effect of Situation Type on the gain ($p<.001$). In the non-problematic situations the gain is smaller than in the potential DE situations. This confirms Hypothesis 2.

Table 4 shows descriptive statistics for the gain as used for Hypothesis 3. We again used a GLM with repeated measures, using two repeated factors: Descriptions Content (that of situations 3 and 5, and that of 4 and 6) and FI Decision (with 2 levels: complete and not complete). We found a highly significant effect of FI Decision on the gain ($p<.001$). The gain is smaller for situations were our algorithm decided to use an incomplete description than in situations were it chose a complete description. This confirms Hypothesis 3.

6 Conclusion

We have discussed generation strategies that facilitate resolution of referring expressions by adding logically redundant information to the descriptions generated. Redundancy has a role to play in different kinds of situation (see Introduction for references), but we have focussed on a class of cases that we believe to be widespread, namely where the domain is hierarchical. We have argued that, in such situations, minimally distinguishing descriptions can sometimes be useless. Various algorithms for generating logically redundant references have been implemented. The extensive experiment of section 5 indicates that these algorithms are fundamentally on the right track.

The new algorithms discussed in this paper are an alternative to classical GRE algorithms. This raises the question how one knows whether to use the new FI or SL instead of one of its competitors? Let us compare the predictions made by our algorithms with those made by Dale and Haddock (1991). Suppose their description *'the bowl on the table'* was said when there are two tables and two bowls, while (only) the table furthest away from the hearer has a bowl on it. In this situation, FI and SL would generate something redundant like *the bowl on the far-away table*. Which of the two descriptions is best? We submit that it depends on the situation: when all the relevant facts are available to the hearer without effort (e.g., all the domain objects are visible at a glance) then minimal descriptions are fine. But in a huge room, where it is not obvious to the hearer what is on each table, search is required. It is this type of situation that there is a need for the kind of 'studied' redundancy embodied in FI and SL, because the minimally *'the bowl on the table'* would not be very helpful. The new algorithms are designed for situations where the hearer may have to make an effort to uncover the relevant facts.

By focussing on the benefits for the reader (in terms of the effort required for identifying the referent), we have not only substantiated the claims in Paraboni and van Deemter (2002), to the effect that it can be good to add logically redundant information to a referring expression; we have also been able to shed light on the *reason* why redundant descriptions are sometimes preferred (compared with the experiment in Paraboni and van Deemter (2002), which did not shed light on the reason for this preference): we can now say with some confidence that, in the circumstances specified, the generated redundant descriptions are resolved with particular ease. By counting the number of clicks that subjects need to find the referent, we believe that we may have achieved a degree of insight into the 'resolution' processes in the head of the reader, not unlike the insights coming out of the kind of eye-tracking experiments that have been popular in psycholinguistics for a number of years now. It would be interesting to see whether our ideas can be confirmed using such a more entrenched experimental paradigm.

7 References

Arts, Anja. 2004. *Overspecification in instructive texts*. PhD. Tilburg University, The Netherlands. Wolf Publishers, Nijmegen.

Cremers, Anita. 1996. *Reference to Objects; an empirically based study of task-oriented dialogues*. Ph.D. thesis, University of Eindhoven.

Dale, Robert and Nicholas Haddock. 1991. Generating Referring Expressions involving Relations. EACL, Berlin, pp.161-166.

Dale, Robert and Ehud Reiter. 1995. Computational Interpretations of the Gricean Maxims in the Generation of Referring Expressions. *Cognitive Science* 18:pp.233-263.

Deutsch, W. 1976. "Sprachliche Redundanz und Objectidentifikation." Unpublished PhD dissertation, University of Marburg.

Edmonds, Philip G. 1994. Collaboration on reference to objects that are not mutually known. COLING-1994, Kyoto, pp.1118-1122.

Krahmer, E. and Theune, M. 2002. Efficient Context-Sensitive Generation of Referring Expressions. In K. van Deemter and R. Kibble (eds.) *Information Sharing*. CSLI Publ., Stanford.

Horacek, Helmut. 2005. Generating referential descriptions under conditions of uncertainty. 10th European workshop on Natural Language Generation (ENLG-2005). Aberdeen, pp.58-67.

Jordan, Pamela W. 2000. Can Nominal Expressions Achieve Multiple Goals?: An Empirical Study. ACL-2000, Hong Kong.

Levelt, W.J.M. 1989. *Speaking: From Intention to Articulation*. MIT Press, Cambridge.

Mangold, Roland. 1986. *Sensorische Faktoren beim Verstehen ueberspezifizierter Objektbenennungen*. Frankfurt: Peter Lang Verlag.

Paraboni, Ivandre. 2000. An algorithm for generating document-deictic references. INLG-2000 Workshop Coherence in Generated Multimedia, Mitzpe Ramon, pp.27-31.

Paraboni, Ivandre and van Deemter, K. (2002). Generating Easy References: the Case of Document Deixis. INLG-2002, New York, pp.113-119.

Sonnenschein, Susan. 1984. The effect of redundant communication on listeners: Why different types may have different effects. *Journal of Psycholinguistic Research* 13, pp.147-166.

van Deemter, Kees. 2004. Finetuning an NLG system through experiments with human subjects: the case of vague descriptions. INLG-04, Brockenhurst, UK, pp.31-40.

van der Sluis, I. 2005. Multimodal Reference, Studies in Automatic Generation of Multimodal Referring Expressions. Ph.D. thesis, Tilburg University, the Netherlands.

Algorithms for Generating Referring Expressions: Do They Do What People Do?

Jette Viethen
Centre for Language Technology
Macquarie University
Sydney NSW 2109
jviethen@ics.mq.edu.au

Robert Dale
Centre for Language Technology
Macquarie University
Sydney NSW 2109
robert.dale@mq.edu.au

Abstract

The natural language generation literature provides many algorithms for the generation of referring expressions. In this paper, we explore the question of whether these algorithms actually produce the kinds of expressions that people produce. We compare the output of three existing algorithms against a data set consisting of human-generated referring expressions, and identify a number of significant differences between what people do and what these algorithms do. On the basis of these observations, we suggest some ways forward that attempt to address these differences.

1 Introduction

The generation of referring expressions (henceforth GRE) — that is, the process of working out what properties of an entity should be used to describe it in such a way as to distinguish it from other entities in the context — is a recurrent theme in the natural language generation literature. The task is discussed informally in some of the earliest work on NLG (in particular, see (Winograd, 1972; McDonald, 1980; Appelt, 1981)), but the first formally explicit algorithm was introduced in (Dale, 1989); this algorithm, often referred to as the Full Brevity (FB) algorithm, has served as a starting point for many subsequent GRE algorithms. To overcome its limitation to one-place predicates, Dale and Haddock (1991) introduced a constraint-based procedure that could generate referring expressions involving relations; and as a response to the computational complexity of 'greedy' algorithms like FB, Reiter and Dale (Reiter and Dale, 1992; Dale and Reiter, 1995) introduced the psycholinguistically motivated Incremental Algorithm (IA). In recent years there have been a number of important extensions to the IA. The Context-Sensitive extension (Krahmer and Theune, 2002) is able to generate referring expressions for the most salient entity in a context; the Boolean Expressions algorithm (van Deemter, 2002) is able to derive expressions containing boolean operators, as in *the cup that does not have a handle*; and the Sets algorithm (van Deemter, 2002) extends the basic approach to references to sets, as in *the red cups*. Some approaches reuse parts of other algorithms: the Branch and Bound algorithm (Krahmer et al., 2003) uses the Full Brevity algorithm, but is able to generate referring expressions with both attributes and relational descriptions using a graph-based technique. There are many other algorithms described in the literature: see, for example, (Horacek, 1997; Bateman, 1999; Stone, 2000; Gardent, 2002). Their general aim is to produce naturalistic referring expressions, often explicitly by means of an attempt to follow the same kinds of principles that we believe people might be following when they produce language — such as the Gricean maxims (Grice, 1975). However, the algorithms have rarely been tested against real data from human referring expression generation.[1]

In this paper, we present a data set containing human-produced referring expressions in a limited domain. Focussing specifically on the algorithms

[1]The only exceptions we know of to this deficit are not directly concerned with the kinds of properties people select, but with phenomena such as how people group entities together (Funakoshi et al., 2004; Gatt, 2006), or with multimodal referring expressions where the linguistic part is not necessarily distinguishing by itself (van der Sluis and Krahmer, 2004).

Proceedings of the Fourth International Natural Language Generation Conference
Sydney, July 2006.

presented in (Dale, 1989), (Dale and Haddock, 1991) and (Reiter and Dale, 1992), we explore how well these algorithms perform in the same context. There are significant differences between the referring expressions produced by humans, and those produced by the algorithms; we explore these differences and consider what it means for work in the generation of referring expressions.

The remainder of this paper is structured as follows. In Section 2, we introduce the data set of human-produced referring expressions we use; in Section 3, we introduce the representational framework we use to model the domain underlying this data; in Section 4 we introduce the three algorithms considered in this paper; in Section 5 we discuss the results of using these algorithms on the data that represents the model of our domain; in Section 6 we discuss the differences between the output of the algorithms and the human-produced data; and in Section 7 we draw some conclusions and suggest some steps towards addressing the issues we have identified.

2 The Data

Our human-produced referring expressions are drawn from a physical experimental setting consisting of four filing cabinets, each of which is four drawers high, located in a fairly typical academic office. The cabinets are positioned directly next to each other, so that the drawers form a four-by-four grid; each drawer is labelled with a number between 1 and 16 and is coloured either blue, pink, yellow, or orange. There are four drawers of each colour which are distributed randomly over the grid, as shown in Figure 1.

Subjects were given a randomly generated number between 1 and 16, and asked to produce a description of the numbered drawer using any properties other than the number. There were 20 participants in the experiment, resulting in a total of 140 referring expressions. Here are some examples of the referring expressions produced:

(1) the top drawer second from the right [d_3]

(2) the orange drawer on the left [d_9]

(3) the orange drawer between two pink ones [d_{12}]

(4) the bottom left drawer [d_{16}]

Since the selection of which drawer to describe was random, we do not have an equal number of

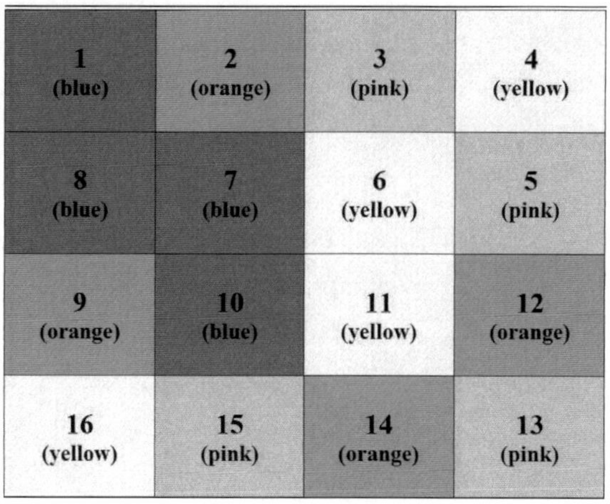

Figure 1: The filing cabinets

descriptions of each drawer; in fact, the data set ranges from two descriptions of Drawer 1 to 12 descriptions of Drawer 16. One of the most obvious things about the data set is that even the same person may refer to the same entity in different ways on different occasions, with the differences being semantic as well as syntactic.

We are interested in comparing how algorithms for referring expression generation differ in their outputs from what people do; since these algorithms produce distinguishing descriptions, we therefore removed from the data set 22 descriptions which were ambiguous or referred to a set of drawers. This resulted in a total of 118 distinct referring expressions, with an average of 7.375 distinct referring expressions per drawer.

As the algorithms under scrutiny here are not concerned with the final syntactic realisation of the referring expression produced, we also normalised the human-produced data to remove superficial variations such as the distinction between relative clauses and reduced relatives, and between different lexical items that were synonymous in context, such as *column* and *cabinet*.

Four absolute properties used for describing the drawers can be identified in the natural data produced by the human participants. These are the colour of the drawer; its row and column; and in those cases where the drawer is situated in one of the corners of the grid, its cornerhood.[2] A number of the natural descriptions also made use of the

[2] A question we will return to below is that of how we decide whether to view a particular property as a one-place predicate or as a relation.

Property	Count	% (out of possible)
Row	95	79.66% (118)
Column	88	73.73% (118)
Colour	63	53.39% (118)
Corner	11	40.74% (27)
Relation	15	12.71% (118)

Table 1: The properties used in descriptions

following relational properties that hold between drawers: above, below, next to, right of, left of and between. In Table 1, Count shows the number of descriptions using each property, and the percentages show the ratio of the number of descriptions using each property to the number of descriptions for drawers that possess this property (hence, only 27 of the descriptions referred to corner drawers). We have combined all uses of relations into one row in this table to save space, since, interestingly, their overall use is far below that of the other properties: 103 descriptions (87.3%) did not use relations.

Most algorithms in the literature aim at generating descriptions that are as short as possible, but will under certain circumstances produce redundancy. Some authors, for example (van Deemter and Halldórsson, 2001), have suggested that human-produced descriptions are often not minimal, and this is an intuition that we would generally agree with. However, a strong tendency towards minimality is evident in the human-produced data here: only 29 out of 118 descriptions (24.6%) contain redundant information. Here are a few examples:

- *the yellow drawer in the third column from the left second from the top* [d_6]
- *the blue drawer in the top left corner* [d_1]
- *the orange drawer below the two yellow drawers* [d_{14}]

In the first case, either the colour or column properties are redundant; in the second, colour and corner, or only the grid information, would have been sufficient; and in the third, it would have been sufficient to mention one of the two yellow drawers.

3 Knowledge Representation

In order to use an algorithm to generate referring expressions in this domain, we must first decide how to represent the domain. It turns out that this raises some interesting questions.

We use the symbols $\{d_1, d_2 \ldots d_{16}\}$ as our unique identifying labels for the 16 drawers. Given some d_i, the goal of any given algorithm is then to produce a distinguishing description of that entity with respect to a context consisting of the other 15 drawers.

As is usual, we represent the properties of the domain in terms of attribute–value pairs. Thus we have, for example:

- d_2: ⟨colour, orange⟩, ⟨row, 1⟩, ⟨column, 2⟩, ⟨right-of, d_1⟩, ⟨left-of, d_3⟩, ⟨next-to, d_1⟩, ⟨next-to, d_3⟩, ⟨above, d_7⟩

This drawer is in the top row, so it does not have a property of the form ⟨below, d_2⟩.

The four corner drawers additionally possess the property ⟨position, corner⟩. Cornerhood can be inferred from the row and column information; however, we added this property explicitly because several of the natural descriptions use the property of cornerhood, and it seems plausible that this is a particularly salient property in its own right.

This raises the question of what properties should be encoded explicitly, and which should be inferred. Note that in the example above, we explicitly encode relational properties that could be computed from others, such as left-of and right-of. Since none of the algorithms explored here uses inference over knowledge base properties, we opted here to 'level the playing field' to enable fairer comparison between human-produced and machine-produced descriptions.

A similar question of the role of inference arises with regard to the transitivity of spatial relations. For example, if d_1 is above d_9 and d_9 is above d_{16} , then it can be inferred that d_1 is transitively above d_{16}. In a more complex domain, the implementation of this kind of knowledge might play an important role in generating usful referring expressions. However, the uniformity of our domain results in this inferred knowledge about transitive relations being of little use; in fact, in most cases, the implementation of transitive inference might even result in the generation of unnatural descriptions, such as *the orange drawer (two) right of the blue drawer* for d_{12}.

Another aspect of the representation of relations that requires a decision is that of generalisation:

next-to is a generalisation of the relations left-of and right-of. The only algorithm of those we examine here that provides a mechanism for exploring a generalisation hierarchy is the Incremental Algorithm (Reiter and Dale, 1992), and this cannot handle relations; so, we take the shortcut of explicitly representing the next-to relation for every left-of and right-of relation in the knowledge base. We then implement special-case handling that ensures that, if one of these facts is used, the more general or more specific case is also deleted from the set of properties still available for the description.[3]

4 The Algorithms

As we have already noted above, there is a considerable literature on the generation of referring expressions, and many papers in the area provide detailed algorithms. We focus here on the following algorithms:

- The Full Brevity algorithm (Dale, 1989) attempts to build a minimal distinguishing description by always selecting the most discriminatory property available; see Algorithm 1.

Let L be the set of properties to be realised in our description; let P be the set of properties known to be true of our intended referent r (we assume that P is non-empty); and let C be the set of distractors (the contrast set). The initial conditions are thus as follows:

- $C = \{\langle \textit{all distractors} \rangle\}$;
- $P = \{\langle \textit{all properties true of } r \rangle\}$;
- $L = \{\}$

In order to describe the intended referent r with respect to the contrast set C, we do the following:

1. Check Success:
   if $|C| = 0$ **then** return L as a distinguishing description
   elseif $P = \emptyset$ **then** fail
   else goto Step 2.
2. Choose Property:
   for each $p_i \in P$ **do**:
   $C_i \leftarrow C \cap \{x | p_i(x)\}$
   Chosen property is p_j, where C_j is the smallest set.
   goto Step 3.
3. Extend Description (wrt the chosen p_j):
   $L \leftarrow L \cup \{p_j\}$
   $C \leftarrow C_j$
   $P \leftarrow P - \{p_j\}$
   goto Step 1.

Algorithm 1: The Full Brevity Algorithm

[3]This is essentially a hack; however, there is clearly a need for some mechanism for handling what we might think of as equivalence classes of properties, and this is effectively a simple approach to this question.

---

1. Check Success
   if Stack is empty **then** return L as a DD
   elseif $|C_v| = 1$ **then** pop Stack & **goto** Step 1
   elseif $P_r = \emptyset$ **then** fail
   else goto Step 2
2. Choose Property
   for each property $p_i \in P_r$ **do**
   $p'_i \leftarrow [r \backslash v] p_i$
   $N_i \leftarrow N \oplus p'_i$
   Chosen prediction is p_j, where N_j contains the smallest set C_v for v.
   goto Step 3
3. Extend Description (w.r.t the chosen p)
   $P_r \leftarrow P_r - \{p\}$
   $p \leftarrow [r \backslash v] p$
   for every other constant r' in p **do**
   associate r' with a new, unique variable v'
   $p \leftarrow [r' \backslash v'] p$
   push `Describe`(r',v') onto `Stack`
   initialise a set P'_r of facts true of r'
   $N \leftarrow N \oplus p$
   goto Step 1

Algorithm 2: The Relational Algorithm

MakeReferringExpression(r, C, P) $L \leftarrow \{\}$
for each member A_i of list P **do**
  V = FindBestValue(r, A_i, *BasicLevelValue*(r, A_i))
  if RulesOut($\langle A_i, V \rangle$) $\neq$ nil
  then $L \leftarrow L \cup \{\langle A_i, V \rangle\}$
      $C \leftarrow C$ − RulesOut($\langle A_i, V \rangle$)
  endif
  if C = {} **then**
    if ⟨type, X⟩ $\in L$ for some X
      then return L
      else return $L \cup \{\langle$type, BasicLevelValue(r, type)$\rangle\}$
      endif
  endif
return failure

FindBestValue(r, A, *initial-value*)
if *UserKnows*(r, ⟨A, *initial-value*⟩) = **true**
then *value* ← *initial-value*
else *value* ← no-value
endif
if (*more-specific-value* ← ***MoreSpecificValue***(r, A, *value*)) $\neq$ nil ∧
  (*new-value* ← ***FindBestValue***(A, *more-specific-value*)) $\neq$ nil ∧
  (|RulesOut(⟨A, *new-value*⟩)| > |RulesOut(⟨A, *value*⟩)|)
then *value* ← *new-value*
endif
return *value*

RulesOut(⟨A, V⟩)
if V = no-value
then return nil
else return $\{x : x \in C \wedge$ ***UserKnows***(x, ⟨A, V⟩) = **false**$\}$
endif

Algorithm 3: The Incremental Algorithm

- The relational algorithm from (Dale and Haddock, 1991) uses constraint satisfaction to incorporate relational properties while avoiding infinite regress; see Algorithm 2.

- the Incremental Algorithm (Reiter and Dale, 1992; Dale and Reiter, 1995) considers the available properties to be used in a description via a preference ordering over those properties; see Algorithm 3.

For the purpose of this study, the algorithms were implemented in Common LISP. The mechanism described in (Dale and Reiter, 1995) to handle generalisation hierarchies for values for the different properties, referred to in the algorithm here as FindBestValue, was not implemented since, as discussed earlier, our representation of the domain does not make use of a hierarchy of properties.

5 The Output of the Algorithms

Using the knowledge base described in Section 3, we applied the algorithms from the previous section to see whether the referring expressions they produced were the same as, or similar to, those produced by the human subjects. This quickly gave rise to some situations not explicitly addressed by some of the algorithms; we discuss these in Section 5.1 below. Section 5.2 discusses the extent to which the behaviour of the algorithms matched that of the human data.

5.1 Preference Orderings

The Incremental Algorithm explicitly encodes a preference ordering over the available properties, in an attempt to model what appear to be semi-conventionalised strategies for description that people use. This also has the consequence of avoiding a problem that faces the other two algorithms: since the Full Brevity Algorithm and the Relational Algorithm choose the most discriminatory property at each step, they have to deal with the case where several properties are equally discriminatory. This turns out to be a common situation in our domain. Both algorithms implicitly assume that the choice will be made randomly in these cases; however, it seems to us more natural to control this process by imposing some selection strategy. We do this here by borrowing the idea of preference ordering from the Incremental Algorithm, and using it as a tie-breaker when multiple properties are equally discriminatory.

Not including type information (i.e., the fact that some d_i is a drawer), which has no discriminatory power and therefore will never be chosen by any of the algorithms,[4] there are only four different properties available for the Full Brevity Algorithm and the Incremental Algorithm: row, column, colour, and position. This gives us 4! = 24 different possible preference orderings. Since some of the human-produced descriptions use all four properties, we tested these two algorithms with all 24 preference orderings.

For the Relational Algorithm, we added the five relations next to, left of, right of, above, and below. This results in 9! = 362,880 possible preference orderings; far too many to test. Since we are primarily interested in whether the algorithm can generate the human-produced descriptions, we restricted our testing to those preference orderings that started with a permutation of the properties used by the participants; in addition to the 24 preference orderings above, there are 12 preference orderings that incorporate the relational properties.

5.2 Coverage of the Human Data

Overall, the Full Brevity Algorithm is able to generate 82 out of the 103 non-relational descriptions from the natural data, providing a recall of 79.6%. The recall score for the Incremental Algorithm is 95.1%, generating 98 of the 103 descriptions. As these algorithms do not attempt to generate relational descriptions, the relational data is not taken into account in evaluating the performance here.

Both algorithms are able to generate all the non-relational minimal descriptions found in the human-produced data. The Full Brevity Algorithm unintentionally replicates the redundancy found in nine descriptions, and the Incremental Algorithm produces all but five of the 29 redundant descriptions.

Perhaps surprisingly, the Relational Algorithm does not generate *any* of the human-produced descriptions. We will return to consider why this is the case in the next section.

6 Discussion

There are two significant differences to be considered here: first, the coverage of redundant descriptions by the Full Brevity and Incremental Algo-

[4]Consistent with much other work in the field, we assume that the head noun will always be added irrespective of whether it has any discriminatory power.

rithms; and second, the inability of the Relational Algorithm to replicate any of the human data.

6.1 Coverage of Redundancy

Neither the Full Brevity Algorithm nor the Incremental Algorithm presumes to be able to generate relational descriptions; however, both algorithms are able to produce each of the minimal descriptions from the set of natural data with at least one of the preference orderings. Both also generate several of the redundant descriptions in the natural data set, but do not capture all of the human-generated redundancies.

The Full Brevity Algorithm has as a primary goal the avoidance of redundant descriptions, so it is a sign of the algorithm being consistent with its specification that it covers fewer of the redundant expressions than the Incremental Algorithm. On the other hand, the fact that it produces *any* redundant descriptions signals that the algorithm doesn't quite meet its specification. The cases where the Full Brevity Algorithm produces redundancy are when an entity shares with another entity at least two property-values and, after choosing one of these properties, the next property to be considered is the other shared one, since it has the same or a higher discriminatory power than all other properties. This is a situation that was not considered in the original algorithm; it is related to the problem of what to do when two properties have the same discriminatory power, as noted earlier. In our domain, the situation arises for corner drawers with the same colour (d_4 and d_{16}), and drawers that are not in a corner but for which there is another drawer of the same colour in each of the same row and column (d_7 and d_8).

The Incremental Algorithm, on the other hand, generates redundancy when an object shares at least two property-values with another object and the two shared properties are the first to be considered in the preference ordering. This is possible for corner drawers with the same colour (d_4 and d_{16}) and for drawers for which there is another drawer of the same colour in either the same row, the same column, or both (d_5, d_6, d_7, d_8, d_{10}, d_{11}, d_{13}, d_{15}).

In these terms, the Incremental Algorithm is clearly a better model of the human behaviour than the Full Brevity Algorithm. However, we may ask why the algorithm does not cover all the redundancy found in the human descriptions. The redundant descriptions which the algorithm does not generate are as follows:

(5) *the blue drawer in the top left corner* [d_1]

(6) *the yellow drawer in the top right corner* [d_4]

(7) *the pink drawer in the top of the column second from the right* [d_3]

(8) *the orange drawer in the bottom second from the right* [d_{14}]

(9) *the orange drawer in the bottom of the second column from the right* [d_{14}]

The Incremental Algorithm stops selecting properties when a distinguishing description has been constructed. In Example (6), for example, the algorithm would select any of the following, depending on the preference ordering used:

(10) *the yellow drawer in the corner*

(11) *the top left yellow drawer*

(12) *the drawer in the top left corner*

The human subject, however, has added information beyond what is required. This could be explained by our modelling of cornerhood: in Examples (5) and (6), one has the intuition that the noun *corner* is being added simply to provide a nominal head to the prepositional phrase in an incrementally-constructed expression of the form *the blue drawer in the top right* ..., in much the same way as the head noun *drawer* is added, whereas we have treated it as a distinct property that adds discriminatory power. This again emphasises the important role the underlying representation plays in the generation of referring expressions: if we want to emulate what people do, then we not only need to design algorithms which mirror their behaviour, but these algorithms have to operate over the same kind of data.

6.2 Relational Descriptions

The fact that the Relational Algorithm generates none of the human-generated descriptions is quite disturbing. On closer examination, it transpires that this is because, in this domain, the discriminatory power of relational properties is generally always greater than that of any other property, so a relational property is chosen first. As noted earlier, relational properties appear to be dispreferred in the human data, so the Relational Algorithm is already disadvantaged. The relatively poor performance of the algorithm is then compounded by its insistence on continuing to use relational properties: an absolute property will only be chosen when either the currently described drawer has no unused relational properties left, or the number of distractors has been reduced so much that the discriminatory power of all remaining relational properties is lower than that of the absolute property, or the absolute property has the same discriminatory power as the best relational one and the absolute property appears before all relations in the preference ordering.

Consequently, whereas a typical human description of drawer d_2 would be *the orange drawer above the blue drawer*, the Relational Algorithm will produce the description *the drawer above the drawer above the drawer above the pink drawer*. Not only are there no descriptions of this form in the human-produced data set, but they also sound more like riddles someone might create to intentionally make it hard for the hearer to figure out what is meant.

There are a variety of ways in which the behaviour of this algorithm might be repaired. We are currently exploring whether Krahmer et al's (2003) graph-based approach to GRE is able to provide a better coverage of the data: this algorithm provides the ability to make use of different search strategies and weighting mechanisms when adding properties to a description, and such a mechanism might be used, for example, to counterbalance the Relational Algorithm's heavy bias towards the relations in this domain.

7 Conclusions and Future Work

We have noted a number of regards in which the algorithms we have explored here do not produce outputs that are the same as those produced by humans. Some comments on the generalisability of these results are appropriate.

First, our results may be idiosyncratic to the specifics of the particular domain of our experiment. We would point out, however, that the domain is more complex, and arguably more realistic, than the much-simplified experimental contexts that have served as intuitions for earlier work in the field; we have in mind here in particular the experiments discussed in (Ford and Olson, 1975), (Sonnenschein, 1985) and (Pechmann, 1989). In the belief that the data provides a good test set for the generation of referring expressions, we are making the data set publicly available [5], so others may try to develop algorithms covering the data.

A second concern is that we have only explored the extent to which three specific algorithms are able to cover the human data. Many of the other algorithms in the literature take these as a base, and so are unlikely to deliver significantly different results. The major exceptions here may be (a) van Deemter's (2002) algorithm for sets; recall that we excluded from the human data used here 16 references that involved sets; and, as noted above, (b) Krahmer et al's (2003) graph-based approach to GRE, which may perform better than the Relational Algorithm on descriptions using relations. In future work, we intend to explore to what extent our findings extend to other algorithms.

In conclusion, we point to two directions where we believe further work is required.

First, as we noted early in this paper, it is clear that there can be many different ways of referring to the same entity. Existing algorithms are all deterministic and therefore produce exactly one 'best' description for each entity; but the human-produced data clearly shows that there are many equally valid ways of describing an entity. We need to find some way to account for this in our algorithms. Our intuition is that this is likely to be best cashed out in terms of different 'reference strategies' that different speakers adopt in different situations; we are reminded here of Carletta's (1992) distinction between risky and cautious strategies for describing objects in the Map Task domain. More experimentation is required in order to determine just what these strategies are: are they, for example, characterisable as things like 'Produce a referring expression that is as short as possible' (the intuition behind the Full Brevity Algorithm), 'Just say what comes to mind first and keep adding information until the description distinguishes the intended referent' (something like the Incremental Algorithm), or perhaps a strategy of minimising the cognitive effort for either the speaker or the hearer? Further psycholinguistic experiments and data analysis are required to determine the answers here.

Our second observation is that the particular results we have presented here are, ultimately, en-

[5] The data set is publicly available from http://www.ics.mq.edu.au/~jviethen/drawers

tirely dependent upon the underlying representations we have used, and the decisions we have made in choosing how to represent the properties and relations in the domain. We believe it is important to draw attention to the fact that precisely how we choose to represent the domain has an impact on what the algorithms will do. If we are aiming for naturalism in our algorithms for referring expression generation, then ideally we would like our representations to mirror those used by humans; but, of course, we don't have direct access to what these are.

There is clearly scope for psychological experimentation, perhaps along the lines initially explored by (Rosch, 1978), to determine some constraints here. In parallel, we are considering further exploration into the variety of representations that can be used, particularly with regard to the question of which properties are considered to be 'primitive', and which are generated by some inference mechanism; this is a much neglected aspect of the referring expression generation task.

References

D. E. Appelt. 1981. *Planning Natural Language Utterances to Satisfy Multiple Goals*. Ph.D. thesis, Stanford University.

J. Bateman. 1999. Using aggregation for selecting content when generating referring expressions. In *Proceedings of the 37th Meeting of the ACL*, pages 127–134.

J. C. Carletta. 1992. *Risk-taking and Recovery in Task-oriented Dialogue*. Ph.D. thesis, University of Edinburgh.

R. Dale and N. Haddock. 1991. Generating referring expressions involving relations. In *Proceedings of the 5th Meeting of the EACL*, pages 161–166, Berlin, Germany.

R. Dale and E. Reiter. 1995. Computational interpretations of the Gricean maxims in the generation of referring expressions. *Cognitive Science*, 19(2):233–263.

R. Dale. 1989. Cooking up referring expressions. In *Proceedings of the 27th Meeting of the ACL*, pages 68–75.

W. Ford and D. Olson. 1975. The elaboration of the noun phrase in children's description of objects. *Journal of Experimental Child Psychology*, 19:371–382.

K. Funakoshi, S. Watanabe, N. Kuriyama, and T. Tokunaga. 2004. Generating referring expressions using perceptual groups. In *Proceedings of the 3rd INLG*, pages 51–60.

C. Gardent. 2002. Generating minimal definite descriptions. In *Proceedings of the 40th Meeting of the ACL*, pages 96–103.

A. Gatt. 2006. Structuring knowledge for reference generation: A clustering algorithm. In *Proceedings of the 11th Meeting of the EACL*.

H. P. Grice. 1975. Logic and conversation. In P. Cole and J. Morgan, editors, *Syntax and Semantics Volume 3: Speech Acts*, pages 43–58. Academic Press.

H. Horacek. 1997. An algorithm for generating referential descriptions with flexible interfaces. In *Proceedings of the 35th Meeting of the ACL*, pages 127–134.

E. Krahmer and M. Theune. 2002. Efficient context-sensitive generation of referring expressions. In K. van Deemter and R. Kibble, editors, *Information Sharing: Reference and Presupposition in Language Generation and Interpretation*, pages 223–264. CSLI.

E. Krahmer, S. van Erk, and A. Verleg. 2003. Graph-based generation of referring expressions. *Computational Linguistics*, 29(1):53–72.

D. D. McDonald. 1980. *Natural Language Generation as a Process of Decision-making Under Constraints*. Ph.D. thesis, Massachusetts Institute of Technology.

T. Pechmann. 1989. Incremental speech production and referential overspecification. *Linguistics*, 27:89–110.

E. Reiter and R. Dale. 1992. A fast algorithm for the generation of referring expressions. In *Proceedings of the 14th Meeting of the ACL*, pages 232–238.

E. Rosch. 1978. Principles of categorization. In *Cognition and Categorization*, pages 27–48. Lawrence Erlbaum, Hillsdale, NJ.

S. Sonnenschein. 1985. The development of referential communication skills: Some situations in which speakers give redundant messages. *Journal of Psycholinguistic Research*, 14:489–508.

M. Stone. 2000. On identifying sets. In *Proceedings of the 1st INLG*, pages 116–123.

K. van Deemter and M. M. Halldórsson. 2001. Logical form equivalence: The case referring expressions generation. In *Proceedings of the 8th ENLG*.

K. van Deemter. 2002. Generating referring expressions: Boolean extensions of the incremental algorithm. *Computational Linguistics*, 28(1):37–52.

I. van der Sluis and E. Krahmer. 2004. Evaluating multimodal NLG using production experiments. In *Proceedings of the 4th LREC*, pages 209–212, 26-28 May.

T. Winograd. 1972. *Understanding Natural Language*. Academic Press.

Group-based Generation of Referring Expressions

Funakoshi Kotaro *　　**Watanabe Satoru** †　　**Tokunaga Takenobu**

Department of Computer Science, Tokyo Institute of Technology
Tokyo Meguro Ôokayama 2-12-1, 152-8552, Japan
take@cl.cs.titech.ac.jp

Abstract

Past work of generating referring expressions mainly utilized attributes of objects and binary relations between objects in order to distinguish the target object from others. However, such an approach does not work well when there is no distinctive attribute among objects. To overcome this limitation, this paper proposes a novel generation method utilizing perceptual groups of objects and n-ary relations among them. The evaluation using 18 subjects showed that the proposed method could effectively generate proper referring expressions.

1 Introduction

In the last two decades, many researchers have studied the generation of referring expressions to enable computers to communicate with humans about objects in the world.

In order to refer to an intended object (the target) among others (distractors), most past work (Appelt, 1985; Dale and Haddock, 1991; Dale, 1992; Dale and Reiter, 1995; Heeman and Hirst, 1995; Horacek, 1997; Krahmer and Theune, 2002; van Deemter, 2002; Krahmer et al., 2003) utilized attributes of the target and binary relations between the target and distractors. Therefore, these methods cannot generate proper referring expressions in situations where there is no significant surface difference between the target and distractors, and no binary relation is useful to distinguish the target. Here, a *proper* referring expression means a concise and natural linguistic expression enabling hearers to identify the target.

For example, consider indicating object b to person P in the situation of Figure 1. Note that labels a, b and c are assigned for explanation to the readers, and person P does not share these labels with the speaker. Because object b is not distinguishable from objects a or c by means of their appearance, one would try to use a binary relation between object b and the table, i.e., "a ball to the right of the table". However, "to the right of" is not a discriminatory relation, for objects a and c are also located to the right of the table. Using a and c as a reference object instead of the table does not make sense, since a and c cannot be uniquely identified because of the same reason that b cannot be identified. Such situations have drawn less attention (Stone, 2000), but can frequently occur in some domains such as object arrangement (Tanaka et al., 2004).

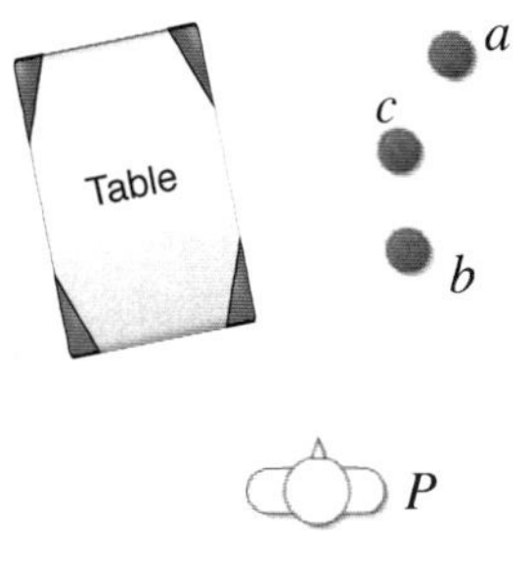

Figure 1: An example of problematic situations

In the situation of Figure 1, the speaker can indicate object b to person P with a simple expression "the front ball". In order to generate such an expression, one must be able to recognize the salient perceptual group of the objects and use the n-ary relative relations in the group.

* Currently at Honda Research Institute Japan Co., Ltd.
† Currently at Hitachi, Ltd.

Proceedings of the Fourth International Natural Language Generation Conference
Sydney, July 2006. ©2006 Association for Computational Linguistics

To overcome the problem described above, Funakoshi et al. (2004) proposed a method of generating Japanese referring expressions that utilizes n-ary relations among members of a group. They, however, dealt with the limited situations where only homogeneous objects are randomly arranged (see Figure 2). Thus, their method could handle only spatial n-ary relation, and could not handle attributes and binary relations between objects which have been the main concern of the past research.

In this paper, we extend the generation method proposed by (Funakoshi et al., 2004) so as to handle object attributes and binary relations between objects as well. In what follows, Section 2 shows an extension of the SOG representation that was proposed in (Funakoshi et al., 2004). Our new method will be described in Section 3 and evaluated in Section 4. Finally we conclude the paper in Section 5.

2 SOG representation

Funakoshi et al. (2004) proposed an intermediate representation between a referring expression and the situation that is referred to by the expression. The intermediate representation represents a course of narrowing down to the target as a sequence of groups from the group of all objects to the singleton group of the target object. Thus it is called SOG (Sequence Of Groups).

The following example shows an expression describing the target x in Figure 2 with the corresponding SOG representation below it. Since Japanese is a head-final language, the order of groups in the SOG representation can be retained in the linguistic expression.

> *hidari oku ni aru*$_{(1)}$ *mittu no tama no uti no*$_{(2)}$ *itiban migi no tama*$_{(3)}$
>
> (the rightmost ball$_{(3)}$ among the three balls$_{(2)}$ at the back left$_{(1)}$)
>
> SOG:$[\{a,b,c,d,e,f,x\},\{a,b,x\},\{x\}]$,
>
> where $\{a,b,c,d,e,f,x\}$ denotes all objects in the situation, $\{a,b,x\}$ denotes the three objects at the back left, and $\{x\}$ denotes the target.

2.1 Extended SOG

As mentioned above, (Funakoshi et al., 2004) supposed the limited situations where only homogeneous objects are randomly arranged, and considered only spatial subsumption relations between consecutive groups. Therefore, relations between

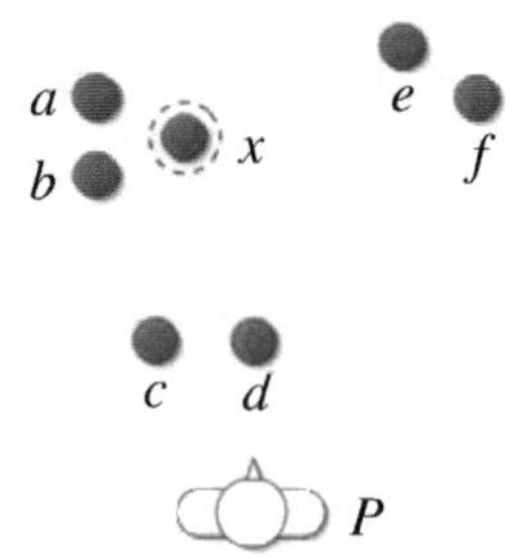

Figure 2: An example from (Funakoshi et al., 2004)

groups are not explicitly denoted in the original SOGs as shown below.

> SOG: $[G_0, G_1, \ldots, G_n]$
> G_i: a group

In this paper, however, other types of relations between groups are also considered. We propose an extended SOG representation where types of relations are explicitly denoted as shown below. In the rest of this paper, we will refer to this extended SOG representation by simply saying "SOG".

> SOG: $[G_0R_0G_1R_1 \ldots G_iR_i \ldots G_n]$
> G_i: a group
> R_i: a relation between G_i and G_{i+1}

2.2 Relations between groups

R_i, a relation between groups G_i and G_{i+1}, denotes a shift of attention from G_i to G_{i+1} with a certain focused *feature*. The feature can be an attribute of objects or a relation between objects. There are two types of relations between groups: *intra-group relation* and *inter-group relation*.

Intra-group relation When R_i is an intra-group relation, G_i subsumes G_{i+1}, that is, $G_i \supset G_{i+1}$. Intra-group relations are further classified into the following subcategories according to the feature used to narrow down G_i to G_{i+1}. We denote these subcategories with the following symbols.

$\xrightarrow{space}$: spatial subsumption
$\xrightarrow{type}$: the object type
$\xrightarrow{shape}$: the shape of objects
$\xrightarrow{color}$: the color of objects
$\xrightarrow{size}$: the size of objects

With respect to this classification, (Funakoshi et al., 2004) dealt with only the $\xrightarrow{space}$ relation.

Inter-group relation When R_i is an inter-group relation, G_i and G_{i+1} are mutually exclusive, that is, $G_i \cap G_{i+1} = \phi$. An inter-group relation is a spatial relation and denoted by symbol $\Rightarrow$.

Example R_i can be one of $\xrightarrow{space}$, $\xrightarrow{type}$, $\xrightarrow{shape}$, $\xrightarrow{color}$, $\xrightarrow{size}$ and $\Rightarrow$. We show a referring expression indicating object $b1$ and the corresponding SOG in the situation of Figure 3. In the SOG, $\{all\}$ denotes the total set of objects in the situation. The indexed underlines denote correspondence between SOG and linguistic expressions. As shown in the figure, we allow objects being on the other objects.

marui$_{(1)}$ *futatu no tukue* *no uti no*$_{(2)}$ *hidari no*$_{(3)}$ *tukue no*$_{(4)}$ *ue no*$_{(5)}$ *tama*$_{(6)}$
(the ball$_{(6)}$ on$_{(5)}$ the left$_{(3)}$ table$_{(4)}$ among the two$_{(2)}$ round$_{(1)}$ tables$_{(2)}$)

SOG: $[\{all\} \xrightarrow{type} \{t1, t2, t3\} \xrightarrow{shape}_{(1)} \{t1, t2\}_{(2)} \xrightarrow{space}_{(3)} \{t1\}_{(4)} \Rightarrow_{(5)} \{b1\}_{(6)}]$

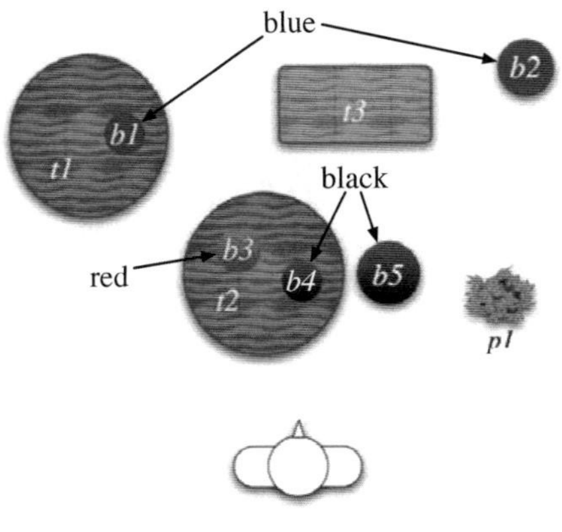

Figure 3: An example situation

3 Generation

Our generation algorithm proposed in this section consists of four steps: perceptual grouping, SOG generation, surface realization and scoring. In the rest of this section, we describe these four steps by using Figure 3 as an example.

3.1 Step 1: Perceptual grouping

Our algorithm starts with identifying groups of objects that are naturally recognized by humans. We adopt Thórisson's perceptual grouping algorithm (Thórisson, 1994) for this purpose. Perceptual grouping is performed with objects in the situation with respect to each of the following features: *type*, *shape*, *color*, *size*, and *proximity*. Three special features, *total*, *singleton*, and *closure* are respectively used to recognize the total set of objects, groups containing each single object, and objects bounded in perceptually significant regions (table tops in the domain of this paper). These three features are handled not by Thòrisson's algorithm but by individual procedures.

Type is the most dominant feature because humans rarely recognize objects of different types as a group. Thus, first we group objects with respect to types, and then group objects of the same type with respect to other features (except for *total*).

Although we adopt Thórisson's grouping algorithm, we use different grouping strategies from the original. Thórisson (1994) lists the following three combinations of features as possible strategies of perceptual grouping.

- *shape* and *proximity*
- *color* and *proximity*
- *size* and *proximity*

However, these strategies are inappropriate to generate referring expressions. For example, because two blue balls $b1$ and $b2$ in Figure 3 are too much distant from each other, Thórisson's algorithm cannot recognize the group consisting of $b1$ and $b2$ with the original strategies. However, the expression like "the left blue ball" can naturally refer to $b1$. When using such an expression, we assume an implicit group consisting of $b1$ and $b2$. Hence, we do not combine features but use them separately.

The results of perceptual grouping of the situation in Figure 3 are shown below. Relation labels are assigned to recognized groups with respect to features used in perceptual grouping. We define six labels: `all`, `type`, `shape`, `color`, `size`, and `space`. Features *singleton*, *proximity* and *closure* share the same label `space`. A group may have several labels.

feature	`label`	recognized groups
total	`all`	$\{t1, t2, t3, p1, b1, b2, b3, b4, b5\}$
singleton	`space`	$\{t1\}$, $\{t2\}$, $\{t3\}$, $\{p1\}$, $\{b1\}$, $\{b2\}$, $\{b3\}$, $\{b4\}$, $\{b5\}$
type	`type`	$\{t1, t2, t3\}, \{p1\}, \{b1, b2, b3, b4, b5\}$
shape	`shape`	$\{t1, t2\}, \{t3\}$
color	`color`	$\{b1, b2\}, \{b3\}, \{b4, b5\}$
size	`size`	$\{b1, b3, b4\}, \{b2, b5\}$
proximity	`space`	$\{t2, t3\}, \{b1, b3, b4, b5\}, \{b3, b4, b5\}$
closure	`space`	$\{b1\}, \{b3, b4\}$

```
Target      # target object
AllGroups   # all generated groups
SOGList     # list of generated SOGs

makeSOG()
 SOG = []; # list of groups and symbols
 All = getAll(); # total set
 add(All, SOG); # add All to SOG
 TypeList = getAllTypes(All);
   # list of all object types
 TargetType = getType(Target);
   # type of the target
 TargetSailency = saliency(TargetType);
   # saliency of the target type
 for each Type in TypeList do
   # {Table, Plant, Ball}
  if saliency(Type) ≥
                   TargetSaliency then
   # saliency: Table > Plant > Ball
    Group = getTypeGroup(Type);
    # get the type group of Type
    extend(SOG, Group);
  end if
 end for
return
```

Figure 4: Function makeSOG

```
extend(SOG, Group)
 Labels = getLabels(Group);
 for each Label in Labels do
   SOGcopy = copy(SOG);
   add(--Label-->, SOGcopy);
   add(Group, SOGcopy);
   search(SOGcopy);
 end for
return
```

Figure 5: Function extend

3.2 Step 2: SOG generation

The next step is generating SOGs. This is so-called *content planning* in natural language generation. Figure 4, Figure 5 and Figure 6 show the algorithm of making SOGs.

Three variables `Target`, `AllGroups`, and `SOGList` defined in Figure 4 are global variables. `Target` holds the target object which the referring expression refers to. `AllGroups` holds the set of all groups recognized in Step 1. Given `Target` and `AllGroups`, function `makeSOG` enumerates possible SOGs in the depth-first manner, and stores them in `SOGList`.

makeSOG (Figure 4) `makeSOG` starts with a list (SOG) that contains the total set of objects in the domain. It chooses groups of objects that are more salient than or equal to the target object and calls function `extend` for each of the groups.

extend (Figure 5) Given an SOG and a group to be added to the SOG, function `extend` extends the SOG with the group for each label attached to the group. This extension is done by creating a copy of the given SOG and adding to its end an intra-group relation symbol defined in Section 2.2 corresponding to the given label and group. Finally it calls `search` with the copy.

search (Figure 6) This function takes an SOG as its argument. According to the last group in the SOG (`LastGroup`), it extends the SOG as described below.

1. If `LastGroup` is a singleton of the target object, append `SOG` to `SOGList` and return.
2. If `LastGroup` is a singleton of a non-target object, find the groups that contain the target object and satisfy the following three conditions: (a), (b) and (c).
   (a) All objects in the group locate in the same direction from the object of `LastGroup` (*the reference*). Possible directions are one of "back", "back right", "right", "front right", "front", "front left", "left", "left back" and "on". The direction is determined on the basis of coordinate values of the objects, and is assigned to the group for the use of surface realization.
   (b) There is no same type object located between the group and the reference.
   (c) The group is not a total set of a certain type of object.

   Then, for each of the groups, make a copy of the SOG, and concatenate "⇒" and the group to the copy, and call `search` recursively with the new SOG.
3. If `LastGroup` contains the target object together with other objects, let the intersection of `LastGroup` and each group in `AllGroups` be `NewG`, and copy the label from each group to `NewG`. If `NewG` contains the target object, call function `extend` unless `Checked` contains `NewG`.
4. If `LastGroup` contains only non-target objects, call function `extend` for each group (`Group`) in `AllGroups` which is subsumed by `LastGroup`.

Figure 7 shows the SOGs generated to refer to object *b*1 in Figure 3.

1. $[\{all\} \xrightarrow{type} \{t1, t2, t3\} \xrightarrow{space} \{t1\} \Rightarrow \{b1\}]$
2. $[\{all\} \xrightarrow{type} \{t1, t2, t3\} \xrightarrow{shape} \{t1, t2\} \xrightarrow{space} \{t1\} \Rightarrow \{b1\}]$
3. $[\{all\} \xrightarrow{type} \{b1, b2, b3, b4, b5\} \xrightarrow{space} \{b1\}]$
4. $[\{all\} \xrightarrow{type} \{b1, b2, b3, b4, b5\} \xrightarrow{color} \{b1, b2\} \xrightarrow{space} \{b1\}]$
5. $[\{all\} \xrightarrow{type} \{b1, b2, b3, b4, b5\} \xrightarrow{color} \{b1, b2\} \xrightarrow{size} \{b1\}]$
6. $[\{all\} \xrightarrow{type} \{b1, b2, b3, b4, b5\} \xrightarrow{size} \{b1, b4, b3\} \xrightarrow{space} \{b1\}]$
7. $[\{all\} \xrightarrow{type} \{b1, b2, b3, b4, b5\} \xrightarrow{size} \{b1, b4, b3\} \xrightarrow{color} \{b1\}]$
8. $[\{all\} \xrightarrow{type} \{b1, b2, b3, b4, b5\} \xrightarrow{space} \{b1, b3, b4, b5\} \xrightarrow{space} \{b1\}]$
9. $[\{all\} \xrightarrow{type} \{b1, b2, b3, b4, b5\} \xrightarrow{space} \{b1, b3, b4, b5\} \xrightarrow{color} \{b1\}]$
10. $[\{all\} \xrightarrow{type} \{b1, b2, b3, b4, b5\} \xrightarrow{space} \{b1, b3, b4, b5\} \xrightarrow{size} \{b1, b3, b4\} \xrightarrow{space} \{b1\}]$
11. $[\{all\} \xrightarrow{type} \{b1, b2, b3, b4, b5\} \xrightarrow{space} \{b1, b3, b4, b5\} \xrightarrow{size} \{b1, b3, b4\} \xrightarrow{color} \{b1\}]$

Figure 7: Generated SOGs from the situation in Figure 3

```
search(SOG)
 LastGroup = getLastElement(SOG);
     # get the rightmost group in SOG
 Card = getCardinality(LastGroup);
 if Card == 1 then
  if containsTarget(LastGroup) then
   # check if LastGroup contains
   # the target
   add(SOG, SOGList);
  else
   GroupList =
       searchTargetGroups(LastGroup);
   # find groups containing the target
   for each Group in GroupList do
    SOGcopy = copy(SOG);
    add(⇒, SOGcopy);
    add(Group, SOGcopy);
    search(SOGcopy);
   end for
  end if
 elsif containsTarget(LastGroup) then
   Checked = [ ];
   for each Group in AllGroups do
    NewG = Intersect(Group, LastGroup);
    # make intersection
    Labels = getLabels(Group);
    setLabels(Labels, NewG);
    # copy labels from Group to NewG
    if containsTarget(NewG) &
      !contains(Checked, NewG) then
     add(NewG, Checked);
     extend(SOG, Group);
    end if
   end for
 else
  for each Group of AllGroups do
   if contains(LastGroup, Group) then
    extend(SOG, Group);
   end if
  end for
 end if
return
```

Figure 6: Function search

3.3 Step 3: Surface realization

A referring expression is generated by deterministically assigning a linguistic expression to each element in an SOG according to Rule 1 and 2. As Japanese is a head-final language, simple concatenation of element expressions makes a well-formed noun phrase[1]. Rule 1 generates expressions for groups and Rule 2 does for relations. Each rule consists of several subrules which are applied in this order.

[Rule 1]: Realization of groups

Rule 1.1 *The total set* ($\{all\}$) *is not realized.*
(Funakoshi et al., 2004) collected referring expressions from human subjects through experiments and found that humans rarely mentioned the total set. According to their observation, we do not realize the total set.

Rule 1.2 *Realize the type name for a singleton.*
Type is realized as a noun and only for a singleton because the *type* feature is used first to narrow down the group, and the succeeding groups consist of the same type objects until reaching the singleton. When the singleton is not the last element of SOG, particle "*no*" is added.

Rule 1.3 *The total set of the same type objects is not realized.*
This is because the same reason as Rule 1.1.

Rule 1.4 *The group followed by the relation* $\xrightarrow{space}$ *is realized as "[cardinality] [type] no-uti (among)", e.g., "futatu-no (two) tukue (desk) no-uti (among)". The group followed by*

[1]Although different languages require different surface realization rules, we presume perceptual grouping and SOG generation (Step 1 and 2) are applicable to other languages as well.

the relation ⇒ is realized as "[cardinality] [type] no".

When consecutive groups are connected by other than spatial relations ($\xrightarrow{space}$ and ⇒), they can be realized as a sequence of relations ahead of the noun (*type* name). For example, expression "the red ball among big balls" can be simplified to "the big red ball".

Rule 1.5 *Other groups are not realized.*

[Rule 2]: Realization of relations

Rule 2.1 *Relation $\xrightarrow{type}$ is not realized.*

See Rule 1.2.

Rule 2.2 *Relations $\xrightarrow{shape}$, $\xrightarrow{color}$ and $\xrightarrow{size}$ are realized as the expressions corresponding to their attribute values. Spatial relations ($\xrightarrow{space}$ and ⇒) are realized as follows, where $|G_i|$ denotes the cardinality of G_i.*

Intra-group relation ($G_i \xrightarrow{space} G_{i+1}$)

If $|G_i| = 2$ (i.e., $|G_{i+1}| = 1$), based on the geometric relations among objects, generate one of four directional expressions "{*migi, hidari, temae, oku*} *no* ({right, left, front, back})".

If $|G_i| \geq 3$ and $|G_{i+1}| = 1$, based on the geometric relations among objects, generate one of eight directional expressions "*itiban* {*migi, hidari, temae, oku, migi temae, hidari temae, migi oku, hidari oku*} *no* ({right, left, front, back, front right, front left, back right, back left}-most)" if applicable. If none of these expressions is applicable, generate expression "*mannaka no* (middle)" if applicable. Otherwise, generate one of four expressions "{*hidari, migi, temae, oku*} *kara j-banme no* (j-th from {left, right, front, back})".

If $|G_{i+1}| \geq 2$, based on the geometric relations among objects, generate one of eight directional expressions "{*migi, hidari, temae, oku, migi temae, hidari temae, migi oku, hidari oku*} *no* ({right, left, front, back, front right, front left, back right, back left})".

Inter-group relation ($G_i \Rightarrow G_{i+1}$)

$|G_i| = 1$ should hold because of `search` in Step 2. According to the direction assigned by `search`, generate one of nine expressions : "{*migi, hidari, temae, oku, migi temae, hidari temaen, migi oku, hidari oku, ue*} *no* ({right, left, front, back, front right, front left, back right, back left, on})".

Figure 8 shows the expressions generated from the first three SOGs shown in Figure 7. The numbers in the parentheses denote coindexes of fragments between the SOGs and the realized expressions.

3.4 Step 4: Scoring

We assign a score to each expression by taking into account the relations used in the expression, and the length of the expression.

First we assign a cost ranging over $[0, 1]$ to each relation in the given SOG. Costs of relations are decided as below. These costs conform to the priorities of features described in (Dale and Reiter, 1995).

$\xrightarrow{type}$	: No cost (to be neglected)
$\xrightarrow{shape}$	: 0.2
$\xrightarrow{color}$	: 0.4
$\xrightarrow{size}$	: big(est): 0.6, small(est): 0.8, middle: 1.0
$\xrightarrow{space}$, ⇒	: Cost functions are defined according to the potential functions proposed in (Tokunaga et al., 2005). The cost for relation "on" is fixed to 0.

Then, the average cost of the relations is calculated to obtain the relation cost, C_{rel}. The cost of surface length (C_{len}) is calculated by

$$C_{len} = \frac{\mathrm{length(expression)}}{\max_i \mathrm{length(expression_i)}},$$

where the length of an expression is measured by the number of characters.

Using these costs, the score of an expression is calculated by

$$score = \frac{1}{\alpha \times C_{rel} + (1 - \alpha) \times C_{len}}.$$

α was set to 0.5 in the following experiments.

4 Evaluation

4.1 Experiments

We conducted two experiments to evaluate expressions generated by the proposed method.

Both experiments used the same 18 subjects and the same 20 object arrangements which were generated automatically. For each arrangement, all factors (number of objects, positions of objects, attributes of objects, and the target object) were randomly decided in advance to conform to the following conditions: (1) the proposed method can generate more than five expressions for the given target and (2) more than two other objects exist which are the same type as the target.

1. SOG: $[\{all\} \xrightarrow{type} \{t1, t2, t3\} \xrightarrow{space}_{(1)} \underline{\{t1\}}_{(2)} \Rrightarrow_{(3)} \underline{\{b1\}}_{(4)}]$
   $\underline{\textit{itiban hidari no}}_{(1)}$ $\underline{\textit{tukue no}}_{(2)}$ $\underline{\textit{ue no}}_{(3)}$ $\underline{\textit{tama}}_{(4)}$ ($\underline{\text{the ball}}_{(4)}$ $\underline{\text{on}}_{(3)}$ the $\underline{\text{leftmost}}_{(1)}$ $\underline{\text{table}}_{(2)}$)
2. SOG: $[\{all\} \xrightarrow{type} \{t1, t2, t3\} \xrightarrow{shape}_{(1)} \underline{\{t1, t2\}}_{(2)} \xrightarrow{space}_{(3)} \underline{\{t1\}}_{(4)} \Rrightarrow_{(5)} \underline{\{b1\}}_{(6)}]$
   $\underline{\textit{marui}}_{(1)}$ $\underline{\textit{futatu no tukue no uti}}_{(2)}$ $\underline{\textit{hidari no}}_{(3)}$ $\underline{\textit{tukue no}}_{(4)}$ $\underline{\textit{ue no}}_{(5)}$ $\underline{\textit{tama}}_{(6)}$
   ($\underline{\text{the ball}}_{(6)}$ $\underline{\text{on}}_{(5)}$ the $\underline{\text{left}}_{(3)}$ $\underline{\text{table}}_{(4)}$ $\underline{\text{among}}_{(2)}$ the $\underline{\text{round}}_{(1)}$ $\underline{\text{two tables}}_{(2)}$)
3. SOG: $[\{all\} \xrightarrow{type} \{b1, b2, b3, b4, b5\} \xrightarrow{space}_{(1)} \underline{\{b1\}}_{(2)}]$
   $\underline{\textit{itiban hidari no}}_{(1)}$ $\underline{\textit{tama}}_{(2)}$ (the $\underline{\text{leftmost}}_{(1)}$ $\underline{\text{ball}}_{(2)}$)

Figure 8: Realized expressions

Figure 9: An example stimulus of Experiment 1

Figure 10: An example stimulus of Experiment 2

Experiment 1 Experiment 1 was designed to evaluate the ability of expressions to identify the targets. The subjects were presented an arrangement with a generated referring expression which gained the highest score at a time, and were instructed to choose the object referred to by the expression. Figure 9 is an example of visual stimuli used in Experiment 1. Each subject responded to all 20 arrangements.

Experiment 2 Experiment 2 was designed to evaluate validity of the scoring function described in Section 3.4. The subjects were presented an arrangement with a marked target together with the best five generated expressions referring to the target at a time. Then the subjects were asked to choose the best one from the five expressions. Figure 10 is an example of visual stimuli used in Experiment 2. Each subject responded to the all 20 arrangements. The expressions used in Experiment 2 include those used in Experiment 1.

4.2 Results

Table 1 shows the results of Experiment 1. The average accuracy of target identification is 95%. This shows a good performance of the generation algorithm proposed in this paper.

The expression generated for arrangement No. 20 (shown in Figure 9) resulted in the exceptionally poor accuracy. To refer to object $b1$, our algorithm generated expression "*itiban temae no tama* (the most front ball)" because $b1$ is the most close object to person P in terms of the vertical axis. Humans, however, chose the object that is the closest to P in terms of Euclidean distance. Some psychological investigation is necessary to build a more precise geometrical calculation model to solve this problem (Landragin et al., 2001).

Table 2 shows the results of Experiment 2. The first row shows the rank of expressions based on their score. The second row shows the count of human votes for the expression. The third row shows the ratio of the votes. The top two expressions occupy 72% of the total. This concludes that our scoring function works well.

5 Conclusion

This paper extended the SOG representation proposed in (Funakoshi et al., 2004) to generate refer-

Table 1: Result of Experiment 1

Arrangement No.	1	2	3	4	5	6	7	8	9	10	
Accuracy	0.89	1.0	1.0	1.0	1.0	1.0	1.0	0.94	1.0	1.0	
	11	12	13	14	15	16	17	18	19	20	Ave.
	1.0	0.94	1.0	1.0	1.0	1.0	1.0	1.0	1.0	0.17	0.95

Table 2: Result of Experiment 2

Rank	1	2	3	4	5	Total
Vote	134	125	59	22	20	360
Share	0.37	0.35	0.16	0.06	0.06	1

ring expressions in more general situations.

The proposed method was implemented and evaluated through two psychological experiments using 18 subjects. The experiments showed that generated expressions had enough discrimination ability and that the scoring function conforms to human preference well.

The proposed method would be able to handle other attributes and relations as far as they can be represented in terms of features as described in section 3. Corresponding surface realization rules might be added in that case.

In the implementation, we introduced rather *ad hoc* parameters, particularly in the scoring function. Although this worked well in our experiments, further psychological validation is indispensable.

This paper assumed a fixed reference frame is shared by all participants in a situation. However, when we apply our method to conversational agent systems, e.g., (Tanaka et al., 2004), reference frames change dynamically and they must be properly determined each time when generating referring expressions.

In this paper, we focused on two dimensional situations. To apply our method to three dimensional worlds, more investigation on human perception of spatial relations are required. We acknowledge that a simple application of the current method does not work well enough in three dimensional worlds.

References

Douglas E. Appelt. 1985. Planning English referring expressions. *Artificial Intelligence*, 26:1–33.

Robert Dale and Nicholas Haddock. 1991. Generating referring expressions involving relations. In *Proceedings of the Fifth Conference of the European Chapter of the Association for Computational Linguistics(EACL'91)*, pages 161–166.

Robert Dale and Ehud Reiter. 1995. Computational interpretations of the Gricean maxims in the generation of referring expressions. *Cognitive Science*, 19(2):233–263.

Robert Dale. 1992. Generating referring expressions: Constructing descriptions in a domain of objects and processes. MIT Press, Cambridge.

Kotaro Funakoshi, Satoru Watanabe, Naoko Kuriyama, and Takenobu Tokunaga. 2004. Generating referring expressions using perceptual groups. In *Proceedings of the 3rd International Conference on Natural Language Generation: INLG04*, pages 51–60.

Peter Heeman and Graeme Hirst. 1995. Collaborating referring expressions. *Computational Linguistics*, 21(3):351–382.

Helmut Horacek. 1997. An algorithm for generating referential descriptions with flexible interfaces. In *Proceedings of the 35th Annual Meeting of the Association for Computational Linguistics*, pages 206–213.

Emiel Krahmer and Mariët Theune. 2002. Efficient context-sensitive generation of descriptions. In Kees van Deemter and Rodger Kibble, editors, Information Sharing: Givenness and Newness in Language Processing. CSLI Publications, Stanford, California.

Emiel Krahmer, Sebastiaan van Erk, and André Verleg. 2003. Graph-based generation of referring expressions. *Computational Linguistics*, 29(1):53–72.

Frédéric Landragin, Nadia Bellalem, and Laurent Romary. 2001. Visual salience and perceptual grouping in multimodal interactivity. In *Proceedings of International Workshop on Information Presentation and Natural Multimodal Dialogue (IPNMD)*, pages 151–155.

Matthew Stone. 2000. On identifying sets. In *Proceedings of the 1st International Conference on Natural Language Generation: INLG00*, pages 116–123.

Hozumi Tanaka, Takenobu Tokunaga, and Yusuke Shinyama. 2004. Animated agents capable of understanding natural language and performing actions. In Helmut Prendinger and Mituru Ishizuka, editors, *Life-Like Characters*, pages 429–444. Springer.

Kristinn R. Thórisson. 1994. Simulated perceptual grouping: An application to human-computer interaction. In *Proceedings of the Sixteenth Annual Conference of the Cognitive Science Society*, pages 876–881.

Takenobu Tokunaga, Tomofumi Koyama, and Suguru Saito. 2005. Meaning of Japanese spatial nouns. In *Proceedings of the Second ACL-SIGSEM Workshop on the Linguistic Dimentions of Prepositions and their Use in Computational Linguistics: Formalisms and Applications*, pages 93–100.

Kees van Deemter. 2002. Generating referring expressions: Boolean extensions of the incremental algorithm. *Computational Linguistics*, 28(1):37–52.

Noun Phrase Generation for Situated Dialogs

Laura Stoia and **Darla Magdalene Shockley** and **Donna K. Byron** and **Eric Fosler-Lussier**
The Ohio State University
Computer Science and Engineering
2015 Neil Ave., Columbus, Ohio 43210
stoia|shockley|dbyron|fosler@cse.ohio-state.edu

Abstract

We report on a study examining the generation of noun phrases within a spoken dialog agent for a navigation domain. The task is to provide real-time instructions that direct the user to move between a series of destinations within a large interior space. A subtask within sentence planning is determining what form to choose for noun phrases. This choice is driven by both the discourse history and spatial context features derived from the direction-follower's position, e.g. his view angle, distance from the target referent and the number of similar items in view. The algorithm was developed as a decision tree and its output was evaluated by a group of human judges who rated 62.6% of the expressions generated by the system to be as good as or better than the language originally produced by human dialog partners.

1 Introduction

In today's world of mobile, context-aware computing, intelligent software agents are being deployed in a wide variety of domains to aid humans in performing navigation tasks. Examples include hand-held tourist information portals (Johnston et al., 2002) campus tour guides (Yang et al., 1999; Long et al., 1996; Striegnitz et al., 2005), direction-giving avatars for visitors to a building (Cassell et al., 2002; Chou et al., 2005), in-car driving direction systems (Dale et al., 2003; Wahlster et al., 2001), and pedestrian navigation systems (Muller, 2002). These applications present an exciting and challenging new frontier for dialog agents, since attributes of the real-world setting must be combined with other contextual factors for the agent to communicate successfully.

In the current work, we focus on a scenario in which the system provides incremental directions to a mobile user who is following the instructions as they are produced. Unlike the rigid directions produced by applications like Mapquest,[1] which describes the entire route from start to finish, this task requires realtime instructions issued while monitoring the user's progress. Instructions are based on dynamic local context variables such as the visibility of and distance to reference points. In referring to items in the setting, human speakers produce a wide variety of noun phrase forms, including descriptions that are headed by a common noun and that employ a definite, indefinite, or demonstrative determiner, *one* anaphors, and pronouns such as *it*, *this* and *that*. Our goal in the current work is to model that entire space of variation, which makes the task more difficult than the noun phrase generation task defined in many previous studies that simplify the alternatives down to *description* or *pronoun*.

In order to study this process, we developed a task domain in which a human partner is directed through an interior space (a graphically-presented 3D virtual world) to perform a sequence of manipulation tasks. In the first stages of the work, we collected and annotated a corpus of human-human dialogs from this domain. Then, using this data, we trained a decision-tree classifier to utilize context variables such as distance, target object visibility, discourse history, etc., to determine lexical properties of referring expressions to be produced by the generation component of our dialog system.

2 Generation for Situated Tasks

Many previous projects, such as (Lauria et al., 2001; Moratz and Tenbrink, 2003; Skubic et al., 2002), *inter alia*, study interpretation of situated language, e.g. for giving directions to a robot. The focus of our work is rather on generating navigation instructions for a human partner to follow.

Linguistic studies have shown that speakers select noun phrase forms to refer to entities based on a variety of factors. Some of the factors are intrinsic to the object being described, while others are features of the context in which the expression is spoken. The entity's status within the discourse,

[1] www.mapquest.com

Proceedings of the Fourth International Natural Language Generation Conference
Sydney, July 2006. ©2006 Association for Computational Linguistics

spatial position, and the presence of similar items from which the target referent must be distinguished, have all been found to cause changes to the lexical properties chosen for a particular referring expression (i.e. (Gundel et al., 1993; Prince, 1981; Grosz et al., 1995)). This variation is expressed in terms of the determiner chosen (e.g. *that/a*), the head noun (e.g. *that/door/one*), and the presence of additional modifiers such as pre-nominal adjectives or prepositional phrases.

In natural language generation, the process of generating referring expressions occurs in stages (Reiter and Dale, 1992). The process we explore in this paper is the sentence planning stage, which determines whether the context supports generating a particular referring expression as a pronoun, description, one-anaphor, etc.

There has been extensive research in both automatic route description and on general noun phrase (NP) generation, but few projects consider extra-linguistic information as part of the context that influences dialog behavior. (Poesio et al., 1999) applies statistical techniques for the problem of NP generation. However, even though the corpus used in that study contains descriptions of museum items visually accessible to the user, the features used in generation were mostly linguistic, and included little information about the visual or spatial properties of the referent. Another related study in statistical NP generation (Cheng et al., 2001) focuses on choosing the modifiers to be included. Again, no features derived from the situated world were used in that study. (Maass et al., 1995) use features from the world, including objects' color, height, width, and visibility, as well as the user's direction of travel and distance from objects, for generating instructions in a situated task. However, their focus is on selecting landmarks and descriptions under time pressure, rather than selecting the linguistic form to be produced.

3 Data Collection

Our task setup is designed to elicit natural, spontaneous situated language examples from human partners. The experimental platform employs a virtual-reality (VR) world in which one partner, the direction-follower (DF), moves about to perform a series of tasks, such as pushing buttons to re-arrange objects in the room, finding and picking up treasures, etc. The simulated world was presented from first-person perspective on a desk-top computer monitor. The DF had no knowledge of the world map or tasks.

DG:	you can currently see **three buttons**... there's actually **a fourth button that's kind of hidden**
DF:	yeah
DG:	by **this cabinet on the right**
DF:	I know, yeah
DG:	ok, um, so what you wanna do is you want to go in and you're gonna press **one of the buttons that's on the right hand wall**, so you wanna go all the way straight into the room and then face the wall
DF:	mhm
DG:	there with **the two buttons**
DF:	yep
DG:	um and you wanna push **the one that's on the left**

Figure 1: Sample dialog fragment and accompanying video frame

His partner, the direction-giver (DG), had a paper 2D map of the world and a list of tasks to complete. As they performed the task, the DG had instant feedback about the DF's location in the VR world, via mirroring of the DF's computer screen on the DG's computer monitor. The partners communicated through headset microphones. Our paid participants were self-identified native speakers of North American English. Figure 1 shows an example view of the world and the accompanying dialog fragment.

The video output of DF's computer was captured to a camera, along with the audio from both microphones. A logfile created by the VR software recorded the DF's coordinates, gaze angle, and the position of objects in the world 10 times per second. These data sources were synchronized using calibration markers. A technical report is available that describes the recording equipment and software used (Byron, 2005).

3.1 Corpus and Annotation Scheme

Using the above-described setup, we created a corpus consisting of 15 dialogs containing a total of 221 minutes of speech. It was transcribed and word-aligned using Praat [2] and SONIC.[3] The dialogs were further annotated using the Anvil software (Kipp, 2004) to identify a set of target referring expressions in the corpus. Because we are in-

[2]http://www.praat.org

[3]http://cslr.colorado.edu/beginweb/speech_recognition/sonic.html/

terested in the spatial properties of the referents of these target referring expressions, the items of interest in this experiment were restricted to objects with a defined spatial position.

Each object in the virtual world was assigned a symbolic id, and the id of each target referring expression was added to the annotation. Referring expressions with plural referents were marked as **Set**, and were labeled with a list of the members in the set. Expressions were also annotated as either *vague* when the referent was not clear at the time of utterance or *abandoned* in case the utterance was cut short. Items that did not contain a surface realization of the head of the NP (e.g., *on the left*), were marked with the tag *empty*.

The corpus contains 1736 target expressions, of which 221 were **Vague**, 45 were **Empty**, and 228 were **Set**s. The remaining 1242 form the set of test items in the experiment described below. **Vague** items were excluded since we do not wish for the algorithm we develop to reproduce this behavior. **Set** items were excluded in order to avoid the more complex calculation of spatial properties associated with plural entities.

The data used in the experiments is a consensus version on which both annotators, two of the authors, agreed on the set of target expressions and their properties. Due to the constraints introduced by the task, referent annotation achieved almost perfect agreement. The data used in this study is only the DG's language.

4 Algorithm Development

Our ultimate goal is to provide input to a surface realization component for NP generation, given the ID of a target referent and a vector of context features. It is desirable for these context features to be automatically derived, to limit the reliance on human annotation, so we restricted out study to features that either were derived automatically, or required minimal human annotation.

One impact of this decision is that even though the linguistic literature predicts that syntactic features such as grammatical role are important in selecting NP forms, these features were difficult to obtain. Our corpus contains spontaneous spoken discourse, which has no sentence boundaries and relaxed structural constraints. Thus, automatic parsing was problematic. With improved parsing techniques, we may include syntactic information in the decision process for NP generation in future, but this was not included in the current study.

Following (Poesio et al., 1999), we consider the

`det`	a, the, that, none
`head`	it, that, one, noun, none
`mod`	+, -

The possible values of each NP frame slot

$$\begin{bmatrix} \texttt{det:} & \text{none} \\ \texttt{head:} & \text{it} \\ \texttt{mod:} & - \end{bmatrix} \qquad \begin{bmatrix} \texttt{det:} & \text{that} \\ \texttt{head:} & \text{noun} \\ \texttt{mod:} & + \end{bmatrix}$$

it   that button on the right

NP frames for *it* and *that button on the right*

Figure 2: NP frame slot values and examples

information conveyed by an NP to be divided into four slots which must be filled to be able to generate the NP form: a determiner/quantifier, a pre or post-modifier and a head noun slot. There were very few examples of premodifiers in the corpus, so we collapsed the modifier feature. Therefore, the output from our algorithm is an NP frame specifying values for the three slots for each target expression. Figure 2 shows the possible values in each slot and example slot values for two NPs. The number of occurrences in the entire corpus for the NP frame slot values are shown in Table 2.[4]

In the experimental VR world developed for this study, all items from the same category were designed to look identical. This was intended to encourage the subjects to use referring expressions that rely on spatial attributes or deictic reference such as *that one*. The spatial properties of target referents and distractors are used as inputs to the content planning algorithm. Their values in this study were calculated automatically based on geometric properties of the virtual world.

To form the training dataset, we processed each target expression with a syntactic chunker.[5] The partial parse it produced was further processed with a regular-expression matcher to isolate the values corresponding to the three slots. Parser errors caused some low-count NP frame values, so we retained only items that occurred at least 10 times in the entire corpus. Any parser errors that remained in the data were not hand corrected, in order to minimize human intervention.

4.1 Context Features

Given the restrictions that we impose over what is accessible to the learning algorithm, we developed a set of features for each referring expression that characterize both the referent and the context in which the expression was spoken. The context

[4] The two possible tags for **Mod** occurred in almost equal proportion (49%/51%)

[5] http://www.ltg.ed.ac.uk/software/chunk/index.html

	Dialog history features	
1.	Count and chainCount	the mention counts for the referent over the dialog and inside a reference chain[a]
2.	DeltaTime and DeltaTimeChain	the time elapsed since it was last mentioned in the dialog overall or in a chain
3.	PrevSpeaker	the previous speaker that mentioned the ID (either DG or DF)
4.	Mod_{i-1}, Det_{i-1}, $Head_{i-1}$	the values of the slots of the NP frame of the prior mention of the same referent
5.	Mod_{i-2}, Det_{i-2}, $Head_{i-2}$	the previous-1 values of the slots
6.	WordDistance and chainWordDistance	the number of words spoken by both speakers since the last mention of the ID overall or in the chain
7.	$Type_{i-1}$	indicates if the previous mention was in a Set, was Vague, or was a test item
	Spatial/Visual features[b]	
8.	Distance	the distance between the referent and the DF's VR coordinates
9.	Angle	the angle between the center of the DF's view angle and the center of the referent
10.	Visible	a boolean value which indicates if the object is visible
	Relation to other objects in the world	
11.	Visible Distractors	the number of other objects besides the target referent in the field of view
12.	SameCatVisDistractors	the number of visible distractors of the same type as the referent
	Object category and its information status	
13.	Cat	the semantic category of the referent: door/cabinet/button
14.	First Locate	indicates if this is the first expression that allowed the DF to identify the object in the world. The point where joint spatial reference is accomplished.

Table 1: The Context Features Used by the Algorithm

[a] mention counts are not considered over vague or ambiguous tags, or over sets.
[b] note that an **Angle** value smaller than 50^0 ensures the object is **visible**

Det			Head		
Value	Count	Percent	Value	Count	Percent
the	364	39%	noun	558	60%
that/this	264	29%	one	166	18%
none	253	27%	it	116	13%
a	46	5%	that	57	6%
			none	30	3%

Table 2: Distribution of **Det** and **Head** values in the corpus

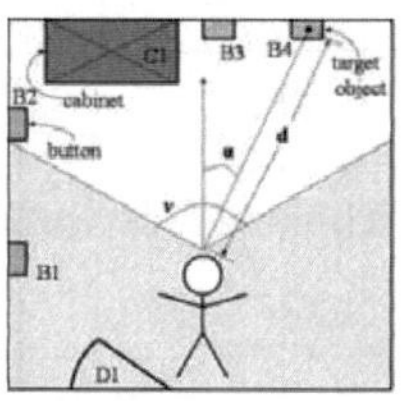

v = Visible area(100°)
α = Angle to target
d = distance to target
In this scene:
VisDistr =3 {B2, B3, C1}
VisSemDistr =2 {B2, B3}

Figure 3: An example configuration with spatial context features. The target object is B4.

features are not only linguistic but also derived from the extralinguistic situation, including spatial relations between the referent and the DF's position and orientation at that instant. The context feature for each target expression includes these automatically-calculated attributes as well as features from the annotation described above. Table 1 describes the full set of context features, and Figure 3 shows a schematic of the spatial context features.

The mention history of any target referent is important for determining the form to use in a subsequent referring expression. Ideally, the discourse history feature should indicate whether a referent has already been discussed, and the distance between a new mention and its antecedent. But determining the discourse status of items in this world was complicated by two factors. All objects in the world of the same semantic category had identical visual features, and the VR world in which the task is conducted is a maze, which required the subjects to perform tasks, move to a different portion of the maze, and possibly return to a previously visited room. Due to the visual and spatial confusion possible in this setting, there is no guarantee that our subjects could accurately calculate whether they were discussing the same object they had encountered before, or remember whether that object had been discussed. While the subjects were focused on a task in a particular room, however, it is reasonable to expect that they could remember which items had been discussed. Therefore, the discourse histories of target objects were calculated using a re-initialization process. Each time the subjects left a VR room to pursue a different task, if more than $25s$ elapsed before the next mention of objects in that room, those subsequent expressions were considered to be in new coreference chains. This time constant was established by examining pronominal referring expressions in the training dialogs.

These features were used as input to develop a classifier to determine NP frames for unseen target referents in context. We chose decision trees due to their ease of interpretation, but we plan to test other machine learning techniques in the future. 5 dialogs were held out as unseen data and the remaining 10 were used to train and adjust the parameters of the decision process. The first procedure was to test whether the three slot values are interdependent. In contrast to previous work, which focused on predicting the values for one of the slots at a time, we hold that due to their interdependence, these decisions should not be made separately. For example, a noun form that has the pronoun *it* as the head will never have a modifier or a determiner. If the three slots are independent, training three separate classifiers and then combining their decisions will yield better results. On the other hand, if they are dependent, better results will be obtained through training a single classifier on the combined label. Unfortunately, combining the labels is problematic due to data sparsity. To test these dependencies, we trained several decision trees, varying the independence assumptions:

Independent - a decision tree was trained for each slot and their outputs combined at the end.

Joint - a decision tree was trained for the combined label for all three slots

Conditional - three decision trees were trained in sequence, each having access to the output of the previous tree. For example, **Mod-Det-Head** means that first the **Mod** tree was trained, then a tree to classify **Det**, using the output from **Mod**, and finally a tree for **Head** , using both the **Det** and **Mod** values.

All possible orderings between **Mod**, **Head** and **Det** were tested. The best result obtained was from the ordering **Mod-Det-Head**, but the differences between the orderings were not significant. The 10 fold cross-validation results are shown in Table 3. There were 632 items in the data set. The Conditional trees outperformed the Independent trees by 9%, which is significant at the level of ($p < .0002$).

As our training data suggests, we test the **Mod-Det-Head** trees against our held out data. We decided to use a leave one out method of training/testing due to the sparsity of data.

Independent	Joint	Mod-Det-Head
22.0 %	28.8 %	31.0 %

Table 3: Testing independence of the slot values

Decision tree classifiers offer the opportunity to examine the relevance of particular features in the final decision. Algorithm 1 and 2 show example trees derived for the **Mod** and **Det** features (the **Head** tree is not shown due to space limitations). We found that there are significant dependencies between the slots in the NP form. Each time one of the slots' values was available to the decision process, it was selected as most informative feature in the next tree. The spatial features were selected as informative in all the trees, most prevelantly in the

Algorithm 1 An example decision tree for **Mod**

```
if FirstLocate = True then
  if VisibleDistractors = 0 then
    if Distance ≤ 116 then
      return Mod: -
    else
      return Mod:+
  else
    if SameCatVisDistractors = 0 then
      if VisibleDistractors ≤ 2 then
        if Angle ≤ 38 then
          return Mod: -
        else
          return Mod: +
      else
        return Mod: +
    else
      return Mod: +
else
  if chainWordDistance = 0 then
    if prevMention ≠ Set/AllVague then
      if firstMention = True then
        return Mod: +
      else
        if Angle ≤ 27 then
          return Mod: -
        else
          return Mod: +
    else
      if noprevMention then
        return Mod: +
      else {prevMention = Set/AllVague}
        return Mod: -
  else
    return Mod: -
```

Algorithm 2 An example decision tree for **Det**

```
if Mod : − then
  if FirstLocate = True then
    return Det:that
  else
    if prevMention ≠ Set/AllVague then
      if notVisible then
        if Cat = Button/Cabinet then
          return Det:none
        else {Cat = Door}
          return Det:that
      else {isVisible}
        if Head_{i−1} = it then
          return Det:none
        else if Head_{i−1} = noun then
          if DeltaTime ≤ 6.3 then
            if Cat = Button/Cabinet then
              return Det:none
            else {Cat = Door}
              return Det:that
          else
            return Det:the
        else if Head_{i−1} = one/none/low then
          return Det:that
        else {Head_{i−1} = that}
          return Det:none
    else if noprevMention then
      return Det:that
    else {prevMention = Set/AllVague}
      return Det:none
else {target has modifier}
  return Det:the
```

decision tree for **Mod**, suggesting that the decision of including extra information is driven largely by the spatial configuration. The information status features and discourse history, such as **First Locate**, **Type**, and attributes of the prior mention, were selected as good predictors for the **Det** slot.

5 Evaluation

We report several methods of evaluating the NP frames produced using the process given by the decision trees. First, we report the results of a strict evaluation in which the system's output must exactly match expressions produced by the human subjects. We also compare this result with a hand-crafted Centering-style generation algorithm. Requiring the algorithm to exactly match human performance is an overly-strict criterion, since in many contexts several possible referring expression forms could be equally felicitous in a given context, so we also conducted a human judgment study. The 5 test dialogs contain 295 target expressions.

5.1 Exact Match Evaluation

The output of the decision tree classifier was compared to the expressions observed in the test dialog. Table 4 reports the results of this evaluation. The accuracy obtained was 31.2%. The most frequent tag gives a 20.0% baseline performance using this strict match criterion.

Exact match results

Predicted	All three features	**det**	**mod**	**head**
Correct	31%	48%	72%	56%

Exact match: head feature per value

Predicted	noun	it	none	one	that
Correct	65%	64%	0%	30%	38%

Exact match: det feature per value

Predicted	a	none	that	the
Correct	0%	49%	36%	66%

Table 4: Classifier results using Exact-match criterion

5.2 Comparison to Centering

For purposes of comparing the performance of our generation algorithm to existing work on generation of NPs, we performed a manual evaluation of the centering-style generation algorithm described in (Kibble and Power, 2000) against our dialog corpus. Algorithms developed according to the centering framework use discourse coherence to make decisions about pronominalization (Grosz et al., 1995), where coherence is measured in terms of topical continuity from one sentence to the next. Centering designates the *backward-looking center (Cb)* as the item in the current sentence that was most topical in the previous sentence. Therefore, to perform a centering-style evaluation, the dialogs must be broken into sentence-like units, and a ranking procedure must be devised for the items mentioned in each unit.

The current evaluation corpus, being a spoken dialog, has not been parsed to automatically determine the syntactic or dependency structure, but rather was manually segmented into utterance units, where each unit contained a main predicate and its satellites. The items mentioned in each unit were ranked according to thematic roles, using the ranking $\{$AGENT $>$ PATIENT $>$ COMP $>$ ADJUNCT$\}$, and excluding references to the speakers themselves, which often appear in AGENT position (Byron and Stent, 1998). The Cb in each unit, if there is one, is the highest-ranked item from the prior unit's list that is repeated in the current unit's list. Following a procedure similar to that reported by Kibble and Power, our decision procedure recommends pronominalizing an item if it is the Cb of its unit and if it is in Subject position, otherwise a description is generated. Based on this rule, all items that are being mentioned for the first time in the discourse are predicted to require a description.

Although most prior studies take the recommendation to pronominalize to mean that a personal pronoun (e.g. *it*) should be generated, due to the demonstrative nature of our domain, the decision to produce a pronoun can result in either a demonstrative or a personal pronoun. Therefore, we considered the algorithm's output to match human production when the target expression in the human corpus was either a personal or demonstrative pronoun, and the algorithm generated either category of pronoun. Table 5 shows the comparison of our system's output and the output from the centering algorithm on anaphoric mentions. The 5 dialogs used for testing in this study contained 145 such items. Both algorithms obtained a similar accuracy (64.8% our system vs. 64.1% centering) and over-generated pronoouns. Although our algorithm does not outperform centering, it assumes less structural analysis of the input text.

5.3 Human Judgment Evaluation

Evaluating generation studies by calculating their similarity to human spontaneous speech may not be the ideal performance metric, since several different realizations may be equally felicitous in a

	Pron	Desc	Total
Human Production	28	117	145
Predicted by Our Algorithm	55	90	
Predicted by Centering	64	81	

Table 5: Comparison to Coherence-based Generation

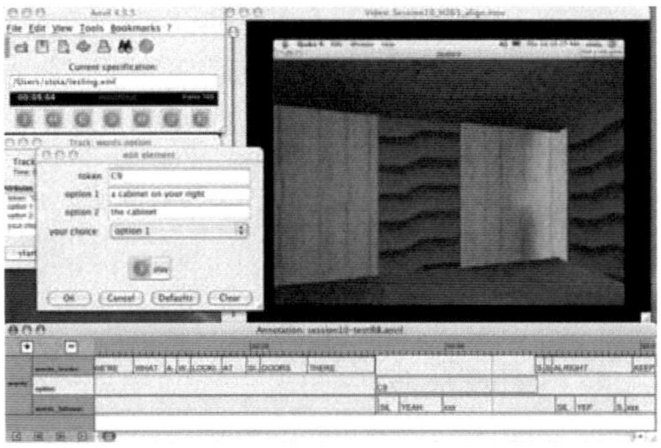

Figure 4: The Anvil software tool used for judging

All Items	
System compared to Human	Trials: 577
equal	45.9%
system preferred	16.6%
(system equal or preferred to human)	**(62.6%)**
human preferred	37.4%
System compared to Random	Trials: 289
equal	24.2%
system preferred	53.3%
(system equal or preferred to random)	**(77.5%)**
random preferred	22.5%
Random compared to Human	Trials: 292
equal	23.3%
random preferred	13.0%
(random equal or preferred to human)	**(36.3%)**
human preferred	65.7%

Items with two judges & judges agreed	
System against Human	Trials: 197
equal	37.3%
system preferred	19.8%
(system equal or preferred to human)	**(57.1%)**
human preferred	36.6%

Table 6: Results of Human Judging

given context. Therefore, we also performed a human judgement evaluation. In this evaluation, judges compared the NPs generated by our algorithm to the NPs produced by human subjects, and to NPs with randomly generated feature assignments. Judges viewed test NPs in the context of the original test corpus.

To re-create the context in which the original expression was produced, the video, audio, and dialog transcript were played for the judges using the Anvil annotation tool (Kipp, 2004). The judges could play or pause the video as they wished. Using the word-alignments established during the data annotation phase, the audio of the test NPs was replaced by silence, and the words were removed in the transcript shown in the timeline viewer. For each test item, the judges were presented with a selection box showing two possible referring expressions that they were asked to compare using a qualitative ranking (option 1 is better, option 2 is better, or they are equal), given a particular target ID and the context. Figure 4 shows a screen-shot of the judges' annotation tool. The judges did not know the source of the expressions they evaluated (system, human production, or random). The 10 judges were volunteers from the university community who were self-identified native speakers of English. They were not compensated for their time.

The decision tree selected NP-frame slot values which were converted into realized NPs. The **Det** and **Head** choices were directly translated into surface forms (for **Head=noun** we chose a consistent common noun for each semantic class: *button*, *door* or *cabinet*. If the system's selection of **Mod** feature matched the value from the corpus, we used the expression produced by the original speaker. If the original expression did not include a modifier, but the system selected **Mod:+**, we lexicalized this feature to a simple but correct spatial description like *on the right*, *on the left* or *in front*.

Table 6 shows the results of human judging. The system's output was either equal or preferred to the original spontaneous language in 62.6% of cases where these two choices were compared directly. Interestingly, the randomly-generated choice was preferred over the original spontaneous language in 13.0% of trials, and was preferred over the system's output in 22.5% of trials. Aggregating over all judges, the system's performance was judged to be much better than random, but not as good as the original human language.

Trials were balanced among judges so that each target item was seen by four judges: with two comparing the system's response to the original human language, one comparing the system to random, and one comparing the human to random. There were 282 trials for which 2 judges saw the identical pair of choices. Out of these, the two judges' responses agreed in 197 cases, producing an inter-annotator reliability (kappa score) of 0.51, with raw agreement of 69% and expected agreement of 37%. Although this is a relatively low kappa value, we believe that the aggregate judgments of all of the judges over all of the test items are still informative, since the scores of items for which we have two judgements follow a very similar pattern to the overal distribution of responses. The low inter-annotator agreement may be due to the substitutability of the expressions.

6 Conclusions and Future Work

In this paper we describe a generation study for situated dialog and a novel evaluation setup of the system's output. The algorithm decides upon the determiner, head and modifier values to be produced in a noun phrase describing an object in a particular moment in the dialog. The decision is influenced by dialog history, spatial and visual relations and information status of the ID to be described. Our algorithm achieved 31.2% exact match with human language, but human evaluators judged the output as good as or better than the original human language 62.6% of the time.

For our future work, we intend to develop the generation module of a dialog system that performs the direction giver's role. We plan to incorporate the results of this study in an extension of (Reiter and Dale, 1992) algorithm that would take into account other types of properties of the objects like visual salience, temporal attributes (for example time elapsed between mentions), if it participated in an action (like the case of a door opening, or a button being pushed) or its importance to the overall task completion.

Acknowledgments

The authors would like to thank our undergraduate RA, Bradley Mellen, for building the virtual world, the 11 judges who rated the system output, and the anonymous reviewers.

References

D. Byron and A. Stent. 1998. A preliminary model of centering in dialog. In *Proceedings of ACL '98*, pp. 1475–1477.

D. Byron. 2005. The OSU Quake 2004 corpus of two-party situated problem-solving dialogs. Technical Report OSU-CISRC-805-TR57, The Ohio State University Computer Science and Engineering Department, September.

J. Cassell, T. Stocky, T. Bickmore, Y. Gao, Y. Nakano, K. Ryokai, D. Tversky, C. Vaucelle, and H. Vilhjalmsson. 2002. MACK: Media lab Autonomous Conversational Kiosk. In *Proceedings of IMAGINA'02*, Monte Carlo, January.

H. Cheng, M. Poesio, R. Henschel, and C. Mellish. 2001. Corpus-based NP modifier generation. In *NAACL '01*, pp. 1–8, Morristown, NJ, USA. Association for Computational Linguistics.

S. Chou, W. Hsieh, F. Gandon, and N. Sadeh. 2005. Semantic web technologies for context-aware museum tour guide applications. In *Proceedings of the 2005 International Workshop on Web and Mobile Information Systems*.

R. Dale, S. Geldof, and J. Prost. 2003. CORAL: Using natural language generation for navigational assistance. In M. Oudshoorn, editor, *Proceedings of the 26th Australasian Computer Science Conference*, Adelaide, Australia.

B. Grosz, A. Joshi, and S. Weinstein. 1995. Centering: A framework for modeling the local coherence of discourse. *Computational Linguistics*, 21(2):203–226.

J. Gundel, N. Hedberg, and R. Zacharski. 1993. Cognitive status and the form of referring expressions in discourse. *Language*, 69(2):274–307.

M. Johnston, S. Bangalore, G. Vasireddy, A. Stent, P. Ehlen, M. Walker, S. Whittaker, and P. Maloor. 2002. MATCH: An architecture for multimodal dialogue systems. In *Proceedings of ACL '02*, pp. 376–383.

R. Kibble and R. Power. 2000. An integrated framework for text planning and pronominalisation. In *Proceedings of INLG'2000*, pp. 77–84.

M. Kipp. 2004. *Gesture Generation by Imitation - From Human Behavior to Computer Character Animation*. Dissertation.com.

S. Lauria, G. Bugmann, T. Kyriacou, J. Bos, and E. Klein. 2001. Training personal robots using natural langauge instruction. *IEEE Intelligent Systems*, 16(5):2–9.

S. Long, R. Kooper, G. Abowd, and C. Atkesonet. 1996. Rapid prototyping of mobile context-aware applications: The cyberguide case study. In *2nd ACM International Conference on Mobile Computing and Networking (MobiCom'96)*, November 10-12.

W. Maass, J. Baus, and J. Paul. 1995. Visual grounding of route descriptions in dynamic environments.

R. Moratz and T. Tenbrink. 2003. Instruction modes for joint spatial reference between naive users and a mobile robot. In *Proc. RISSP 2003 IEEE International Conference on Robotics, Intelligent Systems and Signal Processing, Special Session on New Methods in Human Robot Interaction*.

C. Muller. 2002. Multimodal dialog in a pedestrian navigation system. In *Proceedings of ISCA Tutorial and Research Workshop on Multi-Modal Dialogue in Mobile Environments*.

M. Poesio, R. Henschel, J. Hitzeman, and R. Kibble. 1999. Statistical NP generation: A first report. Utrecht, August.

E. Prince. 1981. On the inferencing of indefinite *this* NPs. In Aravind K. Joshi, Bonnie Lynn Webber, and Ivan Sag, editors, *Elements of Discourse Understanding*, pp. 231–250. Cambridge University Press.

E. Reiter and R. Dale. 1992. A fast algorithm for the generations referring expressions. In *Proceedings of COLING '92*, pp. 232–238.

M. Skubic, D. Perzanowski, A. Schultz, and W. Adams. 2002. Using spatial language in a human-robot dialog. In *2002 IEEE International Conference on Robotics and Automation*, Washington, D.C.

K. Striegnitz, P. Tepper, A. Lovett, and J. Cassell. 2005. Knowledge representation for generating locating gestures in route directions. In *Proceedings of Workshop on Spatial Language and Dialogue (5th Workshop on Language and Space)*, Delmenhorst, Germany, October.

W. Wahlster, N. Reithinger, and A. Blocher. 2001. Smartkom: Towards multimodal dialogues with anthropomorphic interface agents. In *International Status Conference: Lead Projects HumanComputer -Interaction*, Saarbruecken, Germany.

J. Yang, W. Yang, M. Denecke, and A. Waibel. 1999. Smart sight: a tourist assistant system. In *Proceedings of the 3rd International Symposium on Wearable Computers*, pp. 73–78, San Francisco, California, 18-19 October.

The Clarity-Brevity Trade-off in Generating Referring Expressions *

Imtiaz Hussain Khan and **Graeme Ritchie** and **Kees van Deemter**
Department of Computing Science
University of Aberdeen
Aberdeen AB24 3UE, U.K.
{ikhan,gritchie,kvdeemte}@csd.abdn.ac.uk

Abstract

Existing algorithms for the Generation of Referring Expressions (GRE) aim at generating descriptions that allow a hearer to identify its intended referent uniquely; the length of the expression is also considered, usually as a secondary issue. We explore the possibility of making the trade-off between these two factors more explicit, via a general cost function which scores these two aspects separately. We sketch some more complex phenomena which might be amenable to this treatment.

1 Introduction

Until recently, GRE algorithms have focussed on the generation of distinguishing descriptions that are either as short as possible (e.g. (Dale, 1992; Gardent, 2002)) or almost as short as possible (e.g. (Dale and Reiter, 1995)). Since reductions in ambiguity are achieved by increases in length, there is a tension between these factors, and algorithms usually resolve this in some fixed way. However, the need for a distinguishing description is usually assumed, and typically built in to GRE algorithms. We will suggest a way to make explicit this balance between *clarity* (i.e. lack of ambiguity) and *brevity*, and we indicate some phenomena which we believe may be illuminated by this approach. The ideas in this paper can be seen as a loosening of some of the many simplifying assumptions often made in GRE work.

*This work is supported by a University of Aberdeen Sixth Century Studentship, and the TUNA project (EPSRC, UK) under grant number GR/S13330/01. We thank Ielka van der Sluis and Albert Gatt for valuable comments.

2 Clarity, Brevity and Cost

We consider only simple GRE, where the aim is to construct a conjunction of unary properties which distinguish a single target object from a set of potential distractors. Our notation is as follows. A domain consists of a set **D** of objects, and a set **P** of properties applicable to objects in **D**. A *description* is a subset of **P**. The *denotation* of S, written $[\![S]\!]$, is $\{x \in \mathbf{D} \mid \forall p \in S : p(x)\}$.

(Krahmer et al., 2003) describe an approach to GRE in which a *cost function* guides search for a suitable description, and show that some existing GRE algorithms fit into this framework. However, they follow the practice of concentrating solely on distinguishing descriptions, treating cost as a matter of brevity. We suggest that decomposing cost into two components, for the clarity and brevity of descriptions, permits the examination of trade-offs. For now, we will take the cost of a description S to be the sum of two terms:

$$cost(S) = f_C(S) + f_B(S).$$

where f_C counts ambiguity (lack of clarity) and f_B counts size (lack of brevity). Even with this decomposition of cost, some existing algorithms can still be seen as cost-minimisation. For example, the cost functions:

$$f_C(S) = \mid \mathbf{P} \mid \times \mid [\![S]\!] \mid$$
$$f_B(S) = \mid S \mid$$

allow the Full Brevity algorithm (Dale, 1992) to be viewed as minimising $cost(S)$, and the incremental algorithm (Dale and Reiter, 1995) as hill-climbing (strictly, hill-descending), guided by the property-ordering which that algorithm requires. Whereas Krahmer et al.'s cost functions are (brevity-based) heuristic guidance functions, our alternative here is a global quantity for optimisation. Hence their simulation of Full Brevity

Proceedings of the Fourth International Natural Language Generation Conference
Sydney, July 2006.

relies on the details of their algorithm (rather than cost) to ensure clarity, while our own cost function ensures both brevity and clarity.

3 Exploring the Trade-off

3.1 Varying penalties for distractors

Imagine the following situation. You are preparing a meal in a friend's house, and you wish to obtain, from your own kitchen, a bottle of Italian extra virgin olive oil which you know is there. The only way open to you is to phone home and ask your young child to bring it round for you. You know that also in your kitchen cupboard are some distractors: one bottle each of Spanish extra virgin olive oil, Italian non-virgin olive oil, cheap vegetable oil, linseed oil (for varnishing) and camphorated oil (medicinal). It is imperative that you do not get the linseed or camphorated oil, and preferable that you receive olive oil. A full expression, *Italian extra virgin olive oil*, guarantees clarity, but may overload your helper's abilities. A very short expression, *oil*, is risky. You might well settle for the intermediate *olive oil*.

To model this situation, f_C could take a much higher value if $[\![S]\!]$ contains a distractor which must not be selected (e.g. varnish rather than cooking oil). That is, instead of a simple linear function of the size of $[\![S]\!]$, there is a curve where the cost drops more steeply as the more undesirable distractors are excluded. For example, each object could be assigned a numerical rating of how undesirable it is, with the target having a score of zero, and the f_C value for a set A could be the *maximum* rating of any element of A. (This would, of course, require a suitably rich domain model.)

The brevity cost function f_B could still be a relatively simple linear function, providing f_B values do not mask the effect of the shape of the f_C curve.

3.2 Fuzziness of target

Suppose Mrs X has dropped a piece of raw chicken meat on the kitchen table, and immediately removed the meat. She would now like Mr X to wipe the area clean. The meat leaves no visible stain, so she has to explain where it was. In this case, it appears that there is no such thing as a distinguishing description (i.e. a description that pins down the area precisely), although Mrs X can arbitrarily increase precision, by adding properties:

– *the edge of the table,*
– *the edge of the table, on the left* (etc.)

The ideal description would describe the dirty area and nothing more, but a larger area will also do, if not too large. Here, the domain **D** is implicitly defined as all conceivable subareas of the table, the target is again one element of **D**, but – unlike the traditional set-up with discrete elements – a description (fuzzily) defines *one* such area, not a disjoint collection of individual items. Our f_C operates on the description S, not just on the number of distractors, so it can assess the aptness of the denotation of any potential S. However, it has to ensure that this denotation (subarea of the surface) contains the target (contaminated area), and does not contain too much beyond that. Hence, we may need to augment our clarity cost function with another argument: the target itself. In general, more complex domains may need more complicated functions.

3.3 Underspecification in dialogue

Standard GRE algorithms assume that the speaker knows what the hearer knows (Dale and Reiter, 1995). In practice, speakers can often only guess. It has been observed that speakers sometimes produce referring expressions that are only disambiguated through negotiation with the hearer, as exemplified in the following excerpt (quoted in (Hirst, 2002)).

1. A: What's that weird creature over there?
2. B: In the corner?
3. A: *[affirmative noise]*
4. B: It's just a fern plant.
5. A: No, the one to the left of it.
6. B: That's the television aerial. It pulls out.

A and B are in the same room, in an informal setting, so A can be relatively interactive in conveying information. Also, the situation does not appear to be highly critical, in comparison to a military officer directing gunfire, or a surgeon guiding an incision. Initially, A produces an expression which is not very detailed. It may be that he thinks this is adequate (the object is sufficiently salient that B will uniquely determine the referent), or he doesn't really know, but is willing to make an opening bid in a negotiation to reach the goal of reference. In the former case, a GRE algorithm which took account of salience (e.g. (Krahmer and Theune, 1999)), operating with A's model of B's knowledge, should produce this sort of effect. (A dialogue model might also be needed.) In the latter case, we need an algorithm which can relax the need for complete clarity. This could be arranged by having f_C give similar scores to denotations where there are no distractors and to denotations where there are just a few distractors, with f_B making a large contribution to the cost.

3.4 Over-specification

Recently, interest has been growing in 'overspecified' referring expressions, which contain more information than is required to identify their intended referent. Some of this work is mainly or exclusively experimental (Jordan and Walker, 2000; Arts, 2004), but algorithmic consequences are also being explored (Horacek, 2005; Paraboni and van Deemter, 2002; van der Sluis and Krahmer, 2005). Over-specification could also arise in a dialogue situation (comparable to that in Section 3.3) if a speaker is unclear about the hearer's knowledge, and so over-specifies (relative to his own knowledge) to increase the chances of success.

This goes beyond the classical algorithms, where the main goal is total clarity, with no reason for the algorithm to add further properties to an already unambiguous expression. That is, such algorithms assume that every description S for which $|\ [\![S]\!]\ | = 1$ has the same level of clarity (f_C value). This assumption could be relaxed. For example, the approach of (Horacek, 2005) to GRE allows degrees of uncertainty about the effectiveness of properties to affect their selection. Within such a framework, one could separately compute costs for clarity (e.g. likelihood of being understood) and brevity (which might include the complexity of expressing the properties).

4 Conclusion and Future Work

We have argued that the GRE task becomes very different when some commonly-made assumptions are abandoned: some distractors might be worse than others (section 3.1); the target may be impossible to distinguish precisely (section 3.2); the speaker may be unsure what the hearer knows (section 3.3); or there may be a need for over-specification (section 3.4)). As a result, it may be necessary to consider other aspects of the descriptions and their denotations, not simply counting distractors or numbers of properties. Some effects could perhaps be modelled using costs which are not simple linear functions, but which give varying importance to particular aspects of the denotation of a description, or of its content. We hope that this approach will ultimately shed light not only on the effect of the discourse situation, but also some aspects of generating *indefinite* descriptions.

References

Anja Arts. 2004. *Overspecification in Instructive Text*. Ph.D. thesis, Tilburg University, The Netherlands.

Robert Dale and Ehud Reiter. 1995. Computational interpretations of the Gricean maxims in the generation of referring expressions. *Cognitive Science*, 18:233–263.

Robert Dale. 1992. *Generating Referring Expressions: Building Descriptions in a Domain of Objects and Processes*. MIT Press.

Claire Gardent. 2002. Generating minimal distinguishing descriptions. In *Proceedings of the 40th Annual Meeting of the ACL (ACL'02)*, Philadelphia, USA.

Graeme Hirst. 2002. Negotiation, compromise, and collaboration in interpersonal and human–computer conversations. In *Proceedings of Workshop on Meaning Negotiation, 18th National Conference on Artificial Intelligence*, pages 1–4, Edmonton, Canada.

Helmut Horacek. 2005. Generating referential descriptions under conditions of uncertainty. In Graham Wilcock, Kristiina Jokinen, Chris Mellish, and Ehud Reiter, editors, *Proceedings of the 10th European Workshop on Natural Language Generation (ENLG-05)*, pages 58–67.

Pamela Jordan and Marilyn Walker. 2000. Learning attribute selections for non-pronominal expressions. In *Proceedings of the 38th Annual Meeting of the ACL (ACL-00)*, pages 181–190.

Emiel Krahmer and Mariët Theune. 1999. Efficient generation of descriptions in context. In *Proceedings of the ESSLLI workshop on the generation of nominals*, Utrecht, The Netherlands.

Emiel Krahmer, Sebastiaan van Erk, and André Verleg. 2003. Graph-based generation of referring expressions. *Computational Linguistics*, 29(1):53–72.

Ivandré Paraboni and Kees van Deemter. 2002. Generating easy references: the case of document deixis. In *Proceedings of the Second International Conference on Natural Language Generation*, New York, USA.

Ielka van der Sluis and Emiel Krahmer. 2005. Towards the generation of overspecified multimodal referring expressions. In *Proceedings of the Symposium on Dialogue Modelling and Generation at the 15th Annual Meeting of the ST & D (STD-05)*, Amsterdam, The Netherlands.

Generic Querying of Relational Databases using Natural Language Generation Techniques

Catalina Hallett
Center for Research in Computing
The Open University
Walton Hall, Milton Keynes
United Kingdom
c.hallett@open.ac.uk

Abstract

This paper presents a method of querying databases by means of a natural language-like interface which offers the advantage of minimal configuration necessary for porting the system. The method allows us to first automatically infer the set of possible queries that can apply to a given database, automatically generate a lexicon and grammar rules for expressing these queries, and then provide users with an interface that allows them to pose these queries in natural language without the well-known limitations of most natural language interfaces to databases. The way the queries are inferred and constructed means that semantic translation is performed with perfect reliability.

1 Introduction

Natural Language interfaces to databases (hereafter NLIDBs) have long held an appeal to both the databases and NLP communities. However, difficulties associated with text processing, semantic encoding, translation to database querying languages and, above all, portability, have meant that, despite recent advances in the field, NLIDBs are still more a research topic than a commercial solution.

Broadly, research in NLIDBs has focused on addressing the following fundamental, interdependent issues[1]:

- domain knowledge aquisition (Frank et al., 2005);
- interpretation of the input query, including parsing and semantic disambiguation, semantic interpretation and transformation of the query to an intermediary logical form (Hendrix et al., 1978; Zhang et al., 1999; Tang and Mooney, 2001; Popescu et al., 2003; Kate et al., 2005);
- translation to a database query language (Lowden et al., 1991; Androutsopoulos, 1992);
- portability (Templeton and Burger, 1983; Kaplan, 1984; Hafner and Godden, 1985; Androutsopoulos et al., 1993; Popescu et al., 2003)

In order to recover from errors in any either of these steps, most advanced NLIDB systems will also incorporate some sort of cooperative user feedback module that will inform the user of the inability of the system to construct their query and ask for clarification.

We report here on a generic method we have developed to automatically infer the set of possible queries that can apply to a given database, and an interface that allows users to pose these questions in natural language but without the previously mentioned drawbacks of most NLIDBs . Our work is substantially different from previous research in that it does not require the user to input free text queries, but it assists the user in composing query through a natural language-like interface. Consequently, the necessity for syntactic parsing and semantic interpretation is eliminated. Also, since users are in control of the meaning of the query they compose, ambiguity is not an issue.

Our work builds primarily on two directions of research: conceptual authoring of queries via

[1]The extent of NLIDB research is such that it is beyond the scope of this paper to reference a comprehensive list of projects in this area. For reviews on various NLIDBs , the reader is referred to (Androutsopoulos et al., 1995).

Proceedings of the Fourth International Natural Language Generation Conference
Sydney, July 2006.

WYSIWYM interfaces, as described in section 2, and NLIDB portability research. From the perspective of the query composing technique, our system resembles early menu-based techniques, such as Mueckstein (1985), NL-Menu (Tennant et al., 1983) and its more recent re-development Lingo-Logic (Thompson et al., 2005). This resemblance is however only superficial. Our query editing interface employs natural language generation techniques for rendering queries in fluent language; it also allows the editing of the semantic content of a query rather than its surface form, which allows seamless translation to SQL .

As in (Zhang et al., 1999), our system makes use of a semantic graph as a mean of representing the database model. However, whilst Zhang et al (1999) use the Semantic Graph as a resource for providing and interpreting keywords in the input query, we use this information as the main means of automatically generating query frames.

2 WYSIWYM interfaces for database querying

Conceptual authoring through WYSIWYM editing alleviates the need for expensive syntactic and semantic processing of the queries by providing the users with an interface for editing the conceptual meaning of a query instead of the surface text (Power and Scott, 1998).

The WYSIWYM interface presents the contents of a knowledge base to the user in the form of a natural language feedback text. In the case of query editing, the content of the knowledge base is a yet to be completed formal representation of the users query. The interface presents the user with a natural language text that corresponds to the incomplete query and guides them towards editing a semantically consistent and complete query. In this way, the users are able to control the interpretation that the system gives to their queries. The user starts by editing a basic query frame, where concepts to be instantiated (anchors) are clickable spans of text with associated pop-up menus containing options for expanding the query.

Previously, WYSIWYM interfaces have proved valid solutions to querying databases of legal documents and medical records (Piwek et al., 2000), (Piwek, 2002), (Hallett et al., 2005).

As a query-formulation method, WYSIWYM provides most of the advantages of NLIDBs , but overcomes the problems associated with natural language interpretation and of users attempting to pose questions that are beyond the capability of the system or, conversely, refraining from asking useful questions that are in fact within the system's capability. However, one of the disadvantages of the WYSIWYM method is the fact that domain knowledge has to be manually encoded. In order to construct a querying interface for a new database, one has to analyse the database and manually model the queries that can be posed, then implement grammar rules for the construction of these queries. Also, the process of transforming WYSIWYM queries into SQL or another database querying language has previously been database-specific. These issues have made it expensive to port the interface to new databases and new domains.

The research reported here addresses both these shortcomings by providing a way of automatically inferring the type of possible queries from a graph representation of the database model and by developing a generic way of translating internal representations of WYSIWYM constructed queries into SQL .

3 Current approach

In the rest of the paper, we will use the following terms: a *query frame* refers to a system-generated query that has not been yet edited by the user, therefore containing only unfilled WYSIWYM anchors. An *anchor* is part of the WYSIWYM terminology and means a span of text in a partially formulated query, that can be edited by the user to expand a concept. Anchors are displayed in square brackets (see examples in section 3.3).

To exemplify the system behaviour, we will use as a case study the MEDIGAP database, which is a freely downloadable repository of information concerning medical insurance companies in the United States. We have chosen this particular database because it contains a relatively wide range of entity and relation types and can yield a large number of types of queries. In practice we have often noticed that large databases tend to be far less complex.

3.1 System architecture

Figure 1 shows the architecture of the querying system. It receives as input a model of the database semantics (the semantic graph) and it automatically generates some of the compo-

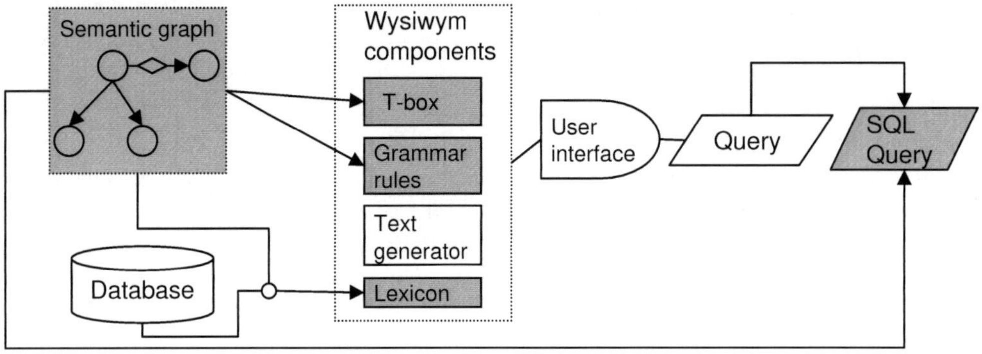

Figure 1: System architecture

nents and resources (highlighted in grey) that in previous WYSIWYM querying systems were constructed manually. Finally, it implements a module that translates the user-composed query into SQL .

The components highlighted in grey are those that are constructed by the current system.

The **T-box** describes the high-level components of the queries. It is represented in Profit notation (Erbach, 1995) and describes the composition of the query frames (the elements that contribute to a query and their type) . A fragment of the semantic graph displayed in 2 will generate the following fragment of t-box:

```
query > [about_company, about_state,
about_phone, about_ext].
about_company > [company_state, company_phone,
company_ext].
company_state intro [company:company_desc].
company_desc intro [comp:comp_desc, phone:phone_desc,
ext:ext_desc].
state_desc > external('dbo_vwOrgsByState_StateName').
comp_desc > external('dbo_vwOrgsByState_org_name').
phone_desc > external('dbo_vwOrgsByState_org_phone').
ext_desc > external('dbo_vwOrgsByState_org_ext').
```

The **grammar rules** are also expressed in Profit, and they describe the query formulation procedure. For example, the following rule will be generated automatically to represent the construction procedure for the query in Example (1.1):

```
rule(english, company_state,
   meaning!(<description &
            predicate!company_state &
            properties![attribute!comp & value!Comp]) &
   layout!level!question &
   cset![meaning!in &
         syntax!category!prep &
         layout!level!word,

         meaning!which &
         syntax!category!int &
         layout!level!word,

         meaning!state &
         syntax!category!np &
         layout!level!word,

         meaning!be &
         syntax!(category!vb & form!pres),
         layout!level!word,

         meaning!Comp &
         syntax!category!np &
         layout!level!phrase,

         meaning!locate &
         syntax!(category!vb & form!part),
         layout!level!word]).
```

In addition to the grammar rules automatically generated by the system, the WYSIWYM package also contains a set of English grammar rules (for example, rules for the construction of definite noun phrases or attachment of prepositional phrases). These rules are domain independent, and therefore a constant resource for the system.

The **lexicon** consists of a list of concepts together with their lexical form and syntactic category. For example, the lexicon entry for *insurance company* will look like:

```
word(english, meaning!company &
syntax!(category!noun & form!name) &
cset!'insurance company')).
```

3.2 Semantic graph

The semantics of a relational database is specified as a directed graph where the nodes represent elements and the edges represent relations between elements. Each table in the database can be seen as a subgraph, with edges between subgraphs representing a special type of join relation.

Each node has to be described in terms of its semantics and, at least for the present, in terms of its linguistic realisation. The semantic type of a node is restricted by the data type of the corresponding entity in the database. A database entity of type *String* can belong to one of the following semantic categories: *person, organization, location (town, country), address (street or complete address), telephone number, other name, other object*. Similarly, numerical entities can have the semantic type: *age, time (year, month, hour), length,*

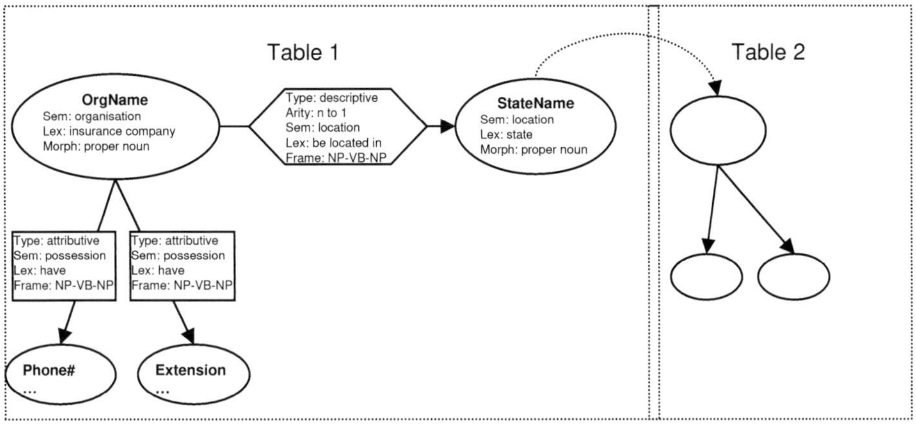

Figure 2: Example of a semantic graph

weight, value, height. The data type *date* has only one possible semantic type, which is *date*. These semantic types have proved sufficient in our experiments, however this list can be expanded if necessary.

Apart from the semantic type, each node must specify the linguistic form used to express that node in a query. For example, in our case study, the field *StateName* will be realised as *state*, with the semantic category *location*. Additionally, each node will contain the name of the table it belongs to and the name of the column it describes.

Relations in the semantic graph are also described in terms of their semantic type. Since relations are always realised as verbs, their semantic type also defines the subcategorisation frame associated with that verb. For the moment, subcategorisation frames are imported from a locally compiled dictionary of 50 frequent verbs. The user only needs to specify the semantic type of the verb and, optionally, the verb to use. The system automatically retrieves from the dictionary the appropriate subcategorisation frame. The dictionary has the disadvantage of being rather restricted in coverage, however it alleviates the need for the user to enter subcategorisation frames manually, a task which may prove tedious for a user without the necessary linguistic knowledge. However, we allow users to enter new frames in the dictionary, should their verb or category of choice not be present. A relation must also specify its arity.

This model of the database semantics is partially constructed automatically by extracting database metadata information such as data types and value ranges and foreign keys. The manual effort involved in creating the semantic graph is reduced to the input of semantic and linguistic information.

3.3 Constructing queries

We focus our attention in this paper to the construction of the most difficult type of queries: complex wh-queries over multiple database tables and containing logical operators. The only restriction on the range of wh-queries we currently construct is that we omit queries that require inferences over numerical and date types.

Each node in the semantic graph can be used to generate a number of query frames equal to the number of nodes it is connected to in the graph. Each query frame is constructed by pairing the current node with each other of the nodes it is linked to. By *generation of query frames* we designate the process of automatically generating Profit code for the grammar rule or set of rules used by WYSIWYM , together with the T-box entries required by that particular rule.

If we consider the graph presented in Fig.2, and focus on the node *orgName*, the system will construct the query frames:

```
Example (1):
1.  In which state is [some insurance
company] located?
2.  What phone number does [some
insurance company] have?
3.  What extension does [some insurance
company] have?
```

If we consider the first query in the example above, the user can further specify details about the company by selecting the *[some insurance company]* anchor and choosing one of the options available (which themselves are automatically generated from the database in question). This information may come from one or more tables. For example, one table in our database contains information about the insurance companies contact details, whilst another describes the services provided by the insurance companies. Therefore, the user can choose between three options: *contact details*, *services* and *all*. Each selection triggers a text regeneration process, where the feedback text is transformed to reflect the user selection, as in the example below:

```
Example (2):
1.  In which state is [some insurance
company] that has [some phone number]
and [some extension] located?
2.  In which state is [some insurance
company] that offers [some medical
insurance plan] and [is available] to
people over 65 located?
3.  In which state is the insurance
company with the following features
located:
• It has [some phone number] and [some
extension]
and
• It offers [some medical insurance
plan] and [is available] to people over
65
```

Figure 3 shows a snapshot of the query editing interface where query (2.1) is being composed.

Each query frame is syntactically realised by using specially designed grammar rules. The generation of high level queries such as those in Example (1.1) relies on basic query syntax rules. The semantic type of each linked element determines the type of wh-question that will be constructed. For example, if the element has the semantic type *location*, we will construct *where* questions, whilst a node with the semantic type *PERSON* will give rise to a *who*-question. In order to avoid ambiguities, we impose further restrictions on the realisation of the query frames. If there is more than one *location*-type element linked to a node, the system will not generate two *where* query frames, which would be ambiguous, but more specific *which* queries. For example, our database contains two nodes of semantic type *location* linked to the node *OrgName*. The first describes the state where an insurance company is located, the second its address. The query frames generated will be:

```
Example (3):
1.  In which states is some insurance
company located?
2.  At what addresses is some insurance
company located?
```

The basic grammar rule pattern for queries based on one table only states that elements linked to a particular node will be realised in relative clauses modifying that node. For example, in Example (2.1), the nodes *phones* and *ext* are accessible from the node *orgName*, therefore will be realised in a relative clause that modifies *insurance company*.

In the case where the information comes from more than one table, it is necessary to introduce more complex layout features in order to make the query readable. For each table that provides information about the focused element we generate bulleted lines as in Example (2.3).

Each question frame consists of a bound element[2], i.e., the user cannot edit any values for that particular element. This corresponds to the information that represents the answer to the questions. In example (2), the bound element is *state*. All other nodes will be realised in the feedback text as anchors, that are editable by users. One exception is represented by nodes that correspond to database elements of boolean type. In this case, the anchor will not be associated to a node, but to a relation, as in Example (2.3) (the availability of an insurance plan is a boolean value). This is to allow the verb to take negative form - in our example, one can have *is available to people over 65* or *is not available to people over 65*.

Since not all anchors have to be filled in, one query frame can in fact represent more than one real-life question. In example (4), one can edit the query to compose any of the following corresponding natural language questions:

```
Example (4):
1.  In which state is the insurance
company with the phone number 8008474836
located?
2.  In which state is the insurance
```

[2]In fact, a single element can be replaced of any number of elements of the same type linked by conjunctions or disjunctions. However, we will refer to a single element by way of simplification. The process of inferring queries remains esentially the same.

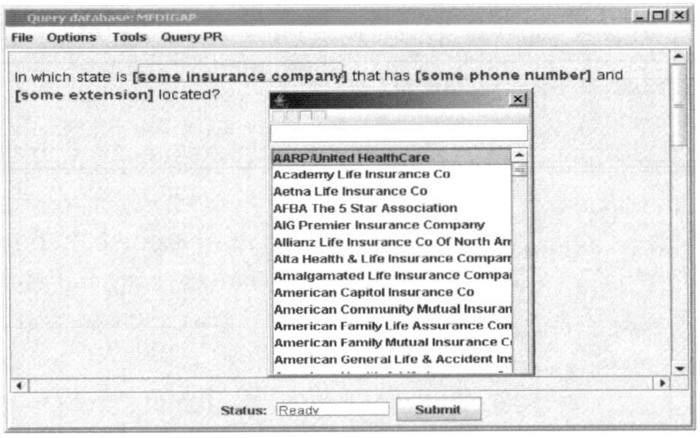

Figure 3: Query editing interface snapshot

```
company Thrivent Financial for Lutherans
with the phone number 8008474836
located?
3. In which state is the insurance
company Thrivent Financial for Lutherans
with the phone number 8008474836 and
extension 8469 located?
```

The actual values of anchors are extracted from the database and transformed into correct lexicon entries on a per-need basis. The strings associated with a value (e.g. *Thrivent Financial for Lutherans*) are retrieved from the database table and column indicated in the description of the node that was used for generating the anchor (e.g. *orgName*) and the syntactic role (e.g. *proper noun*) is given by the syntactic information associated with the node.

3.4 Query translation module

Once a query has been constructed, it is represented internally as a directed acyclic graph. Moreover, each node in the graph can be mapped into a node in the semantic graph of the database. The translation module transforms a contructed query to an SQL statement by parsing the query graph and combining it with the corresponding elements in the semantic graph.

The SELECT portion of the statement contains the focused element. The WHERE portion contains those nodes in the question graph that correspond to edited anchors. For constructing the FROM portion of the statement, we extract, from the semantic graph, for each SELECTED element information about their corresponding database table.

For example, if we assume that in Example (2.1) the user has specified the name of the company and its phone number, the SQL statement generated will be:

```
SELECT dbo_vwOrgsByState.StateName
FROM dbo_vwOrgsByState
WHERE org_name="Thrivent Financial for
                Lutherans"
  And org_phone="8008474836";
```

4 Evaluation

4.1 Usability

A recent study of the usability of a WYSIWYM type of interface for querying databases (Hallett et al., 2006) has shown that users can learn how to use the interface after a very brief training and succeed in composing queries of quite a high level of complexity. They achieve near-perfect query construction after the first query they compose. The study also showed that the queries as they appear in the WYSIWYM feedback text are unambiguous — not only to the back-end system — but also to the user, i.e., users are not misled into constructing queries that may have a different meaning than the one intended. Additionally, it appears that expert users of SQL , with expert knowledge of the underlying database, find the query interface easier to use than querying the database directly in SQL . We consider that most of the conclusions drawn in (Hallett et al., 2006) apply to the current system. The only difference may appear in assessing the ambiguity of the feedback text. Since the query construction rules used for our system are generated automatically, it is likely that the feedback text may be less fluent and, potentially, more ambiguous than a feedback text generated using manually constructed rules, as in (Hallett et al., 2006). We have not yet addressed this issue in a formal evaluation of the current system.

4.2 Coverage

We have assessed the coverage of the system using as our test set a set of English questions posed over a database of geographical information GEOBASE, as in (Tang and Mooney, 2001) and (Popescu et al., 2003). Our first step was to convert the original Prolog database (containing about 800 facts) into a relational database. Then we tested how many of the 250 human produced questions in the test set can be constructed using our system.

There are several issues in using this particular dataset for testing. Since we do not provide a pure natural language interface, the queries our system can construct are not necessarily expressed in the same way or using the same words as the questions in the test set. For example, the question "*How high is Mount McKinley?*" in the test set is equivalent to "*What is the height of Mount McKinley?*" produced by our system. Similarly, "*Name all the rivers in Colorado.*" is equivalent to "*Which rivers flow through Colorado?*". Also, since the above test set was designed for testing and evaluating natural language interfaces, many of the questions have equivalent semantic content. For example, "*How many people live in California?*" is semantically equivalent to "*What is the population of California?*". Similarly, there is no difference in composing and analysing "*What is the population of Utah?*" and "*What is the population of New York City?*".

Out of 250 test questions, 100 had duplicate semantic content and the remaining 150 had original content. On the whole test set of 250 questions, our system was able to generate query frames that allow the construction of 145 questions, therefore 58%. The remaining 42% of questions belong to a single type of questions that our current implementation cannot handle, which is questions that require inferences over numerical types, such as *Which is the highest point in Alaska?* or *What is the combined area of all 50 states?*.

Similar results are achieved when testing the system on the 150 relevant questions only: 60% of the questions can be formulated, while the remaining 40% cannot.

4.3 Correctness

The correctness of the SQL generated queries was assessed on the subset of queries that our system can formulate out of the total number of queries in the test set. We found that the correct SQL was produced for all the generated WYSIWYM queries produced.

5 Conclusions & Further work

Our method presents three main advantages over other natural language interfaces to databases:
1. It is easily customizable for new domains and databases.
2. It eliminates errors in parsing and query-to-SQL translation.
3. It makes clear to the user the full range of possible queries that can be posed to any given database.

From a user's point of view, one could argue that our method is less natural to use than one that allows unconstrained (or less constrained) natural language input. It could also be said that while syntactically correct, the queries as presented to the user may not be as fluent as human-authored questions. These possible disadvantages are, in our opinion, outweighed by the clarity of the query composition process, since the user is fully in control of the *semantic content* of the query she composes; they are unambiguous to both the user and the back-end system.

We are currently extending this work to cover more complex queries that require inferences and ones that contain elements linked through temporal relations. We will also refine the query layout procedures to allow complex queries to be presented in a more intuitive way. Additionally, we are about to begin work on automating the the construction of the semantic graph. We expect that some of the semantic and syntactic information that, at the moment, has to be manually entered in the description of the semantic graph can be inferred automatically from the database content.

Acknowledgement

The work described in this paper is part of the Clinical E-Science Framework (CLEF) project, funded by the Medical Research Council grant G0100852 under the E-Science Initiative. We gratefully acknowledge the contribution of our clinical collaborators at the Royal Marsden and Royal Free hospitals, colleagues at the National Cancer Research Institute (NCRI) and NTRAC and to the CLEF industrial collaborators.

References

I. Androutsopoulos, G.Ritchie, and P.Thanitsch. 1993. An effcient and portable natural language query interface for relational databases. In *Proceedings of the 6th International Conference on Industrial Engineering Applications of Artificial Intelligence and Expert Systems Edinburgh*, pages 327–330.

I. Androutsopoulos, G.D. Ritchie, and P.Thanisch. 1995. Natural language interfaces to databases - an introduction. *Natural Language Engineering*, 2(1):29–81.

I. Androutsopoulos. 1992. Interfacing a natural language front end to a relational database. Master's thesis, Department of Artificial Intelligence University of Edinburgh.

Gregor Erbach. 1995. ProFIT – prolog with features, inheritance, and templates. In *Proceedings of the 7th Conference of the European Chapter of the Asscociation for Computational Linguistics, EACL-95*, Dublin, Ireland.

A. Frank, Hans-Ulrich Krieger, Feiyu Xu, Hans Uszkoreit, Berthold Crysmann, Brigitte Jorg, and Ulrich Schafer. 2005. Querying structured knowledge sources. In *AAAI-05 Workshop on Question Answering in Restricted Domains*, Pittsburgh, Pennsylvania.

Carole D. Hafner and Kurt Godden. 1985. Portability of syntax and semantics in datalog. *ACM Trans. Inf. Syst.*, 3(2):141–164.

C. Hallett, D. Scott, and R.Power. 2005. Intuitive querying of ehealth data repositories. In *Proceedings of the UK E-Science All-Hands Meeting*, Nottingham, UK.

C. Hallett, D. Scott, and R.Power. 2006. Evaluation of the clef query interface. Technical Report 2006/01, Department of Computing, The Open University.

Gary G. Hendrix, Earl D. Sacerdoti, Daniel Sagalowicz, and Jonathan Slocum. 1978. Developing a natural language interface to complex data. *ACM Trans. Database Syst.*, 3(2):105–147.

S. Jerrold Kaplan. 1984. Designing a portable natural language database query system. *ACM Trans. Database Syst.*, 9(1):1–19.

R.J. Kate, Y.W. Wong, and R.J. Mooney. 2005. Learning to transform natural to formal languages. In *Proceedings of the Twentieth National Conference on Artificial Intelligence (AAAI-05)*, pages 1062–1068, Pittsburgh, PA.

B.G.T. Lowden, B.R. Walls, A. De Roeck, C.J. Fox, and R. Turner. 1991. A formal approach to translating english into sql. In Jackson and Robinson, editors, *Proceedings of the 9th British National Conference on Databases*.

Eva-Martin Mueckstein. 1985. Controlled natural language interfaces (extended abstract): the best of three worlds. In *CSC '85: Proceedings of the 1985 ACM thirteenth annual conference on Computer Science*, pages 176–178, New York, NY, USA. ACM Press.

P. Piwek, R. Evans, L. Cahill, and N. Tipper. 2000. Natural language generation in the mile system. In *Proceedings of the IMPACTS in NLG Workshop*, Schloss Dagstuhl, Germany.

P. Piwek. 2002. Requirements definition, validation, verification and evaluation of the clime interface and language processing technology. Technical Report ITRI-02-03, ITRI, University of Brighton.

Ana-Maria Popescu, Oren Etzioni, and Henry Kautz. 2003. Towards a theory of natural language interfaces to databases. In *IUI '03: Proceedings of the 8th international conference on Intelligent user interfaces*, pages 149–157, New York, NY, USA. ACM Press.

Richard Power and Donia Scott. 1998. Multilingual authoring using feedback texts. In *Proceedings of 17th International Conference on Computational Linguistics and 36th Annual Meeting of the Association for Computational Linguistics (COLING-ACL 98)*, pages 1053–1059, Montreal, Canada.

Lappoon R. Tang and Raymond J. Mooney. 2001. Using multiple clause constructors in inductive logic programming for semantic parsing. In *EMCL '01: Proceedings of the 12th European Conference on Machine Learning*, pages 466–477, London, UK. Springer-Verlag.

Marjorie Templeton and John Burger. 1983. Problems in natural-language interface to dbms with examples from eufid. In *Proceedings of the first conference on Applied natural language processing*, pages 3–16, Morristown, NJ, USA. Association for Computational Linguistics.

Harry R. Tennant, Kenneth M. Ross, and Craig W. Thompson. 1983. Usable natural language interfaces through menu-based natural language understanding. In *CHI '83: Proceedings of the SIGCHI conference on Human Factors in Computing Systems*, pages 154–160, New York, NY, USA. ACM Press.

C. Thompson, P. Pazandak, and H. Tennant. 2005. Talk to your semantic web. *IEEE Internet Computing*, 9:75–78.

Guogen Zhang, Wesley W. Chu, Frank Meng, and Gladys Kong. 1999. Query formulation from high-level concepts for relational databases. In *UIDIS '99: Proceedings of the 1999 User Interfaces to Data Intensive Systems*, page 64, Washington, DC, USA. IEEE Computer Society.

Generating Intelligent Numerical Answers in a Question-Answering System

Véronique Moriceau
Institut de Recherche en Informatique de Toulouse
118, route de Narbonne, 31062 Toulouse, France
moriceau@irit.fr

Abstract

In this paper, we present a question-answering system on the Web which aims at generating intelligent answers to numerical questions. These answers are generated in a cooperative way: besides a direct answer, comments are generated to explain to the user the variation of numerical data extracted from the Web. We present the content determination and realisation tasks. We also present some elements of evaluation with respect to end-users.

1 Introduction

Search engines on the Web and most existing question-answering (QA) systems provide the user with a set of hyperlinks and/or Web page extracts containing answer(s) to a question. These answers may be incoherent to a certain degree: they may be equivalent, complementary, contradictory, at different levels of precision or specificity, etc. It is then quite difficult for the user to know which answer is the correct one. Thus, an analysis of relevance and coherence of candidate answers is essential.

1.1 Related work

Search engines on the Web produce a set of answers to a question in the form of hyperlinks or page extracts, ranked according to content or popularity criteria (Salton, 1989; Page et al., 1998). Some QA systems on the Web use other techniques: candidate answers are ranked according to a score which takes into account lexical relations between questions and answers, semantic categories of concepts, distance between words, etc. (Moldovan et al., 2003), (Narayanan and Harabagiu, 2004), (Radev and McKeown, 1998).

Recently, advanced QA systems defined relationships (equivalence, contradiction, ...) between Web page extracts or texts containing possible answers in order to combine them and to produce a single answer (Radev and McKeown, 1998), (Harabagiu and Lacatusu, 2004), (Webber et al., 2002).

Most systems provide the user with either a set of potential answers (ranked or not), or the "best" answer according to some relevance criteria. They do not provide answers which take into account **information from a set of candidate answers** or answer inconsistencies. As for logical approaches used for database query, they are based on majority approach or on source reliability. But, contrary to the assumption of (Motro et al., 2004), we noted that reliability information (information about the author, date of Web pages, ...) is rather difficult to obtain, so we assume that all Web pages are equally reliable.

1.2 Motivations and goals

Our framework is advanced QA systems over open domains. Our main goals are to model and to evaluate a system which, from a factoid question in natural language (in French), selects a set of candidate answers on the Web and generates cooperative answers in natural language. Our challenge is (1) to generate a synthetic answer instead of a list of potential answers (in order to avoid providing the user with too much information), and (2) to generate relevant comments which explain the variety of answers extracted from the Web (in order to avoid misleading the user) (Grice, 1975). In a cooperative perspective, we propose an approach for answer generation which uses answer **integration**. When several possible answers are extracted from the Web, the goal is to define a coherent core

Proceedings of the Fourth International Natural Language Generation Conference
Sydney, July 2006. ©2006 Association for Computational Linguistics

from candidate answers and to generate a **cooperative answer**, i.e. an answer with explanations.

In this paper, we focus on the integration of numerical data in order to generate natural language cooperative answers to numerical questions. We first present some motivational problems for the generation of numerical answers in a QA system. Then, we present the content determination and realization processes. Finally, we give some elements of evaluation of our system outputs, with respect to end-users.

2 On numerical data

We focus on the integration of numerical data for the generation of natural language cooperative numerical answers. We first present some related work on generation from numerical data sets. Then we propose a model for the generation of cooperative numerical answers.

2.1 Related work

The generation of summaries from numerical data has been developed in some NLG systems. For example, the system ANA (Kukich, 1983) generates stock market reports by computing fluctuations for a day. FoG (Goldberg et al, 1994) produces weather forecasts from forecast data. More recently, StockReporter (Dale, 2003) was developed to generate summaries describing how a stock performs over a period. Yu et al. (2005) propose a system which generates summaries of sensor data from gas turbines.

Those systems have input data analysis components which are more or less efficient and describe numerical time-series data. In the framework of QA systems, there are other major problems that the previous systems do not deal with. When a numerical question is submitted to a QA system, a set of numerical data is extracted from the Web. Then, the goal is not to describe the whole data set but to find an appropriate answer, dealing with the user expectations (for example, contraints in the question) or data inconsistencies. Another important point is the analysis of numerical input data in order to identify causes (besides time) of variation.

2.2 A typology of numerical answers

Our challenge is to develop a formal framework for the integration of numerical data extracted from Web pages in order to produce cooperative numerical answers.

To define the different types of numerical answers, we collected a set of 80 question-answer pairs about prices, quantities, age, time, weight, temperature, speed and distance. The goal is to identify for each question-answer pair why extracted numerical values are different (is this an inconsistency? an evolution?).

A numerical question may accept several answers when numerical values vary according to some criteria. Let us consider the following examples.

Example 1 :
How many inhabitants are there in France?
- Population census in France (1999): 60184186.
- 61.7: number of inhabitants in France in 2004.

Example 2 :
What is the average age of marriage of women in 2004?
- In Iran, the average age of marriage of women was 21 years in 2004.
- In 2004, Moroccan women get married at the age of 27.

Example 3 :
At what temperature should I serve wine?
- Red wine must be served at room temperature.
- Champagne: between 8 and 10 °C.
- White wine: between 8 and 11 °C.

The corpus analysis allows us to identify 3 main variation criteria, namely *time* (ex.1), *place* (ex.2) and *restriction* (ex.3: restriction on the focus, for example: Champagne/wine). These criteria can be combined: some numerical values vary according to time and place, to time and restrictions, etc. (for example, the average age of marriage vary according to time, place and restrictions on men/women).

2.3 A model for cooperative numerical answer generation

The system has to generate an answer from a set of numerical data. In order to identify the different problems, let us consider the following example :
What is the average age of marriage in France?
- In 1972, the average age of marriage was 24.5 for men and 22.4 for women. In 2005, it is 30 for men and 28 for women.
- The average age of marriage in France increased from 24.5 to 26.9 for women and from 26.5 to 29 for men between 1986 and 1995.

This set of potential answers may seem incoherent but their internal coherence can be made apparent once a variation criterion is identified. In a cooperative perspective, an answer can be for example:
In 2005, the average age of marriage in France was 30 for men and 28 for women.
It increased by about 5.5 years between 1972 and 2005.
This answer is composed of:

1. a direct answer to the question,
2. an explanation characterizing the variation mode of the numerical value.

To generate this kind of answer, it is necessary (1) to integrate candidate answers in order to elaborate a direct answer (for example by solving inconsistencies), and (2) to integrate candidate answers characteristics in order to generate an explanation.

Figure 1 presents the general architecture of our system which allows us to generate answers and explanations from several different numerical answers. Questions are submitted in natural language to QRISTAL[1] which analyses them and selects potential answers from the Web. Then, a grammar is applied to extract information needed for the generation of an appropriate cooperative answer. This information is mainly:
- the searched numerical value (*val*),
- the *unit* of measure,
- the question *focus*,
- the *date* and *place* of the information,
- the *restriction(s)* on the question focus ,
- the *precision* of the numerical value (for example adverbs or prepositions such as in *about 700, ...*),
- linguistic clues indicating a *variation* of the value (temporal adverbs, verbs of change/movement as in *the price* **increased** *to 200 euro*).

For the extraction of restrictions, a set of basic properties is defined (colors, form, material, etc.). Ontologies are also necessary. For example, for the question *how many inhabitants are there in France?*, population of *overseas regions* and *metropolitan* population are restrictions of *France* because they are daughters of the concept *France* in the ontology. On the contrary, prison population of France is not a restriction because *prison* is not a daughter of *France*. Several ontologies are available[2] but the lack of available knowledge for some domains obviously influences the quality of answers.

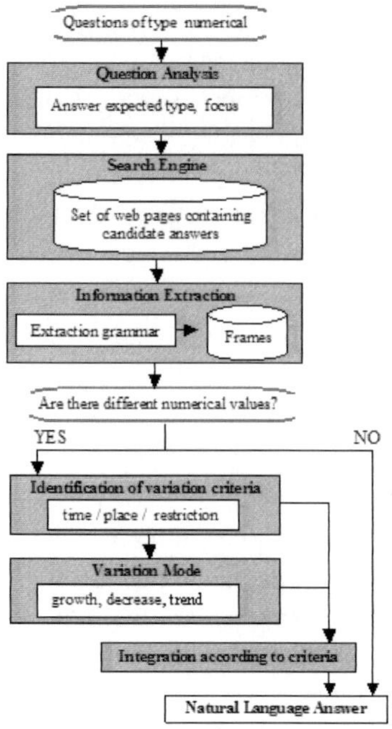

Figure 1: Architecture

We define the set $A = \{a_1, ..., a_N\}$, with a_i a frame which gathers all this information for a numerical value. Figure 2 shows an extraction result.

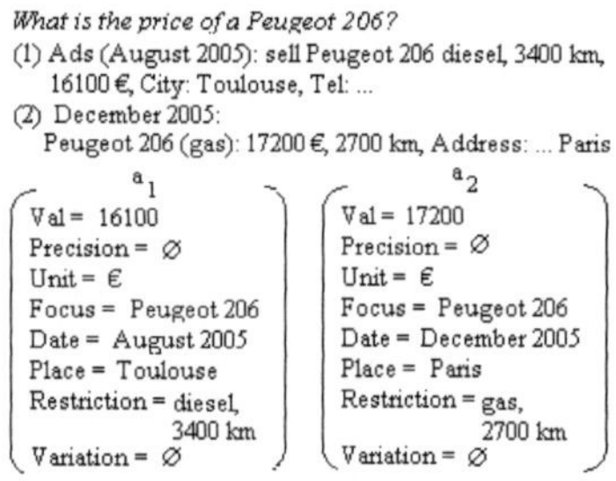

Figure 2: Extraction results

From the frame set, the variation criteria and mode of the searched numerical value are identified: these components perform content determination. Finally, a natural language answer is generated explaining those characteristics. Each of these stages is presented in the next sections.

3 Content determination for explanations

In order to produce explanations for data variation, the system must have a data analysis component

[1] www.qristal.fr, Synapse Développement
[2] http://www.daml.org/ontologies/

which can infer, from extracted information, the variation phenomena, criteria and mode.

3.1 Variation criteria

Once we have the frames representing the different numerical values, the goal is to determine if there is a variation and to identify the variation criteria of the value. We assume that there is a variation if there is at least k different numerical values with different criteria (time, place, restriction) among the N frames (for the moment, we arbitrarily set $k = N/4$, but this has to be evaluated). Thus, a numerical value varies according to:

1. **time** if $T = \{a_i(Val),\ \exists\, a_j \in A,$ such as $a_i(Val) \neq a_j(Val)$ $\wedge\ a_i(Unit) = a_j(Unit)$ $\wedge\ a_i(Date) \neq a_j(Date)\ \}$ $\wedge\ card(T) \geq k$

2. **place** if $P = \{a_i(Val),\ \exists\, a_j \in A,$ such as $a_i(Val) \neq a_j(Val)$ $\wedge\ a_i(Unit) = a_j(Unit)$ $\wedge\ a_i(Place) \neq a_j(Place)\ \}$ $\wedge\ card(P) \geq k$

3. **restriction** if $Rt = \{a_i(Val),\ \exists\, a_j \in A,$ such as $a_i(Val) \neq a_j(Val)$ $\wedge\ a_i(Unit) = a_j(Unit)$ $\wedge\ a_i(Restriction) \neq a_j(Restriction)\ \}$ $\wedge\ card(Rt) \geq k$

4. **time and place** if $(1) \wedge (2)$

5. **time and restriction** if $(1) \wedge (3)$

6. **place and restriction** if $(2) \wedge (3)$

7. **time, place and restriction** if $(1) \wedge (2) \wedge (3)$

Numerical values can be compared only if they have the same unit of measure. If not, they have to be converted. More details about comparison rules are presented in (Moriceau, 2006).

3.2 Variation mode

In the case of numerical values varying over time, it is possible to characterize more precisely the variation. The idea is to draw a trend (increase, decrease, ...) of variaton over time so that a precise explanation can be generated. For this purpose, we draw a regression line which determines the relationship between the two extracted variables *value* and *date*.
In particular, Pearson's correlation coefficient (r), related to the line slope, reflects the degree of linear relationship between two variables. It ranges from $+1$ to -1. For example, figure 3 shows that a positive Pearson's correlation implies a general increase of values whereas a negative Pearson's correlation implies a general decrease. On the contrary, if r is low ($-0.6 < r < 0.6$), then we consider that the variation is random (Fisher, 1925).

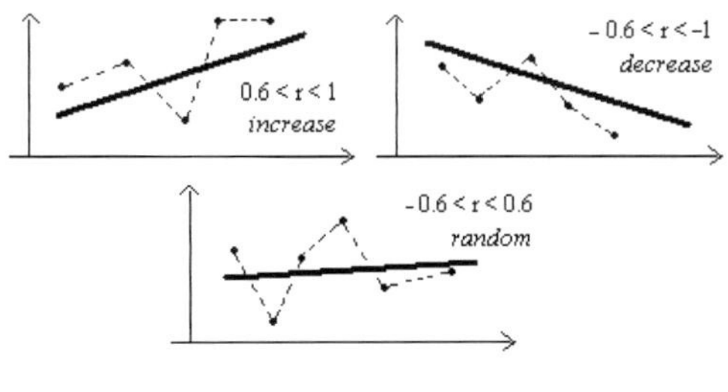

Figure 3: Variation mode

Figure 4 shows the results for the question *How many inhabitants are there in France?* Different numerical values and associated dates are extracted from Web pages. The Pearson's correlation is 0.694 meaning that the number of inhabitants increases over time (between 1999 and 2005).

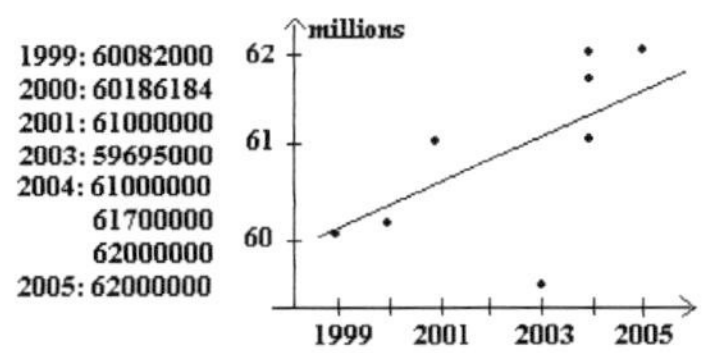

Figure 4: Variation mode: *How many inhabitants are there in France?*

4 Answer generation

Once the searched numerical values have been extracted and characterized by their variation criteria and mode, a cooperative answer is generated in natural language. It is composed of two parts:
- a direct answer if available,
- an explanation of the value variation.

4.1 Direct answer generation

4.1.1 Question constraints

The content determination process for the direct answer generation is mainly guided by constraints which may be explicit or implicit in the question. For example, in the question *how many inhabitants are there in France in 2006?*, there

are explicit constraints on time and place. On the contrary, in *how many inhabitants are there in France?*, there is no constraint on time. Let C be the set of question constraints: $C = \{C_t, C_p, C_r\}$ with :
- C_t: constraint on time ($C_t \in \{exp\_time, \emptyset\}$),
- C_p: constraint on place ($C_p \in \{exp\_place, \emptyset\}$),
- C_r: constraint on restrictions ($C_r \in \{exp\_restr, \emptyset\}$).

For example, in the question *what is the average age of marriage in France?*: $C_t = \emptyset$, $C_p =$ France and $C_r = \emptyset$.

When there is no explicit constraint in the question, we distinguish several cases:
- if there is no explicit constraint on time in the question and if a numerical variation over time has been infered from the data set, then we assume that the user wants to have the most recent information: $C_t = max(\{a_i(date),\ a_i \in A\})$,
- if there is no explicit constraint on place in the question and if a numerical variation according to place has been infered from the data set, then we assume that the user wants to have the information for the closest place to him (the system can have this information for example via a user model),
- if there is no explicit constraint on restrictions in the question and if a numerical variation according to restrictions has been infered from the data set, then we assume that the user wants to have the information for any restrictions.

For example, on figure 5: $C_t = 2000$ (the most recent information), $C_p =$ France and $C_r = \emptyset$.

4.1.2 Candidate answers

Candidate frames for direct answers are those which satisfy the set of constraints C. Let AC be the set of frames which satisfy C (via subsumption):

$$AC = \{a_i \in A, \text{ such as}$$
$$a_i(date) = (C_t \vee \emptyset)\ \wedge\ a_i(place) = (C_p \vee \emptyset) \wedge$$
$$a_i(restriction) = \begin{cases} C_r \vee \emptyset & \text{if } C_r \neq \emptyset \\ exp\_rest \vee \emptyset & \text{if } C_r = \emptyset \end{cases}$$

For figure 5: $AC = \{a_1, a_2, a_3, a_4, a_5, a_6\}$.

4.1.3 Choosing a direct answer

A direct answer has to be generated from the set AC. We define subsets of AC which contain frames having the same restrictions: a direct answer will be generated for each relevant restriction. Let $\mathscr{A}$ be the subsets of frames satisfying the question constraints and having the same restrictions: $\mathscr{A} = \{AC_1, ..., AC_M\}$ with:

$$AC_i = \{a_j, \text{ such as } \forall\ a_j, a_k \in AC,$$
$$a_j(restriction) = a_k(restriction)$$
$$\vee\ \ a_j(restriction) = \emptyset\},$$

and $AC_1, ..., AC_M$ are disjoint.

For figure 5: $\mathscr{A} = \{AC_1, AC_2\}$ with:
$AC_1 = \{a_1, a_3, a_5\}$, subset for restriction *women*,
$AC_2 = \{a_2, a_4, a_6\}$, subset for restriction *men*.

Then, for each element in $\mathscr{A}$, an answer is generated :
$\forall\ AC_i \in \mathscr{A}$, answer = generate_answer(AC_i).

Each element of $\mathscr{A}$ may contain one or several frames, i.e. one or several numerical data. Some of these values may be aberrant (for example, *How high is the Eiffel Tower?* 300m, 324m, *18cm*): they are filtered out via classical statistical methods (use of the standard deviation). Among the remaining frames, values may be equal or not at different degrees (rounded values, for example). Those values have to be integrated so that a synthetic answer can be generated.

There are many operators used in logical approaches for fusion: conjunction, disjunction, average, etc. But, they may produce an answer which is not cooperative: a conjunction or disjunction of all candidates may mislead users; the average of candidates is an "artificial" answer since it has been computed and not extracted from Web pages.

Our approach allows the system to choose a value among the set of possible values, dealing with the problem of rounded or approximative data. Candidate values are represented by an oriented graph whose arcs are weighted with the cost between the two linked values and the weight (w) of the departure value (its number of occurrences). A graph $\mathscr{G}$ of numerical values is defined by $\mathscr{N}$ the set of nodes (set of values) and $\mathscr{A}rc$ the set of arcs. The cost $c(x, y)$ of $arc(x, y)$ is:

$$\frac{|x-y|}{y} \times (w(x) + \sum_{i=1}^{n} w(x_i))\ +\ \sum_{i=1}^{n} c(x_i, x).$$

with $(x_1, ..., x_n, x)$ a path from x_1 to x.

Finally, we define a fusion operator which selects the value which is used for the direct answer. This value is the one which maximizes the difference (*cost(x)*) between the cost to leave this value and the cost to arrive to this value:

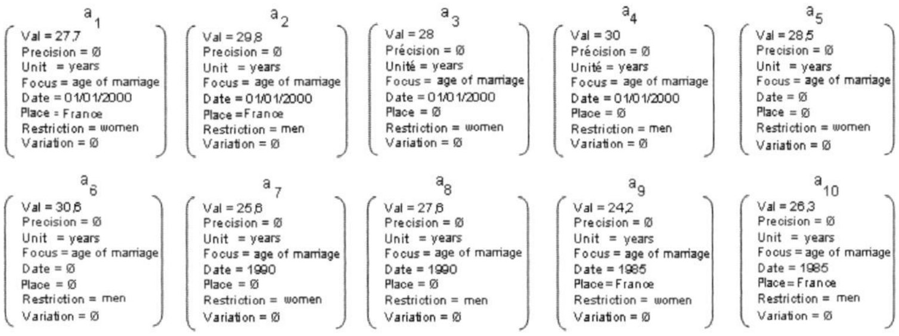

Figure 5: Data set for *What is the average age of marriage in France?*

$$\text{answer} = y \in \mathcal{N}, \text{ such as}$$
$$\text{cost}(y) = \max(\{\ \text{cost}(n), \forall\, n \in \mathcal{N},$$
$$\text{cost}(n) = \text{cost\_leave}(n) - \text{cost\_arrive}(n)\})$$
$$\text{with: } \text{cost\_leave}(x) = \textstyle\sum_i c(x, x_i) \text{ and,}$$
$$\text{cost\_arrive}(x) = \textstyle\sum_i c(x_i, x).$$

Let us consider an example. The following values are candidate for the direct answer to the question *How high is the Mont-Blanc?*: 4800, 4807 (2 occurrences), 4808 (2 occurrences), 4808.75, 4810 (8 occurrences) and 4813. Figure 6 shows the graph of values: in this example, the value which maximizes the costs is 4810.

From the selected value, the system generates a direct answer in natural language in the form of *Focus Verb (Precision) Value*. For example, the generated answer for *How high is the Mont-Blanc?* is *The Mont-Blanc is about 4810 meters high*. Here the preposition *about* indicates to the user that the given value is an approximation.
For the question *what is the average age of marriage in France?*, a direct answer has to be generated for each restriction. For the restriction *men* (AC_2), there are 3 candidate values: 29.8, 30 and 30.6, the value which minimizes the costs being 30. For the restriction *women* (AC_1), there are also 3 candidate values: 27.7, 28 and 28.5, the value which minimizes the costs being 28. After aggregation process, the generated direct answer is: *In 2000, the average age of marriage in France was about 30 years for men and 28 years for women.*

4.2 Explanation generation

The generation of the cooperative part of the answer is complex because it requires lexical knowledge. This part of the answer has to explain to the user variation phenomena of search values: when a variation of values is identified and characterised, an explanation is generated in the form of *X varies according to Criteria*. In the case of variation according to restrictions or properties of the focus, a generalizer is generated. For example, the average age of marriage varies for men and women: the explanation is in the form *the average age of marriage varies according to sex*. The generalizer is the mother concept in the ontology or a property of the mother concept (Benamara, 2004). For numerical value varying over time, if the variation mode (increase or decrease) is identified, a more precise explanation is generated: *X increased/decreased between... and...* instead of *X varies over time*.

Here, verbs are used to express precisely numerical variations. The lexicalisation process needs deep lexical descriptions. We use for that purpose a classification of French verbs (Saint-Dizier, 1999) based on the main classes defined by WordNet. The classes we are interested in for our task are mainly those of verbs of state (*have, be, weight*, etc.), verbs of change (*increase, decrease*, etc.) and verbs of movement (*climb, move forward/backward*, etc.) used metaphorically (Moriceau et al, 2003). From these classes, we selected a set of about 100 verbs which can be applied to numerical values.
From these classes, we characterized sub-classes of growth, decrease, etc., so that the lexicalisation task is constrained by the type of verbs which has to be used according to the variation mode.

A deep semantics of verbs is necessary to generate an answer which takes into account the characteristics of numerical variation as well as possible: for example, the variation mode but also the speed and range of the variation. Thus, for each sub-class of verbs and its associated variation mode, we need a refined description of ontological domains and selectional restrictions so that

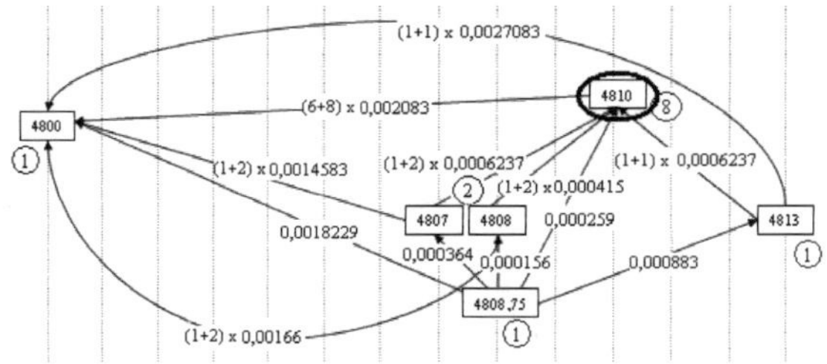

Figure 6: Graph of candidate values for *How high is the Mont-Blanc?*

an appropriate verb lexicalisation can be chosen: which verb can be applied to prices, to age, etc.? (Moriceau et al, 2003). We propose to use proportional series representing verb sub-classes according to the speed and amplitude of variation. For example, the use of *climb* (resp. *drop*) indicates a faster growth (resp. decrease) than *go up* (resp. *go down*): the verb *climb* is prefered for the generation of *Gas prices climb 20.3% in october 2005* whereas *go up* is prefered in *Gas prices went up 7.2% in september 2005.*
Verbs can possibly be associated with a preposition that refines the information (*The average age of marriage increased by* **about** *5.5 years between 1972 and 2005*).

4.3 Answer justification

Our system generates a cooperative answer composed of a direct answer to the question and an explanation for the possible variation of the searched numerical value. But the answer may not be sure because of a too high/low number of candidate values to the direct answer. In this case, it may be useful to add some additional information for the user in order to justify or complete the generated answer.

We propose to add a **know-how** component to our system, which provides the user with one or two relevant Web page extracts besides the generated answer whenever it is necessary. These extracts must contain information about the searched numerical values, and for example some explanations of the causes of numerical variation. Some linguistic clues can be used to select page extracts: number of numerical values concerning the question focus, causal marks (because of, due to, ...), etc. Figure 7 shows an output example of our system.

Question: **How high is the Mont-Blanc?**

Answer: The Mont-Blanc is about 4810 metres high.
The height of the Mont-Blanc varies over time.

Some more details:

> Mont Blanc in the Alps, is the highest mountain in Western Europe. Its height is about 4810 m, but varies from year to year by a few metres, depending on snowfall and climate conditions.
> Mont Blanc has traditionally been considered to be 4807 m high, but GPS-based measurements made in 2002 by the Institut Géographique National and other experts were 4810,40 m. After the heat wave in 2003, new measurements made on September, 6th and 7th were 4808,45 m. These seem to result from fluctuations, caused by the weather. This interpretation is disputed, since the 2003 heat wave didn't significantly affect the glaciers above 4000 meters altitude. It could also be explained by random movements of the summit icecap, due to the violent winds at this altitude.

Figure 7: An ouput example

5 Evaluation

In this section, we present some elements of evaluation of our system with respect to 15 end-users[3].

We first evaluated how users behave when they are faced with different candidate answers to a question. To each user, we presented 5 numerical questions and their candidate answers which vary according to time or restrictions and ask them to produce their own answer from candidate answers. For numerical answers varying according to restrictions, 93% of subjects produce answers explaining the different numerical values for each restriction. For numerical answers varying over time, 80% of subjects produce answers giving the most recent information (20% of subjects produce an answer which a summary of all candidate values). This validates our hypothesis presented in section 4.1.1.

The second point we evaluated is the answer order. Our system produces answers in the form of a direct answer, then an explanation and a justification (page extract) if necessary. We proposed to users answers with these three parts arranged randomly. Contrary to (Yu et al, 2005) which propose first an overview and then a zoom on inter-

[3]Subjects are between 20 and 35 years old and are accustomed to using search engines.

esting phenomena, 73% of subjects prefered the order proposed by our system, perhaps because, in QA systems, users wants to have a direct answer to their question before having explanations.

The last point we evaluated is the quality of the system answers. For this purpose, we asked subjects to choose, for 5 questions, which answer they prefer among: the system answer, an average, an interval and a disjunction of all candidate answers. 91% of subjects prefered the system answer. 75% of subjects found that the explanation produced is useful and only 31% of subjects consulted the Web page extract (28% of these found it useful).

6 Conclusion

We proposed a question-answering system which generates intelligent answers to numerical questions. Candidate answers are first extracted from the Web. Generated answers are composed of three parts: (1) a direct answer: the content determination process "chooses" a direct answer among candidates, dealing with data inconsistencies and approximations, (2) an explanation: the content determination process allows to identify, from data sets, the possible value variations and to infer their variation criteria (time, place or restrictions on the question focus), and (3) a possible Web page extract. This work has several future directions among which we plan:
- to define precisely in which cases it is useful to propose a Web page extract as a justification and,
- to measure the relevance of restrictions on the question focus to avoid generating an enumeration of values corresponding to irrelevant restrictions.

References

F. Benamara. 2004. Generating Intensional Answers in Intelligent Question Answering Systems. *LNAI Series*, volume 3123, Springer.

R. Dale. 2003. http://www.ics.mq.edu.au/ lgt-demo/StockReporter/.

R. A. Fisher 1925. *Statistical Methods for Research Workers*, originally published in London by Oliver and Boyd.

E. Goldberg, N. Driedger, R. Kittredge. 1994. Using natural language processing to produce weather forecasts. *IEEE Expert* 9(2).

H.P. Grice. 1975. Logic and conversation. In P. Cole and J.L. Morgan, (eds.): *Syntax and Semantics*, Vol. 3, Speech Acts, New York, Academic Press.

S. Harabagiu and F. Lacatusu. 2004. *Strategies for Advanced Question Answering*. Proceedings of the Workshop on Pragmatics of Question Answering at HLT-NAACL 2004.

K. Kukich. 1983. Knowledge-based report generation: a knowledge engineering approach to natural language report generation. Ph.D. Thesis, Information Science Department, University of Pittsburgh.

D. Moldovan, C. Clark, S. Harabagiu and S. Maiorano. 2003. *COGEX: A Logic Prover for Question Answering*. Proceedings of HLT-NAACL 2003.

V. Moriceau and P. Saint-Dizier. 2003. *A Conceptual Treatment of Metaphors for NLP*. Proceedings of ICON, Mysore, India.

V. Moriceau. 2006. *Numerical Data Integration for Question-Answering*. Proceedings of EACL-KRAQ'06, Trento, Italy.

A. Motro, P. Anokhin. 2004. Fusionplex: resolution of data inconsistencies in the integration of heterogeneous information sources. *Information Fusion*, Elsevier.

S. Narayanan, S. Harabagiu. 2004. *Answering Questions Using Adcanced Semantics and Probabilistic Inference*. Proceedings of the Workshop on Pragmatics of Question Answering, HLT-NAACL, Boston, USA, 2004.

L. Page, S. Brin, R. Motwani, T. Winograd. 1998. *The PageRank Citation Ranking: Bringing Ordre to the Web*. Technical Report, Computer Science Department, Stanford University.

D.R. Radev and K.R. McKeown. 1998. Generating Natural Language Summaries from Multiple On-Line Sources. *Computational Linguistics*, vol. 24, issue 3 - Natural Language Generation.

P. Saint-Dizier. 1999. Alternations and Verb Semantic Classes for French. *Predicative Forms for NL and LKB*, Kluwer Academic.

P. Saint-Dizier. 2005. *PrepNet: a Framework for Describing Prepositions: preliminary investigation results*. Proceedings of IWCS'05, Tilburg, The Netherlands.

G. Salton. 2002. Automatic Text Processing. *The Transformation, Analysis and Retrieval of Information by Computer*, Addison-Wesley.

B. Webber, C. Gardent and J. Bos. 2002. *Position statement: Inference in Question Answering*. Proceedings of LREC, Las Palmas, Spain.

J. Yu, E. Reiter, J. Hunter, C. Mellish. 2005. Choosing the content of textual summaries of large time-series data sets. *Natural Language Engineering*, 11.

Generating Multiple-Choice Test Items from Medical Text: A Pilot Study

Nikiforos Karamanis
Computer Laboratory
University of Cambridge
CB3 0FD, UK
nk304@cam.ac.uk

Le An Ha and **Ruslan Mitkov**
Computational Linguistics Research Group
University of Wolverhampton
WV1 1SB, UK
{L.A.Ha, R.Mitkov}@wlv.ac.uk

Abstract

We report the results of a pilot study on generating Multiple-Choice Test Items from medical text and discuss the main tasks involved in this process and how our system was evaluated by domain experts.

1 Introduction

Although Multiple-Choice Test Items (MCTIs) are used daily for assessment, authoring them is a laborious task. This gave rise to a relatively new research area within the emerging field of Text-to-Text Generation (TTG) called Multiple-Choice Test Item Generation (MCTIG).[1]

Mitkov et al. (2006) developed a system which detects the important concepts in a text automatically and produces MCTIs testing explicitly conveyed factual knowledge.[2] This differs from most related work in MCTIG such as Brown et al. (2005) and the papers in BEAUNLP-II (2005) which deploy various NLP techniques to produce MCTIs for vocabulary assessment, often using preselected words as the input (see Mitkov et al. for more extensive comparisons).

The approach of Mitkov et al. is semi-automatic since the MCTIs have to be reviewed by domain experts to assess their usability. They report that semi-automatic MCTIG can be more than 3 times quicker than authoring of MCTIs without the aid of their system.

Moreover, analysis of MCTIs produced semi-automatically and used in the classroom reveals that their educational value is not compromised in exchange for time and labour savings. In fact, the semi-automatically produced MCTIs turn out to fare better than MCTIs produced without the aid of the system in certain aspects of item quality.

This paper reports the results of a pilot study on generating MCTIs from medical text which builds on the work of Mitkov et al.

2 Multiple-Choice Test Item Generation

A MCTI such as the one in example (1) typically consists of a question or *stem*, the correct answer or *anchor* (in our example, "chronic hepatitis") and a list of *distractors* (options b to d):

(1) Which disease or syndrome may progress to cirrhosis if it is left untreated?

a) chronic hepatitis

b) hepatic failure

c) hepatic encephalopathy

d) hypersplenism

The MCTI in (1) is based on the following clause from the source text (called the *source clause*; see section 2.3 below):

(2) Chronic hepatitis may progress to cirrhosis if it is left untreated.

We aim to automatically generate (1) from (2) using our simple Rapid Item Generation (RIG) system that combines several components available off-the-shelf. Based on Mitkov et al., we saw MCTIG as consisting of at least the following tasks: a) Parsing b) Key-Term Identification c) Source Clause Selection d) Transformation to Stem e) Distractor Selection. These are discussed in the following sections.

[1]TTG, in which surface text is used as the input to algorithms for text production, contrasts with Concept-to-Text Generation (better known as Natural Language Generation) which is concerned with the automatic production of text from some underlying non-linguistic representation of information (Reiter and Dale, 2000).

[2]Mitkov et al. used an online textbook on Linguistics as their source text. Clearly, their approach is not concerned with concepts or facts derived through inferencing. Neither does it address the problem of compiling a balanced test from the generated MCTIs.

Proceedings of the Fourth International Natural Language Generation Conference
Sydney, July 2006.

2.1 Sentence Parsing

Sentence Parsing is crucial for MCTIG since the other tasks rely greatly on this information. RIG employs Charniak's (1997) parser which appeared to be quite robust in the medical domain.

2.2 Key-Term Identification

One of our main premises is that an appropriate MCTI should have a *key-term* as its anchor rather than irrelevant concepts. For instance, the concepts "chronic hepatitis" and "cirrhosis" are quite prominent in the source text that example (2) comes from, which in turn means that MCTIs containing these terms should be generated using appropriate sentences from that text.

RIG uses the UMLS thesaurus[3] as a domain specific resource to compute an initial set of *potential key terms* such as "hepatitis" from the source text. Similarly to Mitkov et al., the initial set is enlarged with NPs featuring potential key terms as their heads and satisfying certain regular expressions. This step adds terms such as "acute hepatitis" (which was not included in the version of UMLS utilised by our system) to the set.

The `tf.idf` method (that Mitkov et al. did not find particularly effective) is used to promote the 30 most prominent potential key terms within the source text for subsequent processing, ruling out generic terms such as "patient" or "therapy" which are very frequent within a larger collection of medical texts (our reference corpus).

2.3 Source Clause Selection

Mitkov et al. treat a clause in the source text as eligible for MCTIG if it contains at least one key term and is finite as well as of the SV(O) structure. They acknowledge, however, that this strategy gives rise to a lot of inappropriate source clauses, which was the case in our domain too.

To address this problem, we implemented a module which filters out inappropriate structures for MCTIG (see Table 1 for examples). This explains why the number of key terms and MCTIs varies among texts (Table 2).

A finite main clause which contains an NP headed by a key term and functioning as a subject or object with all the subordinate clauses which depend on it is a source clause eligible for MCTIG provided that it satisfies our filters. Example (2) is such an eligible source clause.

[3] http://www.nlm.nih.gov/research/umls/

Structure	Example (key term in italics)
Subordinate clause	Although *asthma* is a lung disease, ...
Negated clause	*Autoimmune hepatitis* should not be treated with interferon.
Coordinated NP	Excessive salt intake causes *hypertension* and hypokalemia.
Initial pronoun	It associates with *hypertension* instead.

Table 1: Inappropriate structures for MCTIG.

Experimentation during development showed that our module improves source clause selection by around 30% compared to the baseline approach of Mitkov et al.

2.4 Transformation to Stem

Once an appropriate source clause is identified, it has to be turned to the stem of a MCTI. This involves getting rid of discourse cues such as "however" and substituting the NP headed by the key term such as "chronic hepatitis" in (1) with a wh-phrase such as "which disease or syndrome". The wh-phrase is headed by the *semantic type* of the key-term derived from UMLS.

RIG utilises a simple transformational component which produces a stem via minimal changes in the ordering of the source clause. The filtering module discussed in the previous section disregards the clauses in which the key term functions as a modifier or adjunct. Additionally, most of the key terms in the eligible source clauses appear in subject position which in turn means that wh-fronting and inversion is performed in just a handful of cases. The following example, again based on the source clause in (2), is one such case:

(3) To which disease or syndrome may chronic hepatitis progress if it is left untreated?

2.5 Selection of Appropriate Distractors

MCTIs aim to test the ability of the student to identify the correct answer among several distractors. An appropriate distractor is a concept semantically close to the anchor which, however, cannot serve as the right answer itself.

RIG computes a set of potential distractors for a key term using the terms with the same semantic type in UMLS (rather than WordNet coordinates employed by Mitkov et al.). Then, we apply a simple measure of distributional similarity derived from our reference corpus to select the best scoring distractors. This strategy means that MCTIs with the same answer feature very similar distractors.

Chapter	Words	# of Key-terms	# of Items	Usable Items	Usable Items w/out post-edited stems	Replaced distractors per term	Total Time	Average Time per Item
Asthma	8,843	9	66	42 (64%)	18 (27%)	2.0	140 mins	3 mins 20 secs
Hepatitis	10,259	17	92	49 (53%)	19 (21%)	0.9	150 mins	3 mins 04 secs
Hypertension	12,941	22	121	59 (49%)	15 (12%)	0.8	200 mins	3 mins 23 secs
Total	32,043	40	279	150 (54%)	52 (19%)	–	490 mins	3 mins 16 secs

Table 2: Usability and efficiency of Multiple-Choice Test Item Generation from medical text.

3 Evaluation

RIG is a simple system which often avoids tough problems such as dealing with key-terms in syntactic positions that might puzzle the parser or might be too difficult to question upon. So how does it actually perform?

Three experts in producing MCTIs for medical assessment jointly reviewed 279 MCTIs (each featuring four distractors) generated by the system. Three chapters from a medical textbook served as the source texts while a much larger collection of MEDLINE texts was used as the reference corpus.

The domain experts regarded a MCTI as *unusable* if it could not be used in a test or required too much revision to do so. The remaining items were considered to be *usable* and could be post-edited by the experts to improve their content and readability or replace inappropriate distractors.

As Table 2 shows, more than half of the items in total were judged to be usable. Additionally, about one fifth of the usable items did not require any editing. The Table also shows the total number of key-terms identified in each chapter as well as the average number of distractors replaced per term.

The last column of Table 2 reports on the efficiency of MCTIG in our domain. This variable is calculated by dividing the total time it took the experts to review all MCTIs by the amount of usable items which represent the actual end-product. This is a bit longer than 3 minutes per usable item across all chapters. Anecdotal evidence and the experts' own estimations suggest that it normally takes them at least 10 minutes to produce an MCTI manually.

Given the distinct domains in which our system and the one of Mitkov et al. were deployed (as well as the differences between them), a direct comparison between them could be misleading. We note, however, that our usability scores are always higher than their worst score (30%) and quite close to their best score (57%). The amount of directly usable items in Mitkov et al. was between just 3.5% and 5%, much lower than what we achieved. They also report an almost 3-fold improvement in efficiency for computer-aided MCTIG, which is very similar to our estimate. These results indicate what our work has contributed to the state of the art in MCTIG.

In our future work, we aim to address the following issues: (a) As in Mitkov et al., the anchor of a MCTI produced by RIG always corresponds to a key-term. However, the domain experts pointed out several cases in which it is better for the key-term to stay in the stem and for another less prominent concept to serve as the answer. (b) Students who simply memorise the input chapter might be able to answer the MCTI if its surface form is too close to the source clause so another interesting suggestion was to paraphrase the stem during MCTIG. (c) We also intend to introduce greater variability in our process for distractor selection by investigating several other measures of semantic similarity.

Acknowledgments

We are grateful to Tony LaDuca, Manfred Straehle and Robert Galbraith from the National Board of Medical Examiners (NBME) for their expert-based feedback and to three anonymous reviewers for their comments.

References

BEAUNLP-II. 2005. Papers on MCTIG by Hoshino and Nakagawa, Liu et al., and Sumita et al. In *Proceedings of the 2nd Workshop on Building Educational Applications Using NLP.*

Jonathan Brown, Gwen Frishkoff, and Maxine Eskenazi. 2005. Automatic question generation for vocabulary assessment. In *Proceedings of HLT-EMNLP 2005*, pages 249–254.

Eugene Charniak. 1997. Statistical parsing with a context-free grammar and word statistics. In *Proceedings of AAAI 1997*, pages 598–603.

Ruslan Mitkov, Le An Ha, and Nikiforos Karamanis. 2006. A computer-aided environment for generating multiple-choice test items. *Natural Language Engineering*, 12(2):177–194.

Ehud Reiter and Robert Dale. 2000. *Building Natural Language Generation Systems.* Cambridge University Press.

Generation of Biomedical Arguments for Lay Readers

Nancy Green
Department of Computer Science
University of North Carolina Greensboro
Greensboro, North Carolina 27402-6170 USA
nlgreen at uncg.edu

Abstract

This paper presents the design of a discourse generator that plans the content and organization of lay-oriented genetic counseling documents containing arguments, and an experiment to evaluate the arguments. Due to the separation of domain, argument, and genre-specific concerns and the methodology used for acquiring a domain model, this approach should be applicable to argument generation in other domains.

1 Introduction

The goal of our research is to develop methods by which intelligent systems can help lay audiences to understand biomedical and other kinds of scientific arguments. We have been studying how one type of lay-communication and biomedical-domain expert, the genetic counselor, presents written arguments in *patient letters*, standard documents summarizing information and services provided to the client (Baker et al., 2002). Clinical genetics involves causal probabilistic reasoning, e.g., diagnosis of a genetic basis for a health problem or prediction of inheritance risks. The patient letter is designed to document the experts' reasoning for medical and legal purposes, as well as to provide an explanation that a lay client can understand.

This paper presents, for the first time, the design of a discourse generator that plans the content and organization of genetic counseling patient letters containing arguments; and an experiment that we performed to evaluate the arguments. The discourse generation process involves three modules: a qualitative causal probabilistic domain model, a normative argument generator, and a genre-specific discourse grammar. In (Green, 2005), we reported a corpus study that produced a reliable biomedical coding scheme. In subsequent workshop papers (Green et al., 2004; 2005), we introduced our use of qualitative probabilistic constraints and provided a brief description of the biomedical domain model. We have also provided informal descriptions of argument patterns in the corpus (Green, to appear; 2006). However, we have not previously published the design of the discourse generator, including the discourse grammar and argument generator, and their relationship to the domain model.

The theoretical significance of this work is three-fold. First, it is empirically based, i.e., based on analysis of arguments in a corpus of genetic counseling patient letters, since the goal is to produce the same kinds of normative arguments as are used in expert-lay communication. Second, the normative argument generator creates an intentional-level representation of the arguments in the text, which provides a foundation for an intelligent system's ability to engage in follow-up discussion about the arguments that have been presented. Finally, due to the separation of domain, argument, and genre-specific concerns in the design, and due to the methodology used to acquire a domain model, it should be possible to apply this approach to lay-oriented argument generation in other domains. The practical significance of this work is that it is major step in the design of a deployable system to generate the first draft of genetic counseling patient letters. As genetics plays an increasingly important role in medicine, there is a need for tools to aid in dissemination of patient-tailored information.

Proceedings of the Fourth International Natural Language Generation Conference
Sydney, July 2006.

In the next section, we give an overview of a prototype generation system, whose main components are described in more detail in sections 3-5; an example of the generation process is given in section 6; an experiment to evaluate the generated arguments is presented in section 7; and related work is summarized in section 8.

2 System Overview

We are developing a prototype system for genetic counselors that will synthesize the first draft of a patient letter. The deployed system will consist of a graphical user interface for the genetic counselor, a domain model/reasoner, an argument generator, a discourse grammar, and a linguistic realizer. Prototypes of all components except the linguistic realizer have been implemented. Although this paper focuses on discourse generation and its relationship to the domain model, as background we now describe the flow of information through the system.

The domain model (section 3) is initialized with generic information on clinical genetics. Through a user interface providing menus and other non-free-text input devices, the counselor will provide standard clinical information such as a patient's symptoms and information about his family tree; test results; preliminary diagnosis (before testing); and final diagnosis (after test results are known). The system uses this information to transform its generic domain model into a specialized domain model of the patient and his family.

In this genre, a patient letter must provide not only the above information, but arguments for the diagnosis and other inferences made by the medical experts. The discourse generation process works as follows. A discourse grammar (section 4) encodes the high-level topic structure of letters in this genre. The discourse grammar rules generate a derivation instantiated from the domain model with information specific to a patient's case. For each of the writer's claims about the case for which a normative argument must be provided according to standard practice, the discourse grammar invokes the argument generator.

The argument generator (section 5) uses non-domain-specific argument strategies that are instantiated with information from the domain model. The argument generator returns a structured representation of an argument in which the communicative function of information, e.g., as data or warrant, is identified. As illustrated in section 6, in future interactive systems knowledge of communicative function could be used to support follow-up discussion. In the current prototype, this knowledge is used to determine presentation order, e.g., that data supporting a claim is to be presented before that claim. One of the goals of the experiment described in section 7 was to evaluate this ordering. In the final system, the output of discourse generation will be transformed by a linguistic realizer into the first draft of a letter.

3 Domain Model

In a previous study of the corpus (Green, 2005), we identified a small set of categories (e.g. *genotype, test result, symptom*) with good inter-rater reliability that can be used to describe the biomedical content of a genetic counseling letter as a causal probabilistic network (Korb and Nicholson, 2004). A prototype domain model has been manually constructed covering representative genetic disorders using only these categories of variables. By restricting a domain model to these categories, the result should reflect the simplified conceptual model of genetics used by genetic counselors in communication with their lay clients; this facilitates generation since the generator will not have to distinguish what information in the domain model is appropriate to communicate to a lay audience. Another benefit of restricting a domain model in this way is that it reduces the knowledge acquisition effort of choosing variables and determining network topology; any genetic disorder in the scope of the coding scheme (over 4500 single-gene autosomal disorders) would be modeled in terms of a small number of variable types and a standard topology. Thus, it should be straightforward to semi-automatically construct a domain model covering many different genetic disorders.

Figure 1 shows part of a domain model after it has been updated with information about a particular patient's case. The nodes labeled *GJB2 (mother), GJB2 (father), GJB2 (child)* are genotype variables, representing the mother's, father's, and child's GBJ2 genotype, respectively. (A genotype is a pair of alleles of a gene; one allele is inherited from each parent. An individual who has two mutated alleles of the GJB2 gene usually experiences hearing loss.) The nodes labeled *hearing loss (child)* and *non-syndromic (child)* are variables representing the child's symptoms. The node labeled *test result (child)* is a variable representing the results of testing the child's GJB2 genotype.

The most likely states of the variables are shown beside the nodes in Figure 1; $\mathbf{T_1}$ and $\mathbf{T_2}$ represent the time at which the (experts') belief is held, before or after the child's genetic test results are known, respectively. The information recorded in the network about this particular case is that the child was observed to have hearing loss and no features of a genetic syndrome; the preliminary diagnosis, i.e. before testing, was that the cause of hearing loss is having two mutated alleles of GJB2; the test results were negative, however; thus, the current diagnosis is some other (unspecified) autosomal recessively inherited genetic condition, represented by the genotype variable labeled *other genotype (child)*. In addition, the parents are hypothesized to be carriers (i.e. to each have one mutated allele) of that genotype, represented by the variables labeled *other genotype (mother)*, *other genotype (father)*.

Although a causal probabilistic network used to perform diagnosis or risk calculation would require specification of numeric probabilities, the role of the network in our system is to qualitatively model the reasoning that the medical experts have performed outside of the system. Also, we found that in the corpus numeric probabilities were provided only when citing epidemiological statistics or risks calculated according to Mendelian inheritance theory (which does not require Bayesian probability computation). Thus, instead of using numeric probabilities for domain reasoning, the domain model uses qualitative constraints based upon formal relations of qualitative influence, product synergy, and additive synergy (Druzdzel and Henrion, 1993).

In addition to being adequate for natural language generation, this approach greatly reduces knowledge acquisition effort; it should be straightforward to semi-automatically acquire the qualitative constraints of a full-scale domain model due to regularities in this domain and the use of a restricted set of variable types as described above. For example, qualitative constraints between genotypes of parents and child would be determined by whether a genotype follows an autosomal dominant or recessive inheritance pattern.

We now describe some of the qualitative domain constraints. An influence relation holds between a node in a causal graph and its direct descendant. **A** has a *positive qualitative influence* on **B**, written $\mathbf{S^+(state(A,V_A), state(B,V_B))}$, if the state of **A** reaching a threshold value $\mathbf{V_A}$ makes it more likely that the state of **B** reaches value $\mathbf{V_B}$. For example, if having two mutated alleles of a genotype A normally results in the appearance of a symptom B, this could be described as $\mathbf{S^+(state(A,2), state(B,yes))}$. Each arc in Figure 1 implicitly represents an $\mathbf{S^+}$ relation.

Product and additive synergy describe converging connections, i.e., the relation between a set of variables **{A, B}** and their direct descendant **C** in a graph. **A** and **B** have *negative product synergy* with respect to state $\mathbf{V_C}$ of **C**, written $\mathbf{X^-(\{state(A,V_A), state(B,V_B)\}, state(C,V_C))}$, if either the state of **A** reaching a threshold $\mathbf{V_A}$ or the state of **B** reaching a threshold $\mathbf{V_B}$ makes it more likely that the state of **C** reaches $\mathbf{V_C}$. This type of relationship characterizes mutually exclusive alternative diagnoses that could account for the same symptom; it also characterizes autosomal dominant inheritance, an inheritance pattern where inheriting one mutated allele of a genotype (from either parent) is usually sufficient to cause health problems. In Figure 1, the possible alternative causes of the symptoms are indicated by the $\mathbf{X^-}$ annotations.

On the other hand, autosomal recessive inheritance, an inheritance pattern where inheriting two mutated alleles (one from each parent) is usually necessary to cause health problems, is characterized by zero product synergy ($\mathbf{X^0}$); **A** and **B** have *zero product synergy* with respect to state $\mathbf{V_C}$ of **C**, $\mathbf{X^0(\{state(A,V_A), state(B,V_B)\}, state(C,V_C))}$, if the state of **A** reaching a threshold $\mathbf{V_A}$ *and* the state of **B** reaching a threshold $\mathbf{V_B}$ makes it more likely that the state of **C** reaches $\mathbf{V_C}$. For example, if the mother's, father's, and child's genotype are represented by variables **A**, **B**, and **C**, respectively, then $\mathbf{X^0(\{state(A,1), state(B,1)\}, state(C,2))}$ can represent the constraint that if the child's genotype **C** has two mutated alleles, then one mutated allele must have come from each parent. In Figure 1, the autosomal recessive inheritance pattern of GJB2 and the other hypothesized genetic disorder are indicated by the $\mathbf{X^0}$ annotations.

Other qualitative constraints used in the domain model are based on negative qualitative influence ($\mathbf{S^-}$), positive product synergy ($\mathbf{X^+}$), and negative additive synergy ($\mathbf{Y^-}$). In addition, the domain model stores epidemiological statistics as probability statements composed of variables used in the network, e.g., the frequency of hearing loss due to GJB2. This type of information can be used as backing in an argument (see section 5) but does not play a role in domain reasoning.

4 Discourse Grammar

A discourse grammar was written based upon our analysis of the corpus and a description of standard practice in genetic counseling (Baker et al., 2002). The current grammar is intended to cover letters on single-factor autosomal genetic disorders. Thanks to the regularities in this domain and in this genre, the grammar consists of a small number of rules. The starting rule of the grammar represents the main sections of a letter in their standard order: opening, referral, preliminary diagnosis, testing, final diagnosis, origin of genetic condition, inheritance implications, prognosis/treatment, and closing. One or more grammar rules describe each of these sections.

Grammar rules may request the domain reasoner for case-specific information to be included in the letter. In addition, when the grammar provides a choice of rules, rule selection is based upon case-specific information provided by the domain reasoner. For example, one rule for reporting the final diagnosis handles cases in which the patient's test results confirm the preliminary diagnosis, and another rule those cases where the preliminary diagnosis has been disconfirmed by test results; the domain reasoner returns the information needed to choose between those two rules.

The process described so far creates an initial outline of the information to be presented (in non-linguistic form), including various claims requiring an argument. Each of those claims is passed to the argument generator described in the next section. For example, the letter shown in Figure 2 contains seven claims labeled C_1 to C_7; argument generation adds information labeled D_1 to D_7, W_1 to W_7, and B_1 to B_4. The information returned by the argument generator is added to the outline, completing the structure that will be transformed by the linguistic realizer into text.

5 Argument Generation

Given a claim, the argument generator uses argument strategies to construct a normative argument for the claim from information provided by the domain reasoner. The strategies are non-domain-specific in the sense that they refer to formal properties of the qualitative causal probabilistic domain model rather than to genetics.

According to Toulmin's model of normative argument structure (1998), an argument for a claim can be analyzed in terms of various functional components: the data, warrant, and backing. The *data* are the facts used to defend a claim. The *warrant* is a principle that licenses the claim given the data. An optional *backing* may be used to justify the warrant, e.g., by giving the facts upon which the warrant is based. To derive the argument strategies used in the system, we analyzed the arguments in the corpus in terms of Toulmin's model; the resulting strategies describe mappings from formal properties of the domain model to the data and warrant supporting a claim and to the backing of a warrant. Several strategies are paraphrased below for illustration.

Strategy 1. *Argument for belief in causal claim, based on effects*: An argument for the *claim* that it is believed to some extent at time T_i that state(A,V_A) holds and that state(A,V_A) is responsible for the states of variables B_1..B_i, i.e., state(B_1,V_{B1}) .. state(B_i,V_{Bi}), consists of the (presupposed) *data* that state(B_1,V_{B1}) .. state(B_i,V_{Bi}) hold, and optionally other *data* that state(B_j,V_{Bj}) .. state(B_k,V_{Bk}) hold, where the *warrant* is a positive influence relation S^+(state(A,V_A), state(B_p,V_{Bp})) for each B_p in $\{ B_1 .. B_i , B_j .. B_k \}$.

Strategy 2. *Argument for decrease in belief to unlikely that state of causal variable is at or over threshold value, based on absence of predicted effect*: An argument for the *claim* that there has been a decrease in belief, from time T_1 to T_2, to the belief at T_2 that it is unlikely that state(A,V_A) holds, consists of the (newly acquired) *data* that it is unlikely that state(C,V_{Ci}) holds for all $V_{Ci} \geq V_C$, where the *warrant* is a positive influence relation S^+(state(A,V_A), state(C,V_C)).

Strategy 3. *Argument for increase in belief in causal claim, based on decrease in belief in alternative cause:* An argument for the *claim* that there has been a increase in belief, from time T_1 to T_2, to the belief at T_2 that it is believed to some extent that state(A,V_A) holds and that state(A,V_A) is responsible for the states of variables state(B_1,V_{B1}) .. state(B_i,V_{Bi}), consists of the (presupposed) *data* that state(B_1,V_{B1}) .. state(B_i,V_{Bi}) hold, and the (newly acquired) *data* that it is unlikely that state(Alt,V_{Alt}) holds for all $V_{Alt} \geq V_{threshold}$, where the *warrant* is a negative product synergy relation X^-({state(A,V_A),state(Alt,$V_{threshold}$)},state(B,V_B)) for each B in {B_1 .. B_i}.

Strategy 4. *Argument for belief in joint responsibility, based on effect.* An argument for the *claim* that it is believed to some extent at time T_i that state(A,V_A) and state(B,V_B) hold and that state(A,V_A) and state(B,V_B) are jointly responsible for state(C,V_C), consists of the (presupposed) *data* that state(C,V_C) holds, where the *warrant* is a zero product synergy relation X^0({state(A,V_A), state(B,V_B)}, state(C,V_C)).

6 Example

This section gives an example of discourse generation for the case in section 3. An outline created by application of the discourse grammar to the domain model in Figure 1 would contain, in addition to basic information about the case not requiring an argument, several claims requiring further support to be provided by the argument generator.

First, the claim that it was believed, before testing, that the child's hearing loss could be due to having two mutated alleles of GJB2 would be supported by an argument constructed using Strategy 1. The data of the argument is the presupposition that the child has hearing loss and the additional finding that she has no syndromic features. The warrant is the positive influence relations (S^+) linking the variable representing the child's GJB2 genotype to each of the two variables representing the child's symptoms. Note that if a reader questioned this argument, an interactive system could provide information on the source of the data or epidemiological statistics backing the warrant.

Second, the claim that it is currently believed, after testing, that it is unlikely that the child's GJB2 genotype has two mutated alleles would be supported by an argument constructed using Strategy 2. The data of the argument is that the child's GJB2 test results were negative. The warrant is the positive influence relation (S^+) from the child's GJB2 genotype to the child's GJB2 test results, which predicts that if the child had this mutation, then the test results would have been positive. If a reader questioned this argument, an interactive system could provide information on the source of the data or back the warrant by providing information about the rate of false negatives.

Third, the claim that it is currently believed, after testing, that it is possible that the child has some other genetic condition that is responsible for her hearing loss would be supported by an argument constructed using Strategy 3. The data of the argument is that she has hearing loss and the current belief that GJB2 is not likely responsible. The warrant is the negative product synergy relation (X^-) between the child's GJB2 genotype and another genotype to hearing loss. If a reader questioned this argument, an interactive system could provide information on the proportion of cases of hearing loss that are due to other genetic conditions as backing for the warrant.

Fourth, the claim that it is currently believed, after testing, that it is possible that the parents are carriers (i.e., each has one mutated allele) of the unspecified genotype claimed to be responsible for the child's hearing loss would be supported by an argument constructed using Strategy 4. The data of the argument is the presupposition that the child has two mutated alleles of the other genotype. The warrant is the zero product synergy relation (X^0) between the two parents' genotype for this alternative to GJB2 and the child's genotype for this same alternative. If a reader questioned this argument, an interactive system could provide an explanation of the warrant, which is based on the theory of Mendelian inheritance; or it could provide the argument for the data, i.e., the belief that the child has two mutated alleles of the other genotype.

Finally, the claim that it is currently believed, after testing, that assuming they are both carriers there is a 25% probability that each future child that the two parents have together will inherit two mutated alleles of the other genotype would be supported by an argument constructed by a strategy not shown in section 5. The data is the assumption that the parents are both carriers, and the warrant is the same zero product synergy relation (X^0) used in the argument for the fourth claim. If a reader questioned this argument, an interactive system could provide an explanation of how the probabilities are determined by zero product synergy.

7 Experiment

Argument generation was evaluated in the following experiment. Five biology graduate students, screened beforehand for writing ability in biology, were shown two patient letters. The letters were created by the experimenter by paraphrasing the output of discourse generation that would be input to the realizer. The paraphrases are similar in syntax and lexical style to letters in the corpus, but the genetic disorders covered in the experiment's letters differ from those covered in the corpus. One letter concerns a child confirmed to have cystic fibrosis (CF); the other a child whose test results for Waardenburg syndrome (WS) were negative. The text of letter CF is given in Figure 2. The first column contains annotations describing the communicative function of the information: C for claim, D for data, W for warrant, and B for backing. Each label is subscripted with an integer referring to the argument. (The row labeled C_2/D_3 functions as both the claim of argument 2 and the data of argument 3.) Annotations were not shown to the experiment's participants. Communicative function was used to determine presentation order within each argument. Letters CF and WS had 23 and 25 segments, respectively, where a *segment* is defined as a unit fulfilling one of the above functions, or a non-argument-related function.

The goal of the experiment was to conduct a preliminary evaluation of the acceptability of the arguments in terms of content, explicitness, and presentation order within arguments. The participants were asked to revise each letter as needed to make it more appropriate for its intended recipients, the biological parents of a patient. Participants were told they could reword, reorder, and make deletions and additions to a letter. The results are summarized in Table 1, which includes the average number of segments to/from which information was added (New) or deleted (Delete), and reordered (Reorder). (Rewordings are not tabulated since it was not our goal to evaluate wording.) New and Delete are measures of acceptability of argument content and explicitness. Reorder is a measure of acceptability of ordering. On average, the number of New, Delete, and Reorder revisions were low: less than two per letter, with most revisions in the category of Reorder. This is encouraging since the system to be built for genetic counselors should provide acceptable arguments requiring a minimum of revision.

To provide more details about the results, first, the only segments to which participants added information are warrants. The deletions of data consist of information presumably already known to the recipients, e.g. D_6 in letter CF; other deletions are of part or all of a warrant or all of a backing. The only deletions of claims consist of information duplicated in another part of the letter; there were no cases where a claim was deleted even though it could be inferred from data and warrant. The reorderings were across-argument, which violates conventional topic structure in the genre, or within-argument. In the latter, half repositioned a claim from final position in an argument to a position before the warrant or backing; the other half repositioned the warrant or backing before the data.

8 Related Work

Due to space limitations, this section focuses on research on generation of *normative* arguments (as opposed to behavior-change and evaluative arguments), and arguments designed for text rather than dialogue. Zukerman et al. have presented several papers on argument generation from Bayesian network domain models (e.g., 2000). The type of domain model used in our work differs in two respects. First, it is based on empirical research since it is intended to represent the simplified conceptual model presented to a lay audience in this genre. Second, it uses qualitative probabilistic constraints. One difference in argument generation is that our system's argument strategies are based on analysis of the corpus. Also, our system creates an intentional-level representation of an argument.

Teufel and Moens (2002) present a coding scheme for scientific argumentation in research articles that is designed for automatic summarization of human-authored text. Thus, it would not be sufficient for generation from a non-linguistic knowledge base. Also, it does not make the finer-grained distinctions of the Toulmin model.

Branting et al. (1999) present the architecture of a legal document drafting system. In it, a discourse grammar applies genre-specific knowledge, while a legal reasoning module creates the illocutionary structure of legal arguments. Branting et al. argue for maintaining a distinct intentional-level representation of arguments to support interactive follow-up discussion. We agree, but our design further distinguishes domain reasoning from argument generation.

As for work on ordering and explicitness, Reed and Long (1997) propose ordering heuristics for arguments of classical deductive logic. Fiedler and Horacek (2001) present a model for deciding what can be omitted from explanations of mathematical proofs. Carenini and Moore (2000) present an experiment to determine how much evidence is optimal in an evaluative argument.

9 Conclusions

This paper presents the design of a discourse generator that plans the content and organization of genetic counseling letters containing arguments. A preliminary evaluation of the arguments was promising. The most important contribution of this work is the design of a non-domain-specific normative argument generator that creates an intentional-level representation of an argument. From the corpus, we formulated argument strategies that map formal properties of qualitative causal probabilistic models to components of Toulmin's model. Due to the separation of domain, argument and genre-specific concerns and the methodology used for acquiring the domain model, this approach should be applicable to lay-oriented normative argument generation in other domains.

Acknowledgments

This material is based upon work supported by the National Science Foundation under CAREER Award No. 0132821.

References

Baker DL, Eash T, Schuette JL, Uhlmann WR. 2002. Guidelines for writing letters to patients. *J Genetic Counseling,* 11(5):399-418.

Branting LK, Callaway CB, Mott BW, Lester JC. 1999. Integrating Discourse and Domain Knowledge for Document Drafting. *Proc ICAIL-99*, 214-220.

Carenini G, Moore J. 2000. An empirical study of the influence of argument conciseness on argument effectiveness. *Proc Ann Meeting of ACL*, 150-7.

Druzdzel MJ, Henrion M. 1993. Efficient reasoning in qualitative probabilistic networks. *Proc 11th Nat Conf on AI,* 548-553.

Fiedler A, Horacek H. 2001. Argumentation in Explanations to Logical Problems. *Computational Models of Natural Language Arguments. Proc ICCS 2001.* Springer LNCS 2073, 969-978.

Green N. 2005. A Bayesian Network Coding Scheme for Annotating Biomedical Information Presented to Genetic Counseling Clients. *J Biomed Inf,* 38: 130-144.

Green N. 2006. Representing Normative Arguments in Genetic Counseling. *AAAI SSS: Argumentation for Consumers of Healthcare.*

Green N. To appear. Argumentation in a Causal Probabilistic Humanistic Domain. *Int J Intell Sys.*

Green N, Britt T, Jirak K. 2004. Communication of Uncertainty in Genetic Counseling Patient Education Systems. *AAAI FSS: Dialog Sys for Health Commun.*

Green N, Britt T, Jirak K, Waizenegger D, Xin X. 2005. User Modeling for Tailored Genomic E-health Information. *User Modeling 2005 Workshop: Personalisation for eHealth,*

Korb K, Nicholson AE. 2004. *Bayesian artificial intelligence.* Chapman Hall/CRC, Boca Raton, Florida.

Reed C, Long D. 1997. Content ordering in the generation of persuasive discourse. *IJCAI-97*, 1022-27.

Teufel S, Moens M. 2002. Summarizing Scientific Articles: Experiments with Relevance and Rhetorical Status. *CL*, 28(4):409-445.

Toulmin SE. 1998. *The uses of argument.* 9th ed. Cambridge Univ. Press, Cambridge, England.

Zukerman I, McConacy R, Korb K. 2000. Using argumentation strategies in automated argument generation. *Proc INLG-2000.*

letter CF	New	Delete	Reorder	letter WS	New	Delete	Reorder
	0	2	1		0	2	4
	0	2	0		0	0	1
	0	0	1		0	1	1
	0	0	6		2	1	1
	0	2	1		1	0	0
AVG	0	1.2	1.8	AVG	0.6	0.8	1.4
STDEV	0	1.1	2.4	STDEV	0.9	0.8	1.5

Table 1. Number of revisions in letters CF and WS. (N=5)

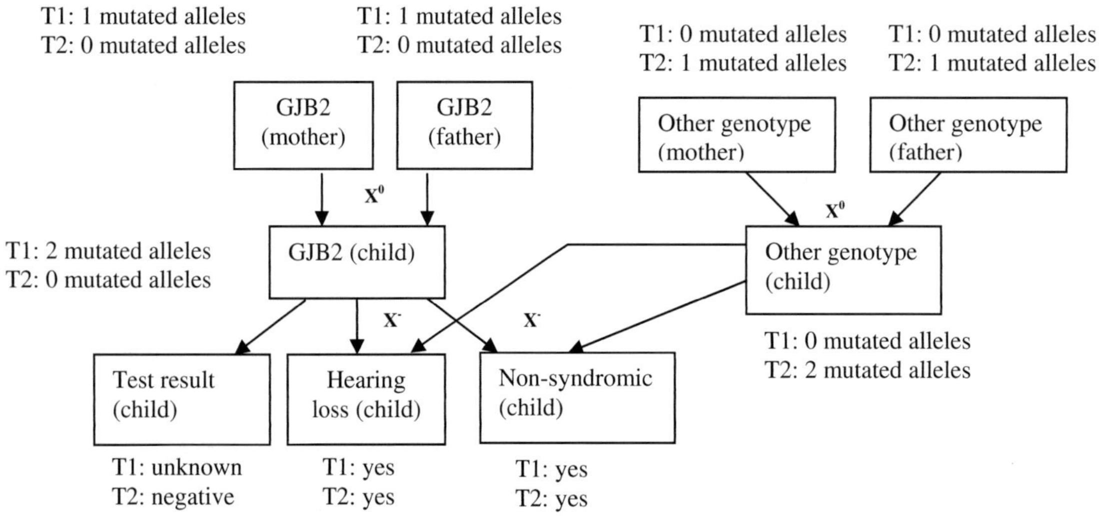

Figure 1. Qualitative causal probabilistic network for hearing loss case.

	[Patient] was referred by [doctor] to [clinic] on [date] for evaluation.
D_1	She has had frequent respiratory infections.
W_1	A genetic condition known as cystic fibrosis (CF) can cause respiratory problems.
B_1	Eighty percent of CF patients have chronic respiratory complaints.
C_1	[Doctor] suspected that CF could be the cause of her respiratory problems.
	Patient was given a sweat chloride test for CF.
D_2	The test showed an abnormal sweat chloride level (75 mmol/L).
W_2	A result over 60 mmol/L is considered positive for CF.
C_2 / D_3	It is very likely that [patient] has CF. This means that cells in [patient's] body contain two altered copies of a gene called CFTR.
W_3	This alteration affects organs that secrete mucous, such as the lungs. The alteration causes excessive secretions, resulting in frequent lung infections.
C_3	This alteration of the CFTR gene is most likely the cause of [patient's] respiratory problems.
D_4	Both of you, [patient's] parents, are of Northern European ancestry.
B_4	One in twenty-five people of N. European ancestry carry one altered copy of the CFTR gene.
C_4	Each of you could carry this alteration.
W_5	Our cells contain two copies of each gene. One copy is inherited from each parent. A child who inherited two altered copies of a gene must have gotten one ... from the mother and one … from the father.
D_5	Since [patient's] cells contain two altered copies of CFTR,
C_5	it is likely that she got one altered copy of CFTR from each of you.
C_6	This is likely
D_6	even though neither of you have cystic fibrosis.
W_6	When a parent has one altered copy and one normal copy of a gene such as CFTR, he or she is not usually affected. Someone who has only one altered copy is called a "carrier". A child who inherits two altered copies will be affected since she has no normal copy.
W_7	A couple in which both are carriers will have a one in four (25%) chance that each child that they conceive will inherit two altered copies and be affected. This also means that they have a three in four (75%) chance that the child will inherit at least one unaltered copy from one parent and not be affected.
D_7	Assuming that you are both carriers,
C_7	the chances for each child that you conceive together is 25% that the child will have CF, and 75% that the child will not have CF.

Figure 2. Letter used in experiment (column 2) with argument annotations (column 1).

Introduction to the INLG'06 Special Session on Sharing Data and Comparative Evaluation

The idea for this special session had its origins in discussions with many different members of the NLG community at the 2005 Workshop on Using Corpora for Natural Language Generation (UCNLG'05, held in conjunction with the Corpus Linguistics 2005 conference at the University of Birmingham in July 2005), and subsequently at the 10th European Natural Language Generation Workshop (ENLG'05, held at the University of Aberdeen in August 2005). At the latter event, the excitement about introducing shared tasks was infectious: the topic hijacked several of the organised discussion groups, it was the focus of conversation at many tables during lunch-breaks, and even the end of the conference didn't put a stop to it, with discussions carrying right on until the taxis to the airport arrived.

There was some common ground: nobody said it wouldn't be a good idea to be able to directly compare different NLG techniques, most people even seemed to agree that sharable data and tasks were the way to go. But opinion was sharply divided about how it was to be achieved. There were—with only a small degree of caricature—two main camps: the bulls argued for a suck-it-and-see approach, for throwing a task at the research community and then sitting back to see what would happen; the bears warned that using one data set was not a good idea until there was community buy-in to a particular data set and a particular task specification over that data set.

Some of the bears were worried that NLG would inevitably emulate MT and end up with a single task, fixed inputs and gold-standard outputs, using a single automatic metric of similarity to assess the quality of generated texts against the gold standard, and moreover, require millions of dollars in direct funding. It would be impossible to decide what the inputs to the task should look like, because after all, as Yorick Wilks had pointed out years before, determining the inputs to NLG was like counting back from infinity to 1 (in contrast to NLU, which, being more akin to counting from 1 to infinity, seemed at least a little more manageable). The community would either become hopelessly mired in the task of trying to agree on an input type and task, or else agree one by dictat and alienate the majority of researchers. Finally, the field would become obsessed with the single task and the scores produced by the single metric, and all true scientific enquiry would be stifled.

The bulls envisaged an entirely different future, where many different tasks and benchmark datasets co-existed peacefully, where some tasks did have associated inputs and outputs, but others had more abstract system specifications. NLG was not inherently different from NLU at all, in fact the output representations used in the latter were just as much there by gentle(wo)man's agreement as any common inputs to NLG would be. The strong NLG traditions of user-oriented and task-based evaluations using human evaluators would be part of the evaluation paradigm in shared-task evaluations, while parallel research might look at—but not impose—bespoke automatic methods for NLG. Money would be needed for data resource creation, but not necessarily for anything else; evidence that this was possible could be found in successful and vibrant shared-task initiatives run on a shoe-string, such as CoNLL and SENSEVAL. The community would create its own forum for reviewing, updating and adding tasks and evaluation methods. NLG would be invigorated, great scientific progress would result, commercial deployment of NLG technology and regular papers in *Computational Linguistics* and ACL proceedings would surely follow.

One thing was clear: opinions abounded, most of them strong ones. Shared-task evaluation had been firmly put on the NLG agenda. So, we thought, what better than to create a larger,

Proceedings of the Fourth International Natural Language Generation Conference
Sydney, July 2006. ©2006 Association for Computational Linguistics

more enduring forum for continuing discussions, in the shape of an INLG special session? We are pleased to say that the response from the NLG community has been very positive, and that the papers in this section of the proceedings and the oral presentations at the special session itself represent both the bullish and the bearish camps. Belz and Kilgarriff present a generally bullish, but occasionally bearish, history of shared-task initiatives in NLP, and the lessons that NLG might learn from it, while Reiter and Belz present a proposal for a series of shared tasks in data-to-text NLG. Van Deemter et al. look at the generation of referring expressions and propose a method for eliciting reference texts for evaluation of GRE algorithms. Paris argues for NLG system evaluation practices similar to the ISO standards for software evaluation, including criteria such as flexibility, portability and maintainability.

Among the oral presentations, Scott and Moore exemplify the bearish position but do argue in favour of a standardised architecture and interface specifications to eventually enable cross-system comparison. Horacek considers the input problem and advocates the gradual and collective development of a generic 'generation specification' formalism. Varges recommends that NLG deliberately take a different route from NLU and encourage a diversity of tasks and representations.

Kathy McKeown's invited talk is perfectly poised between the two camps: from her experience with DUC, TREC and GALE, she concludes that every evaluation programme must expect to have to weather a stormy period of initial disagreement and even hostility, before eventually reaching calmer waters where growing agreement and acceptance enable the true benefits of the programme to take effect.

Consensus-spotters will be able to identify several areas of interest: certainly nobody wants to follow the example of MT and parsing, and become beholden to a single metric and automated gold-standard evaluation; some degree of standardisation in sub-tasks and representations is desirable, but should evolve over time; and perhaps most unanimously, the diversity of current NLG research with its many different tasks and interests must be preserved.

Even a small amount of common ground can be enough for debate to flourish and consensus to grow. We hope that the snapshot of opinion presented at this special session will be the beginning of a long history of comparative evaluation in NLG.

Anja Belz and Robert Dale (Organisers; one bull and one bear)

Evaluations of NLG Systems: common corpus and tasks or common dimensions and metrics?

Cécile Paris, Nathalie Colineau and Ross Wilkinson
CSIRO ICT Centre
Locked Bag 17, North Ryde
NSW 1670, Australia
{Cecile.Paris, Nathalie.Colineau, Ross.Wilkinson}@csiro.au

Abstract

In this position paper, we argue that a common task and corpus are not the only ways to evaluate Natural Language Generation (NLG) systems. It might be, in fact, too narrow a view on evaluation and thus not be the best way to evaluate these systems. The aim of a common task and corpus is to allow for a comparative evaluation of systems, looking at the systems' performances. It is thus a "system-oriented" view of evaluation. We argue here that, if we are to take a system oriented view of evaluation, the community might be better served by enlarging the view of evaluation, defining common dimensions and metrics to evaluate systems and approaches. We also argue that end-user (or usability) evaluations form another important aspect of a system's evaluation and should not be forgotten.

1 Introduction

For this special session, a specific question was asked: what would a shared task and shared corpus be that would enable us to perform comparative evaluations of alternative techniques in natural language generation (NLG)? In this position paper, we question the appropriateness of this specific question and suggest that the community might be better served by (1) looking at a different question: what are the dimensions and metrics that would allow us to compare various techniques and systems and (2) not forgetting but encouraging usability evaluations of specific applications.

The purpose of defining a shared task and a shared corpus is to compare the performance of various systems. It is thus a system-oriented view of evaluation, as opposed to an end-user oriented (or usability) view of evaluation. It is, however, potentially a narrow view of a system-oriented evaluation, as it looks at the performance of an NLG system within a very specific context – thus essentially looking at the performance of a specific application. We argue here that (1), even if we take a system-oriented view of evaluation, the evaluation of NLG systems should not be limited to their performance in a specific context but should take other system's characteristics into account, and that (2) end-user evaluations are crucial.

2 Enlarging the view of system-oriented evaluations

The comparison of NLG systems should not be limited to a particular task in a specific context. Most systems are designed for specific applications in specific domains and tend to be tuned for these applications. Evaluating them in a context of a specific common evaluation task might de-contextualise them and might encourage fine-tuning for this task, which might not be useful in general. Furthermore, the evaluation of a system should not be limited to its performance in a specific context but should address characteristics such as:

- Cost of building (time and effort);
- Ease of extension, maintainability and customisability to handle new requirements (time, effort and expertise required);
- Cost of porting to a new domain or application (time, effort and expertise required);
- Cost of data capture if required (how expensive, expertise required);
- Coverage issues (users, tasks, dimensions of context; and
- Ease of integration with other software.

These dimensions are important if we want the technology to be adopted and if we want poten-

Proceedings of the Fourth International Natural Language Generation Conference
Sydney, July 2006. ©2006 Association for Computational Linguistics

tial users of the technology to be able to make an informed choice as to what approach to choose when.

Most NLG systems are built around a specific application. Using them in the context of a different application or domain might be difficult. While one can argue that basic techniques do not differ from one application to another, the cost of the modifications required and the expertise and skills needed may not be worth the trouble. It may be simply cheaper and more convenient to rebuild everything. However, firstly, this might not be an option, and, secondly, it may increase the cost of using an NLG approach to such an extent as to make it unaffordable. In addition, applications evolve over time and often require a quick deployment. It is thus increasingly desirable to be able to change (update) an application, enabling it to respond appropriately to the new situations which it must now handle: this may require the ability to handle new situations (e.g., generate new texts) or the ability to respond differently than originally envisaged to known situations. This is important for at least two reasons:

(1) We are designers not domain experts. Although we usually carry out a domain/corpus/task analysis beforehand to acquire the domain knowledge and understand the users' needs in terms of the text to be generated, it is almost impossible to become a domain expert and know what is the most appropriate in each situation. Thus, the design of a specific application should allow the experts to take on control and ensure the application is configured appropriately. This imposes the additional constraint that an application should be maintainable directly by a requirement specialist, an author, expert or potentially the reader/listener;

(2) Situations are dynamic – what is satisfactory today may be unsatisfactory tomorrow. We must be prepared to take on board new requirements as they come in.

These requirements, of course, come at a cost. With this in mind, then, we believe that there is another side to system-oriented evaluation which we, as designers of NLG systems, need to consider: the ease or cost of developing flexible applications that can be easily configured and maintained to meet changing requirements. As a start towards this goal, we attempted to look more precisely at one of the characteristics mentioned above, the cost of maintaining and extending an application, attempting to understand what we should take into account to evaluate a system on that dimension. We believe asking the following questions might be useful. When there are new requirements:

(1) What changes are needed and do the modifications require the development of new resources, the implementation of additional functionality to the underlying architecture, or both?

(2) Who can do it and what is the expertise required? – NLG systems are now quite complex and require a lot of expertise that may be shared among several individuals (e.g., software engineering, computational linguistics, domain expertise, etc.).

(3) How hard it is? – How much effort and time would be required to modify/update the system to the new requirements?

In asking these questions, we believe it is also useful to decouple a specific system and its underlying architecture, and ask the appropriate questions to both.

3 Usability Evaluations of NLG Systems

When talking about evaluation of NLG systems, we should also remember that usability evaluations are crucial, as they can confirm the usefulness of a system for its purpose and look at the impact of the generated text on its intended audience. There has been an increasing number of such evaluations – e.g., (Reiter *et al.*, 2001, Paris *et al.*, 2001, Colineau *et al.*, 2002, Kushniruk *et al.*, 2002, Elhadad *et al.*, 2005) – and we should continue to encourage them as well as develop and share methodologies (and pitfalls) for performing these evaluations. It is interesting, in fact, to note that communities that have emphasized common task and corpus evaluations, such as the IR community, are now turning their attention to stakeholder-based evaluations such as task-based evaluations. In looking at ways to evaluate NLG systems, we might again enlarge our view beyond reader/listener-oriented usability evaluations, as readers are not the only persons potentially affected by our technology. When doing our evaluations, then, we must also consider other parties. Considering NLG systems as information systems, we might consider the following stakeholders beyond the reader:

- The **creators** of the information: for some applications, this may refer to the person creating the resources or the information required for the NLG system. This might be, for example, the people writing the fragments of text that will be later assembled automatically. Or it might include the person who will author the discourse rules or the templates required. With respect to these people, we might ask questions such as: "Does employing this NLG system/approach save them time?", "Is it easy for them to update the information?"[1]

- The "**owners**" of the information. We refer here to the organisation choosing to employ an NLG system. Possible questions here might be: "Does the automatically generated text achieve its purpose with respect to the organisation?", "Can the organisation convey similar messages with the automated system? (e.g., branding issues).

4 Discussion

In this short position paper, we have argued that we need to enlarge our view of evaluation to encompass both usability evaluation (and include users beyond readers/listeners) and system-oriented evaluations. While we recognise that it is crucial to have ways to compare systems and approaches (the main advantage of having a common corpus and task), we suggest that we should look for ways to enable these comparisons without narrowing our view on evaluation and de-contextualising the systems under consideration. We have presented some possible dimensions on which approaches and systems could be evaluated. While we understand how to perform usability evaluations, we believe that an important question is whether it is possible to agree on dimensions for system-oriented evaluations and on "metrics" for these dimensions, to allow us to evaluate the different applications and approaches, and allow potential users of the technology to choose the appropriate one for their needs. In our own work, we exploit an NLG architecture to develop adaptive hypermedia applications (Paris *et al.*, 2004), and some of our goals (Colineau *et al.*, 2006) are to:

- Articulate a comprehensive framework for the evaluation of approaches to building tailored information delivery systems and specific applications built using these approaches.
- Identify how an application or an approach measures along some dimensions (in particular for system-oriented evaluation).

We believe these are equally important for the evaluation of NLG systems.

Acknowledgements

We would like to thank the reviewers of the paper for their useful comments.

References

Colineau, N., Paris, C. & Vander Linden, K. 2002. An Evaluation of Procedural Instructional Text. In the *Proceedings of the International Natural Language Generation Conference (INLG) 2002*, NY.

Colineau, N., Paris, C. & Wilkinson, R. 2006. Towards Measuring the Cost of Changing Adaptive Hypermedia Systems. In *Proceedings of the International Conference on Adaptive Hypermedia and Adaptive Web-based Systems (AH2006)*. 259-263, Dublin, Ireland. LNCS 4018.

Elhadad, N. McKeown, K. Kaufman, D. & Jordan, D. 2005. Facilitating physicians' access to information via tailored text summarization. In *AMIA Annual Symposium, 2005*, Washington DC.

Kushniruk, A., Kan, MY, McKeown, K., Klavans, J., Jordan, D., LaFlamme, M. & Patel, V. 2002. Usability evaluation of an experimental text summarization system and three search engines: Implications for the reengineering of health care interfaces. In *Proceedings of the American Medical Informatics Association Annual Symposium (AMIA 2002).*

Paris, C., Wan, S., Wilkinson, R. & Wu, M. 2001. Generating Personalised Travel Guides? And who wants them? In *Proceedings of the 2001 International Conference on User Modelling (UM'01)*, Sondhofen, Germany.

Paris, C., Wu, M., Vander Linden, K., Post, M. & Lu, S. 2004. Myriad: An Architecture for Contextualised Information Retrieval and Delivery. In *Proceedings of the International Conference on Adaptive Hypermedia and Adaptive Web-based Systems (AH2004)*. 205-214, The Netherlands.

Reiter, E., Robertson, R., Lennox A. S. & Osman, L. (2001). Using a randomised controlled clinical trial to evaluate an NLG system. In *Proceedings of ACL'01*, Toulouse, France, 434-441.

[1] We realise that, for some NLG applications, there might be no authors if all the data exploited by the system comes from underlying existing sources, e.g., weather or stock data or existing textual resources.

Building a semantically transparent corpus for the generation of referring expressions

Kees van Deemter and **Ielka van der Sluis** and **Albert Gatt**
Department of Computing Science
University of Aberdeen
{kvdeemte,ivdsluis,agatt}@csd.abdn.ac.uk

Abstract

This paper discusses the construction of a corpus for the evaluation of algorithms that generate referring expressions. It is argued that such an evaluation task requires a semantically transparent corpus, and controlled experiments are the best way to create such a resource. We address a number of issues that have arisen in an ongoing evaluation study, among which is the problem of judging the output of GRE algorithms against a human gold standard.

1 Creating and using a corpus for GRE

A decade ago, Dale and Reiter (1995) published a seminal paper in which they compared a number of GRE algorithms. These algorithms included a Full Brevity (FB) algorithm which generates descriptions of minimal length, a greedy algorithm (GA), and an Incremental Algorithm (IA). The authors argued that the latter was the best model of human referential behaviour, and versions of the IA have since come to represent the state of the art in GRE. Dale and Reiter's hypothesis was motivated by psycholinguistic findings, notably that speakers tend to initiate references before they have completely scanned a domain. However, this finding affords different algorithmic interpretations. Similarly, the finding that basic-level terms in referring expressions allow hearers to form a psychological gestalt could be incorporated into practically any GRE algorithm.[1]

We decided to put Dale and Reiter's hypothesis to the test by an evaluation of the output of different GRE algorithms against human production. However, it is notoriously difficult to obtain suitable corpora for a task that is as semantically intensive as Content Determination (for GRE). Although existing corpora are valuable resources, NLG often requires information that is not available in text. Suppose, for example, that a corpus contained articles about politics, how would the output of a GRE algorithm be evaluated against the corpus? It would be difficult to infer from an article exactly which representatives in the British House of Commons are Liberal Democrats, or Scottish. Combining multiple texts is hazardous, since facts could alter across sources and time. Moreover, the conditions under which such texts were produced (e.g. *fault-critical* or not, as explained below) are hard to determine.

A recent GRE evaluation by Gupta and Stent (2005) focused on dialogue corpora, using MAPTASK and COCONUT, both of which have an associated domain. Their results show that referent identification in MAPTASK often requires no more than a TYPE attribute, so that none of the algorithms performed better than a baseline. In contrast to MAPTASK, COCONUT has a more elaborate domain, but it is characterised by a collaborative task, and references frequently go beyond the identification criterion that is typically invoked in GRE[2]. Mindful of the limitations of existing corpora, and of the extent to which evaluation depends on the corpus under study, we are using controlled experiments to create a corpus whose construction will ensure that existing algorithms can be adequately differentiated on an identification task.

[1]A separate argument for IA involves tractability, but although some alternatives (such as FB) are intractable, others (such as GA) are only polynomial, and can therefore not easily be dismissed on purely computational grounds.

[2]Jordan and Walker (2000) have demonstrated a significantly better match to the human data when task-related constraints are taken into account.

Proceedings of the Fourth International Natural Language Generation Conference
Sydney, July 2006.

2 Setup of the experiment

Like Dale and Reiter (1995), we focused on first-mention descriptions. However, we decided to include simple 'disjunctive' references to sets (as in 'the red chair and the black table'), in addition to conjunctions of atomic properties, since these can be handled by essentially the same algorithms (van Deemter, 2002). For generality, we looked at two very different domains. One of these involved artificially constructed pictures of furniture, where the available attributes and values are relatively easy to determine. The other involved real photographs of individuals, which provide a richer range of options to subjects. To date, data has been collected from 19 participants, and analysis is in progress.

Our first challenge was to make the experiment naturalistic. Subjects were shown 38 randomised trials, each depicting a set of objects, one or two of which were the targets, surrounded by 6 distractors (Figure 1). In each case, a minimal distinguishing description of the targets was available. Subjects were led to believe that they would be describing the targets for an interlocutor. Once a description was typed, the system removed from the screen what it took to be the referents.

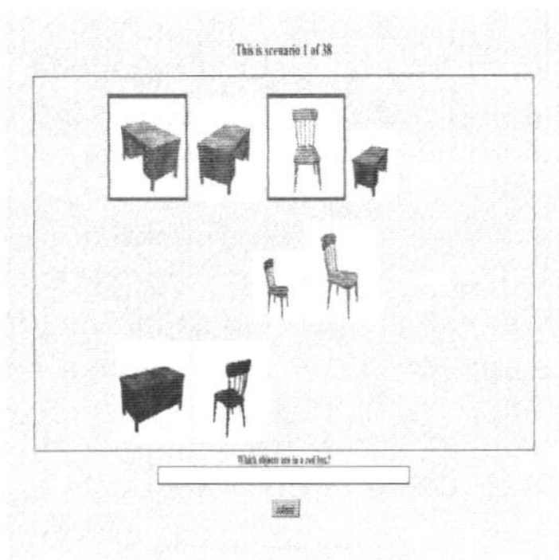

Figure 1: A stimulus example from the furniture domain.

Three groups performed the task in different conditions, namely: $\langle \pm FaultCritical \rangle$, where half the subjects in the $\langle +FaultCritical \rangle$ case could use location ('in the top left corner'). The $\langle +FaultCritical \rangle$ group was told: 'Our program will eventually be used in situations where it is crucial that it understands descriptions accurately. In these situations, there will often be no option to correct mistakes. Therefore, (...) you will not get the chance to revise (your description)'. By contrast, the $\langle -FaultCritical \rangle$ subjects were given the opportunity to revise their description should the system have got it wrong. Subjects in the $\langle -Location \rangle$ condition were told that their interlocutor could see exactly the same pictures as they could, but these had been jumbled up; by contrast, $\langle +Location \rangle$ subjects were led to believe that their addressee could see the pictures in exactly the same position.

The second main challenge was to create trials that would distinguish between all the algorithms. For instance, if trials involved only one attribute, say an object's TYPE (e.g., *chair* or *table*), they would not allow us to distinguish IA from FB, as both would always generate the shortest description. Subtler issues arise with *local brevity* (Reiter, 1990), an optimisation strategy which requires sufficiently complex trials to make a difference.

3 How to analyse the data?

Our semantically transparent corpus can be used for testing various hypotheses, for instance about when an algorithm should overspecify descriptions (e.g. more in $\langle +FaultCritical, +Location \rangle$ (Arts, 2004), and/or when the target is a set). Here, we focus on the issue raised in Section 1, namely, which of the algorithms discussed in Dale and Reiter (1995) matches human behaviour best.

The first problem is determining the relevant algorithms. The IA comes in different flavours, because its output depends on the order in which the different properties are attempted (commonly called the preference order). It is possible to consider *all* different IAs (trying every conceivable preference order), but this would increase the number of statistical hypotheses to be tested, impacting the validity of the results and requiring a Bonferroni correction. Instead, we are using a pretest to find the optimal version of IA, comparing only that version to the other algorithms.

The second question is how to assess algorithm performance. Since our production experiment does not yield a *single* gold standard (GS), an algorithm might match subjects better in one condition (e.g. $\langle +FaultCritical \rangle$, or perform better in one domain (e.g. furniture). Moreover, it might match subjects poorly overall due to sample variation, while evincing a perfect match with a single individual. Using both a *by-subjects* and a *by-items* analysis will partially control for sample dispersion.

How should we calculate the *match* between an algorithm and a GS? Once again, there are two facets to this problem. Since we are focusing on Content Determination, each human description could be viewed as associating, with the relevant trial, a set of properties. Our approach will be to annotate each human description with the set of attributes it contains. However, the real data is often messy. For example, when one subject called an object 'the non-coloured table', and another called it 'the grey desk', both may be expressing the same attributes (i.e. TYPE and COLOUR). Also, while it is often assumed that the output of GRE is a definite noun phrase, this is not always the case in our corpus, which contains indefinite distinguishing descriptions such as *'a red chair, facing to the right'*, and telegraphic messages such as *'red, right-facing'*.

The second aspect to the problem concerns the actual human-algorithm comparison. Suppose the GS equals the output of one subject, and we are comparing two algorithms, x and y. Suppose our subject produced 'the two huge red sofas', which the GS associates with the set $\{sofa, red, large\}$. Suppose our algorithms describe the target as:

Output from x : $\{sofa, red, top\}$
Output from y : $\{sofa, red, large, top\}$

Which of these algorithms matches the GS best? Algorithm y adds a property (perhaps overspecifying even more than the GS). Algorithm x has the same length as the GS, but replaces one property by another. Several reasonable ways of assessing the differences can be devised, one of which is Levenshtein distance (which suggests preferring y over x, since the latter involves a deletion *and* an addition) (Levenshtein, 1966). We also intend to examine how often the GS over- or underspecifies where the algorithm does not.

4 Conclusion

Corpora can be an invaluable resource for NLG as long as the necessary contextual information and the conditions under which the texts in a corpus were produced are known. We believe that controlled and balanced experiments are needed for building semantically transparent resources, whose construction we have discussed. As shown in this paper, evaluation of algorithms against the number of gold standards obtained with such a corpus needs careful consideration.

Evaluation of GRE – and NLG systems more generally – would benefit from more investigation of the differences between readers and producers. In future work, we intend to follow up with a reader-oriented experiment in which we test the speed and/or accuracy with which the output of different GRE algorithms is understood by subjects. The dependent variables here will be nonlinguistic (perhaps involving subjects clicking on pictures of presumed target referents). This illustrates a more general issue in this area, namely that corpora should, in our view, only be a starting point, with which data of different kinds can be associated.

5 Acknowledgments

Thanks to Ehud Reiter, Richard Power and Emiel Krahmer for useful comments. This work is part of the TUNA project (`http://www.csd.abdn.ac.uk/research/tuna/`), funded by the EPSRC in the UK (GR/S13330/01).

References

[Arts2004] A. Arts. 2004. *Overspecification in Instructive Texts*. Ph.D. thesis, Tilburg University.

[Dale and Reiter1995] R. Dale and E. Reiter. 1995. Computational interpretations of the Gricean maxims in the generation of referring expressions. *Cognitive Science*, 18:233–263.

[van Deemter2002] K. van Deemter. 2002. Generating referring expressions: Boolean extensions of the incremental algorithm. *Computational Linguistics*, 28(1):37–52.

[Gupta and Stent2005] S. Gupta and A. J. Stent. 2005. Automatic evaluation of referring expression generation using corpora. In *Proceedings of the 1st Workshop on Using Corpora in NLG, Birmingham, UK.*

[Jordan and Walker2000] P. Jordan and M. Walker. 2000. Learning attribute selections for non-pronominal expressions. In *Proceedings of the 38th Annual Meeting of the Association for Computational Linguistics*.

[Levenshtein1966] V. Levenshtein. 1966. Binary codes capable of correcting deletions, insertions and reversals. *Soviet Physics Doklady*, 10(8):707–710.

[Reiter1990] E. Reiter. 1990. The computational complexity of avoiding conversational implicatures. In *Proceedings of the 28th ACL Meeting*, pages 97–104. MIT Press.

Shared-task Evaluations in HLT: Lessons for NLG

Anja Belz
University of Brighton, UK
A.S.Belz@brighton.ac.uk

Adam Kilgarriff
Lexical Computing Ltd., UK
adam@lexmasterclass.com

1 Introduction

While natural language generation (NLG) has a strong evaluation tradition, in particular in user-based and task-oriented evaluation, it has never evaluated different approaches and techniques by comparing their performance on the same tasks (shared-task evaluation, STE). NLG is characterised by a lack of consolidation of results, and by isolation from the rest of NLP where STE is now standard. It is, moreover, a shrinking field (state-of-the-art MT and summarisation no longer perform generation as a subtask) which lacks the kind of funding and participation that natural language understanding (NLU) has attracted.

Evidence from other NLP fields shows that STE campaigns (STECs) can lead to rapid technological progress and substantially increased participation. The past year has seen a groundswell of interest in comparative evaluation among NLG researchers, the first comparative results are being reported (Belz and Reiter, 2006), and the move towards some form of comparative evaluation seems inevitable. In this paper we look at how two decades of NLP STECs might help us decide how best to make this move.

2 Shared-task evaluation in HLT

Over the past twenty years, virtually every field of research in human language technology (HLT) has introduced STECs. A small selection is presented in the table below[1]. NLG researchers have tended to be somewhat unconvinced of the benefits of comparative evaluation in general, and the kind of competitive, numbers-driven STECs that have been typical of NLU in particular. Yet STECs do not have to be hugely competitive events fixated on one task with associated input/output data and single evaluation metric, static over time.

Tasks: There is a distinction between (i) evaluations designed to help potential users to decide whether the technology will be valuable to them, and (ii) evaluations designed to help system developers improve the core technology (Spärck Jones and Galliers, 1996). In the former, the application context is a critical variable in the task definition; in the latter it is fixed. Developer-oriented evaluation promotes focus on the task in isolation, but if the context is fixed badly, or if the outside world changes but the evaluation does not, then it becomes irrelevant. NLP STECs have so far focused on developer-oriented evaluation, but there are increasing calls for more 'embedded', more task-based types of evaluations[2].

Existing NLP STECs show that tasks need to be broadly based and continuously evolving. To begin with, the task needs to be simple, easy to understand and easy for people to recognise as their task. Over time, as the limitations of the simple task are noted and a more substantial community is 'on board', tasks can multiply, diversify and become more sophisticated. This is something that TREC has been good at (still going strong 14 years on), and the parsing community has failed to achieve (see notes in table).

Evaluation: NLP STECs have tended to use automatic evaluations because of their speed and reproducibility, but some have used human evaluators, in particular in fields where language is generated (MT, summarisation, speech synthesis).

Evaluation scores are not independent of the task and context for which they are calculated. This is clearly true of human-based evaluation, but even scores by a simple metric like word error rate in speech recognition are not comparable unless certain parameters are the same: background-noise, language, whether or not speech is controlled. Development of evaluation methods and benchmark tasks therefore must go hand in hand.

Evaluation methods have to be accepted by the research community as providing a true approxi-

[1] Apologies for omissions, and for bias towards English.

[2] A prominent theme at the 2005 ELRA/ELDA Workshop on HLT Evaluation.

Proceedings of the Fourth International Natural Language Generation Conference
Sydney, July 2006.

Name	Start	Domain	Sponsors	Notes
MUC	1987	Information extraction	US Govt	Rapidly came to define IE; ended 1998.
PARSEVAL	1991	Parsing	—	Only ever defined a metric, no STEC[1].
TREC	1992	Information retrieval	US Govt	Large and long-running, multiple tracks.
SEMEVAL	1994	Semantic interpretation	US Govt	No STEC emerged[2].
NIST-MT	1994	Machine translation	US Govt	Revitalised since 2001 by BLEU[3].
Morpholympics	1994	Morphological analysis	GLDV	German morphological analysis; one-off.
SENSEVAL	1998	Word sense disambiguation	ACL-SIGLEX	Validity of WSD task problematic.
SUMMAC	1998	Text summarization	US Govt	One-off.
CoNLL	1999	Various	ACL-SIGNLL	Focus on learning algorithms.
CLEF	2000	IR across languages	EU Project	
DUC	2001	Document summarization	US Govt	Defines field.
Morfolimpiadas	2003	Morphological analysis	Portuguese Govt	Portuguese language only.
SIGHAN	2003	Chinese tokenization	ACL-SIGHAN	Key benchmark.
Blizzard	2003	Speech synthesis	Festvox project	Building synthetic voice from given data.
HAREM	2005	Named-entity recognition	Portuguese Govt	Portuguese language only.
RTE	2005	Textual entailment	EU Project	
TC-STAR	2005	Speech-to-speech translation	EU integrated project	Black-box and glass-box evaluation[4].

Notes

1. PARSEVAL is an evaluation measure, not a full STEC. This has proved problematic: the parsing community no longer accepts the PARSEVAL measure, but there has been no organisational framework for establishing an alternative.
2. SEMEVAL did not proceed largely because it was too ambitious and agreement between people with different interests and theoretical positions was not achieved. It was eventually reduced in scope and aspects became incorporated in MUC, SUMMAC and SENSEVAL.
3. MT has been transformed by corpus methods, which have shifted MT from a backwater to perhaps the most vibrant area of NLP in the last five years.
4. In TC-STAR, the SST task is broken down into numerous subtasks. The modules and systems that meet the given criteria are exchanged among the participants, lowering the barrier to entry.

mation of quality. E.g. BLEU is strongly disliked in the non-statistical part of the MT community because it is biased in favour of statistical MT systems. PARSEVAL stopped being used when the parsing community moved towards dependency parsing and related approaches.

Sharing: As PARSEVAL shows, measures and resources alone are not enough. Also required are (i) an event (or better, cycle of events) so people can attend and feel part of a community; (ii) a forum for reviewing task definitions and evaluation methods; (iii) a committee which 'owns' the STEC, and organises the next campaign.

Funding is usually needed for gold-standard corpus creation but rarely for anything else (Kilgarriff, 2003). Participants can be expected to cover the cost of system development and workshop attendance. A funded project is best seen as supporting and enabling the STEC (especially during the early stages) rather than being it.

In sum, STECs are good for community building. They produce energy (as we saw when the possibility was raised for NLG at UCNLG'05 and ENLG'05) which can lead to rapid scientific and technological progress. They make the field look like a game and draw people in.

3 Towards an NLG STEC

In 1981, Spärck Jones wrote that IR lacked consolidation and the ability to build new work on old, and that this was substantially because there was no commonly agreed framework for describing and evaluating systems (Spärck Jones, 1981, p. 245). Since 1981, various NLP sub-disciplines have consolidated results and progressed collectively through STECs, and have seen successful commercial deployment of NLP technology (e.g. speech recognition software, document retrieval and dialogue systems).

However, Spärck Jones's 1981 analysis could be said to still hold of NLG today. There has been little consolidation of results or collective progress, and there still is virtually no commercial deployment of NLG systems or components.

We believe that comparative evaluation is key if NLG is to consolidate and progress collectively. Conforming to the evaluation paradigm now common to the rest of NLP will also help re-integration, and open up the field to new researchers.

Tasks: In defining sharable tasks with associated data resources for NLG, the core problem is deciding what inputs should look like. There is a real risk that agreement cannot be achieved on this, so not many groups participate, or the plan never reaches fruition (as happened in SEMEVAL).

There are, however, ways in which this problem can be circumvented. One is to use a more abstract task specification describing system functionality, so that participants can use their own inputs, and systems are compared in task-based evaluations similar to the traditions and standards of software evaluation (as in Morpholympics). An alternative is to approach the issue through tasks with inputs and outputs that 'occur naturally', so that participants can use their own NLG-specific representations. Examples include data-to-text mappings where e.g. time-series data or a data repository are mapped to fault reports, forecasts, etc.

Both data-independent task definitions and tasks with naturally occurring data have promise, but we propose the second as the simpler, easier to organise solution, at least initially. A specific proposal of a set of tasks can be found elsewhere in this volume (Reiter and Belz, 2006). An interesting idea (recommended by ELRA/ELDA) is to break down the input-output mapping into stages (as in the TC-STAR workshops, see table) and then, in a second round of evaluations, to make available intermediate representations from the most successful systems from the first round. In this way, standardised representations might develop almost as a side-effect of STECs.

Evaluation: As in MT there are at least two criteria of quality for NLG systems: language quality (fluency in MT) and correctness of content (adequacy in MT). In NLG, these have mostly been evaluated directly using human scores or preference judgments, although recently automatic metrics such as BLEU have been used. They have also been evaluated indirectly, e.g. by measuring reading speeds and manual post-processing[3]. A more user-oriented type of evaluation has been to assess real-world usefulness, in other words, whether the generated texts achieve their purpose (e.g. whether users learn more with NLG techniques than with cheaper alternatives[4]).

The majority of NLP STECs have used automatic evaluation methods, and the ability to produce results 'at the push of a button', quickly and reproducibly, is ideal in the context of STECs. However, existing metrics are unlikely to be suitable for NLG (Belz and Reiter, 2006), and there is a lot of scepticism among NLG researchers regarding automatic evaluation. We believe that NLG should develop its own automatic metrics (development of such metrics is part of the proposal by Reiter and Belz, this volume), but for the time being an NLG STEC needs to involve human-based evaluations of the intrinsic as well as extrinsic type.

Sharing: A recent survey conducted on the main NLG and corpus-based NLP mailing lists[5] revealed that there are virtually no data resources that could be directly used in shared tasks. Considerable investment has to go into developing such resources, and direct funding is necessary. This points to a funded project, but we recommend direct involvement of the NLG community and SIGGEN. Other aspects of organisation are not NLG-specific, so the general recommendations in the preceding section apply.

4 Conclusion

STECs have been remarkable stimulants to progress in other areas of HLT, through their community-building role, and through 'hothousing' solutions to specific problems. There are also lessons to be learnt about STECs not being overly ambitious, remaining responsive to developments in the broader field and wider world, and having appropriate institutional standing. We believe that NLG can benefit greatly from the introduction of shared tasks, provided that an inclusive and flexible approach is taken which is informed by the specific requirements of NLG.

References

A. Belz and E. Reiter. 2006. Comparing automatic and human evaluation of NLG systems. In *Proc. EACL'06*, pages 313–320.

A. Kilgarriff. 2003. No-bureaucracy evaluation. In *Proc. Workshop on Evaluation Initiatives in NLP, EACL'03*.

E. Reiter and A. Belz. 2006. GENEVAL: A proposal for shared-task evaluation in NLG. In *Proc. INLG'06*.

K. Spärck Jones and J. R. Galliers. 1996. *Evaluating Natural Language Processing Systems: An Analysis and Review*. Springer Verlag.

K. Spärck Jones, 1981. *Information Retrieval Experiment*, chapter 12. Butterworth & Co.

[3]E.g. in the SkillSum and SumTime projects at Aberdeen.

[4]E.g. evaluation of the NL interface of the DIAG intelligent tutoring system, di Eugenio et al.

[5]Belz, March 2006.

GENEVAL: A Proposal for Shared-task Evaluation in NLG

Ehud Reiter
University of Aberdeen, UK
ereiter@csd.abdn.ac.uk

Anja Belz
University of Brighton, UK
a.s.belz@brighton.ac.uk

Abstract

We propose to organise a series of shared-task NLG events, where participants are asked to build systems with similar input/output functionalities, and these systems are evaluated with a range of different evaluation techniques. The main purpose of these events is to allow us to compare different evaluation techniques, by correlating the results of different evaluations on the systems entered in the events.

1 Background

Evaluation is becoming increasingly important in Natural Language Generation (NLG), as in most other areas of Natural Language Processing (NLP). NLG systems can be evaluated in many different ways, with different associated resource requirements. For example, a large-scale task-effectiveness study with human subjects could last over a year and cost more than US$100,000 (Reiter et al., 2003); on the other hand, a small-scale comparison of generated texts to human-written reference texts can be done in a manner of days. However, while the latter kind of study is very appealing in terms of cost and time, and cheap and reliable evaluation techniques would be very useful for people developing and testing new NLG techniques, it is only worth doing if we have reason to believe that its results tell us something about how useful the generated texts are to real human users. It is not obvious that this is the case (Reiter and Sripada, 2002).

Perhaps the best way to study the reliability of different evaluation techniques, and more generally to develop a better empirical understanding of the strengths and problems of different evaluation techniques, is to perform studies where a range of different evaluation techniques are used to evaluate a set of NLG systems with similar functionalities. Correlating the results of the different evaluation techniques will give us empirical insight as to how well these techniques work in practice.

Unfortunately, few such studies have been carried out, perhaps because (to date) few NLG systems have been built with comparable functionality (our own work in this area is discussed below). We hope to surmount this problem, by organising 'shared task' events to which NLG researchers can submit systems based on a supplied data set of inputs and (human-written) text outputs. We will then carry out our evaluation experiments on the submitted systems. We hope that such shared-task events will also make it easier for new researchers to get involved in NLG, by providing data sets and an evaluation framework.

2 Comparative Evaluations in NLG

There is a long history of shared task initiatives in NLP, of which the best known is perhaps MUC (Hirschman, 1998); others include TREC, PARSEVAL, SENSEVAL, and the range of shared tasks organised by CoNLL. Such exercises are now common in most areas of NLP, and have had a major impact on many areas, including machine translation and information extraction (see discussion of history of shared-task initiatives and their impact in Belz and Kilgarriff (2006)).

One of the best-known comparative studies of evaluation techniques was by Papineni et al. (2002) who proposed the BLEU metric for machine translation and showed that BLEU correlated well with human judgements when comparing several machine translation systems. Several other studies of this type have been carried out in the MT and Summarisation communities.

The first comparison of NLG evaluation techniques which we are aware of is by Bangalore et al. (2000). The authors manually created several variants of sentences from the Wall Street Journal, and evaluated these sentences using both human judgements and several corpus-based metrics. They used linear regression to suggest a combination of the corpus-based metrics which they be-

Proceedings of the Fourth International Natural Language Generation Conference
Sydney, July 2006. ©2006 Association for Computational Linguistics

lieve is a better predictor of human judgements than any of the individual metrics.

In our work (Belz and Reiter, 2006), we used several different evaluation techniques (human and corpus-based) to evaluate the output of five NLG systems which generated wind descriptions for weather forecasts. We then analysed how well the corpus-based evaluations correlated with the human-based evaluations. Amongst other things, we concluded that BLEU-type metrics work reasonably well when comparing statistical NLG systems, but less well when comparing statistical NLG systems to knowledge-based NLG systems.

We worked in this domain because of the availability of the SumTime corpus (Sripada et al., 2003), which contains both numerical weather prediction data (i.e., inputs to NLG) and human written forecast texts (i.e., target outputs from NLG). We are not aware of any other NLG-related corpora which contain a large number of texts and corresponding input data sets, and are freely available to the research community.

3 Our Proposal

We intend to apply for funding for a three-year project to create more shared input/output data sets (we are focusing on data-to-text tasks for the reasons discussed in Belz and Kilgarriff (2006)), organise shared task workshops, and create and test a range of methods for evaluating submitted systems.

3.1 Step 1: Create data sets

We intend to create input/output data sets that contain the following types of representations:

- raw non-linguistic input data;
- structured content representations, roughly corresponding to document plans (Reiter and Dale, 2000);
- semantic-level representations, roughly corresponding to text specifications (Reiter and Dale, 2000);
- actual human-authored corpus texts.

The presence of intermediate representations in our data sets means that researchers who are just interested in document planning, microplanning, or surface realisation do not need to build complete NLG systems in order to participate.

We will create the semantic-level representations by parsing the corpus texts, probably using a LinGO parser[1]. We will create the content representations using application-specific analysis tools, similar to a tool we have already created for SumTime wind statements. The actual data sets we currently intend to create are as follows (see also summary in Table 1).

SumTime weather statements: These are brief statements which describe predicted precipitation and cloud over a forecast period. We will extract the texts (and the corresponding input data) from the existing SumTime corpus.

Statistics summaries: We will ask people (probably students) to write paragraph-length textual summaries of statistical data. The actual data will come from opinion polls or national statistics offices. The corpus will also include data about the authors (e.g., age, sex, domain expertise).

Nurses' reports: As part of a new project at Aberdeen, Babytalk[2], we will be acquiring a corpus of texts written by nurses to summarise the status of a baby in a neonatal intensive care unit, along with the raw data this is based on (sensor readings, records of actions taken such as giving medication).

3.2 Step 2: Organise workshops

The second step is to organise workshops. We intend to use a fairly standard organisation (Belz and Kilgarriff, 2006). We will release the data sets (but not the reference texts), give people six months to develop systems, and invite people who submit systems to a workshop. Participants can submit either complete data-to-text NLG systems, or components which just do document planning, microplanning, or realisation.

We are planning to increase the number and complexity of tasks from one round to the next, as this has been useful in other NLP evaluations (Belz and Kilgarriff, 2006); for example, we will add surface realisation as a separate task in round 2 and layout/structuring task in round 3.

We will carry out all evaluation activities (see below) ourselves, workshop participants will not be involved in this.

3.3 Step 3: Evaluation

The final step is to evaluate the systems and components submitted to the workshop. As the main

[1] `http://lingo.stanford.edu/`

[2] `http://www.csd.abdn.ac.uk/research/babytalk/`

Corpus	num texts	num ref (*)	text size	main NLG challenges
Weather statements	3000	300	1-2 sentences	content det, lex choice, aggregation
Statistical summaries	1000	100	paragraph	above plus surface realisation
Nurses' reports	200	50	several paras	above plus text structuring/layout

(*) In addition to the main corpus, we will also gather texts which will be used as reference texts for corpus-based evaluations; 'num ref' is the number of such texts. These texts will not be released.

Table 1: Planned GENEVAL data sets.

purpose of this whole exercise is to see how well different evaluation techniques correlate with each other, we plan to carry out a range of different evaluations, including the following.

Corpus-based evaluations: We will develop new, linguistically grounded evaluation metrics, and compare these to existing metrics including BLEU, NIST, and string-edit distance. We will also investigate how sensitive different metrics are to size and make-up of the reference corpus.

Human-based preference judgements: We will investigate different experimental designs and methods for overcoming respondent bias (e.g. what is known as 'central tendency bias', where some respondents avoid judgements at either end of a scale). As we showed previously (Belz and Reiter, 2006) that there are significant inter-subject differences in ratings, one thing we want to determine is how many subjects are needed to get reliable and reproducible results.

Task performance. This depends on the domain, but e.g. in the nurse-report domain we could use the methodology of (Law et al., 2005), who showed medical professionals the texts, asked them to make a treatment decision, and then rated the correctness of the suggested treatments.

As well as recommendations about the appropriateness of existing evaluation techniques, we hope the above experiments will allow us to suggest new evaluation techniques for NLG.

4 Next Steps

At this point, we encourage NLG researchers to give us their views regarding our plans for the organisation of GENEVAL, the data and evaluation methods we are planning to use, to suggest additional data sets or evaluation techniques, and especially to let us know whether they would be interested in participating.

If our proposal is successful, we hope that the project will start in summer 2007, with the first data set released in late 2007 and the first workshop in summer 2008. ELRA/ELDA have also already agreed to help us with this work, contributing human and data resources.

References

Srinavas Bangalore, Owen Rambow, and Steve Whittaker. 2000. Evaluation metrics for generation. In *Proceedings of INLG-2000*, pages 1–8.

Anja Belz and Adam Kilgarriff. 2006. Shared-task evaluations in HLT: Lessons for NLG. In *Proceedings of INLG-2006*.

Anja Belz and Ehud Reiter. 2006. Comparing automatic and human evaluation of NLG systems. In *Proceedings of EACL-2006*, pages 313–320.

Lynette Hirschman. 1998. The evolution of evaluation: Lessons from the Message Understanding Conferences. *Computer Speech and Language*, 12:283–285.

Anna Law, Yvonne Freer, Jim Hunter, Robert Logie, Neil McIntosh, and John Quinn. 2005. Generating textual summaries of graphical time series data to support medical decision making in the neonatal intensive care unit. *Journal of Clinical Monitoring and Computing*, 19:183–194.

Kishore Papineni, Salim Roukos, Todd Ward, and Wei-Jing Zhu. 2002. Bleu: A method for automatic evaluation of machine translation. In *Proceedings of ACL-2002*, pages 311–318.

Ehud Reiter and Robert Dale. 2000. *Building Natural Language Generation Systems*. Cambridge University Press.

Ehud Reiter and Somayajulu Sripada. 2002. Should corpora texts be gold standards for NLG? In *Proceedings of INLG-2002*, pages 97–104.

Ehud Reiter, Roma Robertson, and Liesl Osman. 2003. Lessons from a failure: Generating tailored smoking cessation letters. *Artificial Intelligence*, 144:41–58.

Somayajulu Sripada, Ehud Reiter, Jim Hunter, and Jin Yu. 2003. Exploiting a parallel text-data corpus. In *Proceedings of Corpus Linguistics 2003*, pages 734–743.

AUTHOR INDEX